D1382751

Chasing the White Whale

Chasing the White Whale

The *Moby-Dick* Marathon; or, What Melville Means Today

by David Dowling

UNIVERSITY OF IOWA PRESS  IOWA CITY

University of Iowa Press, Iowa City 52242
Copyright © 2010 by the University of Iowa Press
www.uiowapress.org
Printed in the United States of America
Design by Sara T. Sauers

The University of Iowa Press is a member of Green Press Initiative
and is committed to preserving natural resources.

Printed on acid-free paper

Library of Congress Cataloging-in-Publication Data
Dowling, David Oakey, 1967–
Chasing the white whale: the Moby-Dick marathon; or, what
Melville means today / by David Dowling.
   p. cm.
Includes bibliographical references and index.
ISBN-13: 978-1-58729-906-3 (pbk.)
ISBN-10: 1-58729-906-2 (pbk.)
ISBN-13: 978-1-58729-940-7 (eBook)
ISBN-10: 1-58729-940-2 (eBook)
1. Melville, Herman, 1819–1891. Moby Dick. 2. Sea stories,
American—History and criticism. 3. Whaling in literature.
4. Whales in literature. I. Title.
PS2384.M62D69 2010
813'.3—dc22   2010010257

·CONTENTS·

· ACKNOWLEDGMENTS ·

$\mathcal{M}$Y IMMEDIATE DEBTS for this book are to the late Irwin Marks, who in 1996 first conceived of an all-night reading of *Moby-Dick* in New Bedford, and President James Russell of the New Bedford Whaling Museum, whose tireless commitment to the annual *Moby-Dick* Marathon reading made the 2009 event the most successful of all thirteen events, breaking records for attendance and demand for reading spots. The success of the event itself was vital to the writing of this book; it was my good fortune to have caught the reading at a particularly high point in its history. In addition to Russell, the people behind that success who kindly and imaginatively supported my research were Melville's great-great grandson Peter Gansevoort Whittemore and Mayor Scott Lang. These gracious hosts generously provided me with invaluable and enlightening insights into the event. Other Melvillians of various stripes who deserve mention here for assisting research for the 2009 reading and making it so memorable include Edward Camara Jr., Richard Tonachel, Nephi Tyler, John O'Connor, and Keith Hilles-Pilant. The Melville Society, ever collegial and embracing of this project, included Wyn Kelley, Mary K. Bercaw Edwards, Timothy Marr, and Christopher Sten.

John Bryant, current keeper of the flame of the Melville Society, and Dan Beachy-Quick, a poet and latter-day Charles Olson in his own right, have served as astute readers of my work on Melville. Their insightful and careful feedback was crucial in directing the course of this book. The research of Hershel Parker, literary archeologist of Melville lore, was essential for providing the nuances of historical detail for several of the chapters. My admiration for Charles Olson grew from David Blake's enthusiasm for his audacious method that redefined how literary criticism might be done in an unbridled and artful way. For their suggestions in support of my research on Melville in popular culture, I want to thank my editor at the University of

Iowa Press, Joseph Parsons; my colleague at the University of Iowa, Michael Chaser; and the host of young Melville scholars led by James Roth in my Hawthorne-Melville course at the University of Iowa.

My long-term debts for this book are to the many Melvillians who have touched my life and inspired me to dive into the works of one of our greatest and most difficult authors. They include Martin Bickman, above all, who generously offered his wisdom and insight regarding New England literary and whaling culture. His guidance was instrumental in the completion of this book, as Marty and I have conversed about Melville since the early 1990s from university halls to the trails of the majestic Front Range of the Colorado Rocky Mountains. Mary Klages, A. Robert Lee, and Giles Gunn, all believers in the White Whale, also provided much energy and insight for the foundation of this book. These were, and continue to be, my model readers of *Moby-Dick*.

John Hale and Jim Donnelley of Western Reserve Academy in Hudson, Ohio, were the scholarly fanatics who first introduced me to the idea of an all-night reading of *Moby-Dick*. Their masterful orchestration of the reading in the late 1990s initially sparked my interest in the event, which bloomed into the idea for this book through the suggestion of Joseph Parsons. His creativity and fearlessness in conceiving of this project are unparalleled in the world of academic press publishing and deserve the highest praise for so perfectly suiting a book to its author. As a result, this has been a labor of love to write, the best circumstance under which any author should work, and I owe it to Joe.

Also behind this book is my love of museums originally inspired by my parents, Oak and Mary Dowling, who introduced me to some of the greatest in the world, showing me at a tender age how a giant heart in Chicago beats with vitality, wonder, and excitement. The support of my partner, Caroline Tolbert, and the enthusiasm of my children, Jacqueline, Eveline, and Edward for this book have made it a source of joy from the start, and for that I owe them my deepest thanks. For them, as Thoreau said, "There is no remedy for love, but to love more."

CHASING THE WHITE WHALE

Introduction

Melville Lives

O NOT CALL ME ISHMAEL. My role in writing this book about the annual *Moby-Dick* Marathon reading—a nonstop, twenty-five-hour immersion in Melville's novel—may echo that of Ishmael aboard the *Pequod*. Like him, I am both a participant and an observer, deeply absorbed in the rituals unfolding and fully wedded to the task of retelling them in all their complexity, mystery, and dynamism. But I do not intend to speak with his voice, channel his spirit, narrate his story. Instead of playing the role of Ishmael, or Melville, for that matter, like Hal Holbrook's lifetime of Disney-esque Mark Twain impersonations, I am interested in finding the Melville who lives today through *Moby-Dick* as showcased in the marathon readings of 2009 and earlier. Rather than serving up "cold pork," as Charles Olson says in *Call Me Ishmael* (1947) while discussing the economic history of whaling in his now classic prose-poem homage to *Moby-Dick, Chasing the White Whale* attempts to weigh, from an insider's vantage point, the *Moby-Dick* Marathon reading— among the most significant events in contemporary print culture—"in the scale of the total society."[1]

It was with trepidation that I traveled, in 2009, to meet with the disciples of Melville; if their obsession were anything like Melville's, this would be an intense crew. As John Bryant, a regular attendee and editor-in-chief of *Leviathan,* the journal of the Melville Society, remarked, "God knows how many lunatics are out there doing this."[2] My initial apprehension would quickly transform to a new appreciation for Melville's influence on New England culture and on the lives of nonacademic aficionados. I met Nephi Tyler, waterfront worker and son of a southern transplant navy man, who wore on his sleeve his admiration for his father's participation in the reading. Theirs was more than an ordinary obsession; the novel was built into the fiber of their souls. I learned of how Tyler's father, who had sculpted whales as a hobby for years, held aloft his greatest creation in a ritual dedication of an antebellum house his other son had rebuilt. Another reader, Mark Wojnar, his obsession for Melville reaching beyond the reasonable, deemed the marathon a greater priority than steady employment, as his attendance at the event was more consistent than his luck on the job market. Wojnar is a man for whom little else matters than Melville, his wisdom of *Moby-Dick* so profound as to win the praise of Melville's great-great-grandson Peter Whittemore as well as the dean of Melville scholarship, Hershel Parker.

People like these are not in it for literary amusement or diversion. The experience of reading the full novel over nearly twenty-five hours is not for the faint of heart, nor does it lend itself to pretension or superficiality. Like an athletic marathon,[3] there is no way to fake it. Like pursuing the whale itself for months on end, reading and listening to twenty-five hours of *Moby-Dick* is equal parts heaven and hell. It becomes a communal experience with the potential for transcendence, a sort of group meditation with language. No reader is here for self-promotion. The objective, rather, is to function as a vessel for the palpitating spirit of Melville. Readers tune in to the music of Melville's soul in the guise of the enigmatic force of vitality that is *Moby-Dick*, the product of one of America's greatest writers surging at the very height of his powers. Here is not so much an intellectual feast, nor a series of one-act plays performed by the top brass of Melville scholarship. Instead the reading is a democratic chorus of voices, crossing national and gender lines with the same manic radical equality as the novel itself. Readers represent a Whitmanian song of occupations, including professors, fishermen, schoolteachers, selectmen, students, journalists, legislators, physicians, and clergy of all denominations. Each reading showcases a world of voices and languages, as selected passages are read in Portuguese, Japanese, Italian, Danish, Spanish, or French, followed by that same passage in English to reflect both the crew's cultural diversity and the global sweep of the *Pequod*'s voyage.

The *Moby-Dick* Marathon is part of Melville's surging cultural relevance today, something well chronicled in the extracts of references to him compiled in the preface of Andew Delbanco's *Melville: His World and Work*. Melville has been referenced everywhere from "The Sopranos" television series to political commentaries on terrorism to *Mad* magazine.[4] More recently, *The Onion* ran a gag under the heading "Stockwatch," complete with graph from the New York Stock Exchange, reporting "New England Whaling Ltd. (NEWH) up $0.39 to $5.20 (up 8.11%)," with the caption: "After 150 years of record lows, stock prices have begun to rebound as whale oil once again becomes a relatively affordable energy source."[5] The joke touches on New Bedford's steep decline, since its whaling glory days of the 1840s when it was referred to as Whaling City, into economic irrelevance.

New Bedford had begun to mine its whaling past for economic purposes as early as 1922 with the world premier of *Down to the Sea in Ships*, a silent film set in 1850 during the golden age of whaling that attempts to capitalize on the modernist renaissance of Melville. In response to its 1990s economic plight, the city hatched a plan to attract tourist dollars by incorporating the area's history into such events as the marathon. In 1996, thirteen blocks of the oldest section of town became the New Bedford Whaling National Historical Park run by the National Park Service.[6] The park stretches from the docks through a residential area that includes nearly a hundred homes that had belonged to the antebellum whaling elite. Among them is 100 Madison Street, owned by Melville's sister in the 1860s and now a bed-and-breakfast. On January 3, 1997, the city and the National Park Service held the inaugural marathon reading that marked New Bedford's greatest effort to make whaling history its main tourist industry. Of course, the menacing inns, like Peter Coffin's, the seedy brothels, and gaming houses are conspicuously absent from the park, while the town's material wealth (the mansions) and Christian piety (the Seamen's Bethel) receive the spotlight. In this sense, New Bedford's whaling stock has rebounded, as the city has transformed into what Saudi Arabia and other oil-rich Middle Eastern nations may become a century from now after our oil reserves vanish.

In academic culture, Melville's significance continues to loom large and is actually growing. The establishment in 1999 of Bryant's *Leviathan*—a much-needed expanded, improved, and sophisticated revamping of the patchwork newsletter *Melville Society Extracts*—is only one example.[7] The Melville Society represents the cutting edge in academic research on the author, reaching into new areas such as oral storytelling culture in Mary K. Bercaw Edwards's *Old Cannibal Me: Spoken Sources in Melville's Early Works* (2009), cultural geography in *"Whole Oceans Away": Melville and the Pacific* (2008) edited by Jill Barnum, Wyn Kelley, and Christopher Sten, and new approaches to the White Whale by editors Bryant, Edwards, and Timothy Marr in *"The Ungraspable Phantom": Essays on* Moby-Dick (2006). The Melville Society is indeed at the heart of the *Moby-Dick* Marathon reading, and their representatives set the tone most years with a lecture that opens the festivities. Their contribution is indeed immeasurable. These scholars are constantly refreshing and invigorating approaches to both the novel and the author with energy and imagination that keeps Melville alive and relevant in ways that have inspired the mass readership.

With Melville firmly rooted in both popular and academic culture,[8] his relevance is readily apparent. But why is it that both professionals (literary critics, educators, curators, creative writers) and amateurs (bibliophiles or "fans") feel moved to conduct a relay reading of *Moby-Dick,* Melville's longest, most ambitious, and most difficult novel? As many American literature instructors have asked themselves in their desire to teach Melville's best prose, wouldn't it be easier to do *Billy Budd?* Is this event, especially for those who remain for the full twenty-five hours of it, "an appropriate occasion for self-discipline in the blessed virtue of patience," as one reviewer noted of the more dutiful listeners at a Melville lecture on the South Seas delivered in 1858?[9] *Moby-Dick* is anything but sedate, somber, or reverent; reflective meditation is consistently shattered in the novel by the cry, "There she blows!" It exudes the threat of fatal, disastrous results, as in the chapters "The Line," "The Monkey-rope," and "The Mast-Head." For those who love it, the novel is frolicsome, rambunctious, and irreverent, much like the forty-barrel bull whales, or undergraduates on spring break, giddy with the future in their eyes: "Like a mob of young collegians, they are full of fight, fun, and wickedness, tumbling around the world at such a reckless and rollicking rate."[10] How can one witness a breaching whale indifferently or not be inspired by the audacious bravado, the sheer exuberance of a writer who rises and swells with his subject, exclaiming, "Give me a Condor's quill! Give me Vesuvius's crater for an inkstand!"[11]

The *Moby-Dick* Marathon reading, thankfully, is not on the syllabus; its sheer force of energy seems to rise in direct proportion to its distance from formal education. Now that the novel is no longer a staple of the undergraduate curriculum and has all but vanished from high schools—where things of beauty too frequently turn into torture devices—it seems that America has now found a new passion for Ishmael's tale. The marathon reading is not required by anyone or any institution (although one blogger suggested that it should be after attending the 2008 reading). Most colleges and universities do not give travel funds to faculty who want to read at the event, let alone attend it, for it does not squarely fit into any of the boxes of the holy academic trinity of teaching, research, and service. It does not present itself as a lucrative enterprise.[12] Any spinoff merchandising opportunities have been taken by the New Bedford Whaling Museum gift shop to go directly into its nonprofit mission. The event is as removed from commercial culture as one can imagine; it is not a purchased experience, and thus has even greater value.

Ironically, much of *Moby-Dick* is a meditation on money and its power to motivate, inspire, and corrupt. "The Doubloon" is especially effective at illustrating the wide-ranging interpretations of capital in light of money's universal appeal, totally unavoidable yet nearly limitless in types of value ascribed to it. The economy of the marathon reading is more a communal literary journey than an entertainment passively consumed. Audience members may be asked, for example, to replace readers who have slept through their assigned passages in the wee hours of the night. The reading can be nonetheless, in the language of the academy, *performative*, though mildly so, with a costumed Ishmael, Father Mapple, and Ahab performing set pieces from "Loomings," "The Sermon," and "The Quarter-Deck," along with a lighthearted children's theatrical staging of "Midnight, Forecastle." No one passes a hat or requests compensation, as the rewards are intrinsic to the readers' voluntary—not forced or dutiful—participation. The management style at New Bedford is dedicated to a non-compulsory feel, with audience and readers free to come and go as they like in a way that is consonant with Ishmael's own wayward flair. In deep accordance with the spirit of Ishmael (who chides how that "urbane activity with which a man receives money is really marvelous, considering that we so earnestly believe money to be the root of all earthly ills, and that on no account can a monied man enter heaven. Ah! How cheerfully we consign ourselves to perdition!"),[13] no exorbitant ticket prices or merchandising mar this otherwise noncommercial event.

Without a commercial or even professional purpose that might serve to justify the uncommon rigor of the event, one is pressed to explore the deeper reasons for its devout following. There is an identifiable groundswell of interest in radical subversive authors, as seen in the recent films *Trumbo* and *Gonzo: The Life and Work of Dr. Hunter S. Thompson*. The subjects of both films were countercultural warriors wrestling with military, police force, and political integrity with every bit of the wit and force of Melville's assault on missionaries and the hypocrisies of organized religion. For example, in *Moby-Dick* Queequeg embodies and lives by a set of core values, with far more integrity than those of the most traditionally religious characters in the novel, such as the cowardly and noncommittal Starbuck and the ruthless capitalists Peleg and Bildad. In fact, Melville's assault on Christianity played a hand in the destruction of his fiction-writing career, evidenced by how the antireligious content of *Pierre* (1852) appalled Evert Duyckinck, his longtime friend and editor, and led Duyckinck to withdraw his support for the author. Melville's "quarrel with fiction," as Nina Baym has called it, is as important as *Melville's Quarrel with God*, the focus of Lawrence Thompson's 1952 work, as formal religion and fictional genre conventions were only two of the sacred cows he subverted in his career. Domesticity and gender were among his other favorite targets.

Beyond Melville's appeal as a literary outlaw, the popularity of a marathon reading of Melville's magnum opus demands investigation. Nearly absurd and without clear purpose in its practical dimensions, the reading defies even the literary-critical reflection that *Moby-Dick* invites, demands, and thrives upon. Twain would laugh at the folly of the marathon reading of *Moby-Dick*, just as he would at the prospect of running 26.2 miles for "exercise." But like the athletic marathon from which this reading borrows its name, the participants come to learn about themselves and their world through a common pursuit enacted and celebrated in a ritual that crystallizes and concentrates through a communal gathering a pursuit that is otherwise solitary—the reading of this gigantic novel—for the purpose of witnessing together its majesty and power to move us, change us, make us grow, and to reflect on our former selves who may have encountered it in the past.

A group reading of *Moby-Dick* is well suited to the innumerable interpretations the book invites and even subverts. Given its depth, each reader and listener perceives a different novel beyond its bare plot line. As such, the reading is a ritual celebration of diversity and its delicate balance with individualism, concepts prominently figured in the novel itself. The chorus of voices brings out the living human bonds contained within the text. By making the novel come alive in an active reading, *Moby-Dick* and Melville himself are reanimated and reified. Indeed, many people come to the reading optimistic that the range and depth of the novel's vision might extend to them. Like Ishmael, audience members and readers frequently expect nothing less than to "see the world" through the experience. "Now then," Peleg asks Ishmael prior to shipping aboard the *Pequod*, "thou not only wantest to go a-whaling, to find out by experience what whaling is, but ye also want to go in order to see the world?" Ishmael nods. "Well then, just step forward there, and take a peep over the weather-bow," quips Peleg, roundly disabusing him of his romantic idealism. "But go a-whaling I must," Ishmael affirms,[14] a romantic at heart, like those who attend the reading in spite of all reason— "but you've read it before," or simply, "why?" the uninitiated protest—and Peleg agrees to ship him.

Some deep, mysterious longing brings us here to see the novel in a different light, to hear its voice spoken in myriad fresh voices, and to feel the full manic narrative wave of the most ambitious American novel ever composed. Peter Whittemore, a theologian, acknowledged in 2000 that he loves "meeting with people who are so entranced by Melville that they come to a meeting like this in an age when the Internet and TV has made reading look like an old-fashioned habit."[15] Such is the feel of the marathon, a postmodern reading event with roots in antebellum oratory (Father Mapple's sermon is read in the historic Seamen's Bethel, a chapel across the street from the museum) and in an ancient whaling industry that paradoxically careens toward the future with the momentum and force of the White Whale himself. The history of the event itself speaks to the readings as comprising the most significant movement outside of formal criticism to accommodate Melville—not as charming nostalgia, but as more urgently relevant to our contemporary world—in literary history at the turn of the twenty-first century.

Etymology: Origins of the Moby-Dick Marathon

THE ORIGINS of the *Moby-Dick* Marathon point to the excitement and magic behind the founding of the event. In 1986, Jan Larson, Director of Museum Education at Mystic Seaport (Mystic, Connecticut), started the *Moby-Dick* Marathon. She was familiar with the *Ulysses* marathon readings[16] and decided that Mystic Seaport and its abundance of whale-history finery would set the perfect stage for a nonstop reading of Melville's *Moby-Dick*. Mystic Seaport, in fact, is home to the most authentic and last surviving American wooden whaling vessel in the world, the *Charles W. Morgan*, the one ship in the world today that most closely resembles the *Acushnet*, on which Melville actually sailed. The fact that Melville never set foot on the *Charles W. Morgan* was thus easily overcome by the ship's historical fidelity to a whaling schooner, a "mystical three dimensional environment where we can put these words back into the wood," as Larson described it in 2001.[17]

The reading blossomed into four sessions over as many days, as the group began moving to areas of the ship corresponding to scenes in the novel. Larson later obtained permission to host the group aboard the ship overnight. The Mystic Seaport reading is held annually on the last day of July, finishing on August 1 to commemorate Melville's birthday. In a sugary finish that speaks to Mystic Seaport's more commercial venue (as compared to the one at the New Bedford Whaling Museum), readers share a White Whale birthday cake. These readings became so popular that crowds pressed the *Charles W. Morgan* beyond its capacity of thirty-three; reservations are now required for overnight berths. Five years after the first reading, Jack Putnam, a Mystic Seaport educator, donned a Herman Melville costume and cavorted about the reading rendering his best impersonation of the great author. Groton school children in a remedial reading program attended one year, and sign language was provided by interpreters from a local school for the deaf.[18] Based on its summer schedule and Mystic Seaport's success as a well-advertised major tourist attraction in the area, Mystic's reading continues to thrive under the direction of Mary K. Bercaw Edwards.

In 1996, New Bedford Whaling Museum volunteer Irwin Marks noticed something amiss about the Mystic Seaport nonstop reading. "Mystic Seaport does this to celebrate Melville's birthday," he said, "and I got to thinking about how Melville has absolutely no connection to Mystic, whereas New Bedford *is* Melville."[19] Pioneering and ingenious as it was to put the words back into the wood of the *Charles W. Morgan*, Marks thought it would be more appropriate to put the words back into the streets of New Bedford, since so much of *Moby-Dick* takes place in and ruminates upon that town, which by 1841 had just eclipsed Nantucket as the whaling capital of the world.[20] "This is where he came to ship out, this is where he worshipped in Seamen's Bethel. He wrote a whole chapter ['The Street'] in which he lauds the city of New Bedford," Marks noted.[21] With historical rationale and justification in place, January 3 became the Whaling Museum's adopted date for the reading, to more directly link the event to the *Acushnet* and thus to *Moby-Dick*'s and the author's history. On that date in 1997 nearly 150 volunteer readers, led by a costumed Ishmael played by former assistant district attorney Raymond Veary, carried the inaugural event to its completion more than twenty-five hours later.

Veary would continue to intone the famous first words of "Loomings," "Call me Ishmael," through the thirteenth annual reading in 2009. While there is a place for the summer camp atmosphere of remedial readers and birthday cakes—"It gets hot. It rains. Bugs come," as Mystic's Melville impersonator

Jack Putnam said[22]—*Moby-Dick* also deserves a more sophisticated reading, and it has found just that in New Bedford. With the emphasis on the town's proud whaling history, which made it the wealthiest city per capita in America in the 1840s and whaling the third largest industry in the U.S. by 1850, it was fitting that the Mayor of New Bedford, Scott Lang, read at the event, a tradition that continues today.[23] Economically, New Bedford may never be as prosperous as it was during the glory days of whaling in the two decades before the Civil War, but beyond the civic significance, of course, is the national importance of this reading that celebrates one of America's greatest authors. There, in 2008, to represent the federal government, was a reading by congressional Representative Barney Frank and a video address from Senator Edward M. Kennedy. Frank would make a return appearance, fashionably late—or "notoriously" so, as one staffer scoffed—in 2009. As the only openly gay member of Congress, Frank had the luck of being assigned to read from Ishmael and Queequeg's awkward roommate scene featuring the cannibal's phallic pipe as its central image, a slice of vintage Melvillian gender folly skewering conventional notions of masculinity.

The whaling town would eventually win out over the authentic whaler as the best setting for a nonstop reading among Melville aficionados. But Mystic Seaport continues its reign as repository of some of the world's best historical maritime artifacts and is distinguished for its exceptional pioneering creativity in initiating the first mass reading of the novel in the U.S. The Mystic reading, like New Bedford's, showcases *Moby-Dick* as a representative of whaling history in general rather than Melville's career. In terms of emphasizing Melville's authorship and the novel's literary composition, a case could also be made for conducting the reading at Arrowhead, Melville's Pittsfield, Massachusetts, country home in the Berkshires, where he wrote the novel in full view of Mount Greylock between 1849 and 1851. This landlocked setting, however, would do little for the history of *Moby-Dick*'s maritime world. The family drama and attendant trauma would likely take center stage; one could imagine a costumed Lizzy Melville and daughters in this case, banging on the door, demanding that Herman obey reason, pull himself out of his obsessive trance, and come down for supper—all while the reading droned on into the wee hours of the night.

There are many histories to this fine book, and Melville's herculean effort to write *Moby-Dick* is certainly one of them. Like the whaling history that undergirds the tale, Melville's personal history does not bespeak the ordinary.

He often locked himself in his room without food, writing in a creative white heat until evening, when his wife and daughters would admonish him to return to the land of the living. The marathon reading itself defies ordinary reason as well. We are supposed to sleep; we are *not* supposed to read nonstop a novel of this length and depth. The history of *Moby-Dick* is the history of such obsessions, which can either be enhanced or muted by the setting of the reading. Museums and libraries provide ideal portals for time travel into Melville's world, much more so than bookstores. An exception would be Canio's Bookstore in Sag Harbor, a historically significant locale for *Moby-Dick* that has hosted nonstop readings. Other hosts include the John Jermain Memorial Library and the University of Kansas, which by contrast are noncommercial public institutions outside of the inexorable web of the marketplace. But unlike the Whaling Museum, these sites have little historical significance to the book. The various locations of the readings bring out particular dimensions of the novel. One site is not more "real" than another; the issue represents an intriguing study in the conundrum of accuracy in literary history: Which site is more true to the spirit of Melville's novel? Of all of them, New Bedford holds a special place in the hearts of dedicated Melvillians.

The first I learned of the New Bedford reading was in Cambridge, Massachusetts, at a bookstore on Harvard Square. I was buying, among other things, Giles Gunn's edited volume on Melville, as well as what appeared to be a local product (an unwieldy dissertation) on Melville bearing the imprint of "Queequeg Press" (I couldn't resist). After ringing up my purchases, the shopkeeper took note of my selections and fixed me with his eye like "The Prophet" in *Moby-Dick* and asked, "Have you been to New Bedford?" I looked up, puzzled.

"The Reading? Have you been?"

I shook my head.

"Ohhh . . .," he said, knowing precisely my fate as a smile spread across his bearded face.

As he continued to talk, I heard my fate spelled out before me, and I knew in my bones I must go. The only worry I had was that there might be someone impersonating Melville at the event. (A colleague recently asked just how a Melville impersonator should act. Depressed?) I couldn't dissociate the idea of a Melville impersonator from the image of a paid actor playing the part of Jesus at the Holy Land theme park in Orlando, Florida, who signs autographs, leads the parade (cross in tow), gets abused by nasty Romans, and does the full "character encounter" circuit. Perhaps I had also been accosted too frequently by "Will," the Shakespeare impersonator at the Colorado Shakespeare Festival. Luckily, I found out that no one would be impersonating Melville at the reading in New Bedford.

Witnessing an actor playing an author may also strike too close to home because my academic research speciality is the professionalization of American authorship, which engages, among other things, the branding of authors as products for sale. I assume that an author has to be dead in order to be impersonated, otherwise actors would be turning up as Stephen King. Yet only classical writers are impersonated, thus it would seem that beyond a place in the *Norton Anthology* perhaps impersonation is the true sign of an author's literary merit, the ultimate canonization in the pop-cultural zeitgeist. Melville himself knew that commercial culture makes every author to some extent an author impersonator. He despised sitting for daguerrotypes[24] — the antebellum equivalent to the publicity head shot—a view he made clear both in an angry letter to Duyckinck and in his portrayal of Queequeg's business of peddling shrunken heads in *Moby-Dick*. The prospect of someone "playing" him would only play into his sense of the sham of professional identity. Melville thus anticipated Kurt Vonnegut's postmodern observation that "We are what we pretend to be. So we should be careful what we pretend to be."[25] Writing, Melville excelled at; impersonating an author, he could have been arrested for.

So if I would admittedly have drawn an arbitrary line at author impersonators, but willingly accepted, say, actors in the roles of *Moby-Dick* characters, how could I possibly justify attending a nonstop reading of this novel, which presents itself as outrageous, impossible, lunatic, and a little silly? It is a state of mind that says anything is possible, a challenge, a dare to read perhaps the greatest novel of all time in just one day. Nonsense, yes, but worthy and wonderful nonsense all the same, as the event, like its athletic counterpart, typifies these ennobling quotes in praise of human aspiration: "I know of no more encouraging fact than the unquestionable ability of man to elevate himself by a conscious endeavor," Henry David Thoreau writes;[26] "Competitive running," like this nonstop reading, "is a metaphor for the unresting aspiration of the human spirit," says Roger Robinson; Ahab's gnashing, frenzied spirit rings out in Bill Rogers's claim that "successful marathoners have to lose their cool, and allow this irrational, animal consciousness to take over"; "Racing," like this reading, "is where I have to face the truth about myself,"

Joe Henderson proclaims; and the ultimate justification for embracing this nonlinear event comes from Clarence Demar's *Marathon*: "Do most of us want life on the same calm level as a geometrical problem? Certainly we want our pleasures more varied with both mountains and valleys of emotional joy, and marathoning furnishes that."[27]

Charting a Course

"I LOVE ALL men who *dive*," Melville said once in a letter praising Emerson. Like the sea, at its greatest depths, the pressure is immense in *Moby-Dick*. Most Melvillians, like hardcore distance runners, do not view their marathon reading activities as a frivolous pastime but as an ancient obsession born out of necessity and survival in antiquity—a hunt, after all, for a vital resource—and linked to the advancement of civilization. They are "thought-divers, that have been diving & coming up again with blood-shot eyes since the world began."[28] However many nonacademic or "fannish" participants there might be at the reading, they are not light readers, just as the Colorado cross-country team members are not joggers out for lighthearted amusement. Professional academics, furthermore, can actually do better work when they apply their scholarly knowledge to the activities and events of author societies. The study of print culture and book history, if done honestly, demands immersion into our own contemporary, even popular, culture.[29] The reading stands as one of the best examples of "town vs. gown" cooperation, showcasing the continuity between classical literature and the lives of real readers.

To this end, I view the readers in this event on equal footing, honoring the wisdom of the Melville Society's academic experts along with noncredentialed readers, and indeed, I seek to find links between professional and amateur reactions to the text. I am not theoretically wedded to any one critical perspective but instead draw from a variety of passionate readings of the novel regardless of paradigm. Hard-core runners and Melvillians congregate in clans and operate according to an ethos, bordering on obsession, largely impenetrable to the mass public. Commitment to the chase and relentless obsession bind Melville's disciples into distinct subcultures that define themselves according to their relation to text, echoing the very characters of *Moby-Dick* itself. The typical *Moby-Dick* Marathon reader attends in order to look into the eyes of and hear the voices of others with utter sincerity and commitment (in a world where these qualities are becoming increasingly scarce) to this voyage, to keeping the wakeful living nightmare—dreamed in Pittsfield in 1850 in full view of the white snow hill of Mount Greylock—vibrating with the fear, weariness, love, obsession, vitality, and insane dreams of this novel. The reading does not fit into the practical commercial world of print culture. Neither did *Moby-Dick* fit into the career plans or mass market poised to receive Melville's work. The reading is an anomaly, as is the novel itself, along with its herculean process of composition.

Just as the prospect of running a marathon is difficult to explain to non-runners, explaining the enthusiasm for and deep significance of this event to nonbelievers is nearly impossible. To the uninitiated, no explanation will suffice, as the Zen saying goes, and to the initiated, no explanation is necessary. Experience is the best teacher to achieve that objective.

Just as Ishmael's malaise is remedied by going to sea and befriending Queequeg, and thus escaping from the disembodied, commodified, and restrained world of land, the reading is not a purchased experience; it is physical, free (aside from the nominal museum admission), and inclusive. As such, it evades the culture's movement toward the increasingly abstract, disembodied human interactions dominated by the Internet, the most common of which is online payment, perhaps the most conspicuous of our civilized hypocrisies and bland deceits.

The New Bedford reading offers a novel alternative to such alienating, isolated consumption. The novel itself reaches outward, away from such common practices associated with land, in a series of searches—both physical and intellectual—striving toward meaning or belief, that are constantly undercut. Sometimes that idealism is fulfilled, sometimes cruelly dashed, at a particular reading. The reality of a live reading is that one's favorite segment has an equal chance of being read terribly, or read by a child, or read by a person who races through the passage or butchers its pronunciation, or by someone who gets cadence and tone just right, in a perfect Massachusetts accent cut with a gravelly brogue that conjures up the creaking wood and the salty sea spray of waves battering the bow.

Everyone's stake in the reading is linked to that individual's claim for the leviathan himself. What do readers and listeners seek in him? What does the reading confirm about the world and ourselves? Answers to these questions reflect on the White Whale as the embodiment of good or evil, on the juxtaposition between Ishmael's reflective thinking, his loomings, and Ahab's business of charting and chasing Moby-Dick on iron rails. All of the participants present seek some aspect of the novel we have known and expect to encounter again, call it a *fast fish*—a scene, an image, a turn of phrase, a metaphysical riff, a key speech, or an interaction between characters. We are all still nonetheless open to what we call the *loose fish*—the unexpected surprises; the illuminations along the way; the new meanings in brit, ambergris, or the work of the specksynder which we may have overlooked before. The experience of the reading thus necessarily avoids, even while offering the narrative pleasures of, an absurdist pursuit where, like Ishmael's first whale chase, all are randomly tossed from the boat. We are like Ahab, waiting for something that we know will arrive, something we remember from our private readings, a life-altering encounter we are revisiting. "Hast seen the White Whale?" is Ahab's mantra through the last third of the novel. Indeed, we all have faced the Whale before and must now, deep in the frosty January night, find him once again. Presentiment reigns. What will he do to us now? How will he affect us in this moment? He changed our lives at least once; will he do it again today?

Much of *Moby-Dick* is inscrutable. Salman Rushdie has said that the novel is a condemnation of fundamentalism, and indeed, absolutist definitions destabilize under Ishmael's scrutiny throughout the novel. "Herman Melville delves into these dark waters," he writes, "in order to offer us a very modern parable: Ahab, gripped by his possession, perishes; Ishmael, a man without strong feeling or powerful affiliations, survives. The self-interested modern man is the sole survivor; those who worship the whale—for pursuit is a form of worship—perish by the whale."[30]

I asked the marathon readers about ambiguity and inscrutability in the text and in the world today. What do readers do with allusions they are not familiar with? Do they search for resolution, pursue further inquiry, or do they prefer the mystery? Does the reading ready them to dig deeper, like Ishmael's probings into Queequeg's past in "Biographical"? To puzzle over the text's ambiguities (the painting in the Spouter Inn, the markings on the whale in "The Blanket") that riddle the interconnected web of transnational contemporary issues of the oil business, terrorism, war, and technology? How, if at all, could a live, continuous reading support a text which demands both quiet reflection—"you cannot run and read it,"[31] Melville said—and rereading of it in context of the broader questions of our contemporary world? The challenge is there: "Read it if you can," Ishmael says of the Whale's brow.[32] But at this pace, an appreciation for minute nuance can only be fleeting.

This is the cost of a new appreciation for the work as an organic whole, for its unifying narrative sweep, for its interconnected chapter clusters and embedded closures.

Many readers bring their own copy of *Moby-Dick* to the reading, clutching it close with spiritual adhesion, holding it as if it were the Bible. Not just any edition, but one that is annotated, marked with the tracks of their lives, bearing various inks and handwritings, observations and responses reflecting the different phases of their lives. It is comfortable, worn in, an extension of themselves. I cradle my tattered 1980 Signet paperback Brentano's Bookstore copy purchased in San Francisco with my father when I was thirteen, my window into the world, my courage-teacher. *Moby-Dick* is a frank and subtle confrontation of the chaos and absurdity of our existence, a novel that refuses the option of shutting down the senses, but rather, inspires us to keep them more acute, more attuned for insight, transcendence, "for wonders supernatural without dying for them," as in the blacksmith's own luminous self-discovery that rescues him from self-annihilation.[33]

The desire to talk back to Melville is social, not solipsistic; the embodied marathon reading, though it does not allow critical intrusion into the narrative flow, still ritualizes the opposite energies of Ahab, whose speech is consistently confessional and self-referential. To bear witness to the novel as a whole is to do something akin to Ishmael's project. Both bear witness to something of profound significance, and rather than carry that weight in silence, they speak it. It is my privilege to be able to speak of the event in this forum of critical and social commentary after taking in Melville's exhausting sweep of all western civilization, which sets up Ishmael's testimony "not as an individual case speaking for a general law," as Eyal Peretz says. Rather, he continues, "it has to establish itself as a witness to the whole history of Western literature, [to its] existence and survival as the keeper and guard of this horrible excess of numerous wounding white events." Moby Dick, the whale, speaks as if "the whole of Western literature requires that the entire body of Western literature, in a way, be understood as testifying to *Moby-Dick*."[34] For most of us, we have never witnessed another such book; it is to the prospect of embarking on the journey of its discovery that we now turn.

PART I

Shipping Out

New Bedford, showing the harbor in 1841. Courtesy MIT Museum.

·1·

That Everlasting Itch

The Allure of Whaling and Marathon Reading

$\mathcal{A}$T THE AGE OF 21 IN 1841, Herman Melville was wayward, restless, recalcitrant, and generally up to no good. Going whaling for him was something like joining the military today for many high school graduates or college dropouts: a last resort and a chance for redemption, even nobility, from a life of dead ends on shore. Whaling at the time was a true adventure; less than half of all crews returned home with the same ship. Most sailors jumped ship at remote locales, eventually joining a series of other vessels, often naval or merchant, and exploring a variety of ports before heading for home. As if he were "hitchhiking throughout the Pacific,"[1] the youthful Melville was something of proto-sixties-era renegade standing beside the highway, thumb extended with cocky assurance.[2]

Like Ishmael, Melville had tried his hand at school teaching, but fate would prevent any future in it. "Herman's School is to be discontinued next week for want of funds until winter," his mother Maria Melville wrote, perturbed at his inability to repay his debts to her. "He thinks of going far-west, as nothing offers for him here—Oh that the Lord may strengthen me to bear all my troubles, & be pleased to sustain me under them."[3] And west he went to seek his fortune. Returning empty-handed, he fell on the support of his tireless advocate and brother Gansevoort, who would later play an instrumental role in the publication of his first novel, *Typee* (1846). As a lawyer and active player in the political world, Gansevoort was highly effective as a publicist and promoter of Melville's early literary career. He would die soon after seeing to the publication of *Typee*, however, leaving Melville on his own in the literary marketplace.

Melville was every bit the wild, proto-hippie upon his return from the West, his hair and beard long and shaggy in contrast to the clean-cut man-about-town image of Gansevoort. Before his brother set sail on the *Acushnet*,

Gansevoort was pleased that "Herman has had his hair sheared & whiskers shaved & looks more like a Christian than usual."[4] But the makeover did not help his job prospects, as he had no marketable skills,[5] unlike Fly (Eli James Murdock), his western traveling companion, who possessed impeccable penmanship. Fly would find work almost immediately in New York City as a copyist, a scrivener much like the protagonist of Melville's 1854 tale, "Bartleby, the Scrivener; A Story of Wall-Street." Melville's misfortune of possessing abominable penmanship, which made him unemployable in the service economy in positions equivalent to those of office assistant or receptionist, would become our great fortune, as it directly led to the experience behind *Moby-Dick*. For Gansevoort's last option at placing his wayward brother in gainful, if temporary, employment fit for a vital, voracious twenty-one-year-old was to ship him out on a whaler.

The Allure of Whaling

MELVILLE EMBRACED the opportunity and was exhilarated at the thought of setting out on an epic journey to match his western one, this time at sea, bound for the South Pacific. Melville would transform this situation with his creative alchemy in *Moby-Dick*. Ishmael gravitates seaward to break free from a depressing, claustrophobic life on land, "a damp, drizzly November in my soul."[6] He gladly exchanges whatever authority he enjoyed as a schoolmaster, "making the tallest boys stand in awe of" him, to "go as a simple sailor."[7] Whaling offers renewal of body ("the wholesome exercise and pure air on the forecastle deck") and mind ("meditation and water are wedded forever")[8] more as a psychological last resort than an occupational one. Ishmael is already gainfully employed as a schoolteacher while Melville, much to the chagrin of Gansevoort, was not.[9] Embarking on a whaling voyage means leaving behind much more than the lee shore; it also means leaving behind one's routines and sense of identity. The close quarters and extended time at sea, sometimes up to three years, present an all-consuming yet hardly one-dimensional world for the whaleman and provide all the allure of full physical and mental immersion. For common sailors, the profits are negligible, as Ishmael acknowledges. Though a green hand whaleman, Melville himself was no foreigner to the sea or to low payment as a common sailor, since he had sailed on a merchant ship in that capacity to Liverpool, England, in 1839. (His novel *Redburn* draws directly from his experience of this first voyage.) But aboard a whaler, the physical risks are considerably higher and the work far more dangerous and dirty than on a merchant ship; the Spartan self-denial of fine food, physical comfort, and female companionship are significant compromises. But the nearness to the elemental core that weds nature and commerce and to the prospect of exploration, discovery, and adventure, for Melville and Ishmael, outweigh those considerable costs.

As marathon readers, we also are drawn toward full immersion in an adventure that brings us in close quarters with others. We embrace the opportunity to make this novel's sublime nightmare come true through the inspiration of the very readers who breathe life into the tale. The vocal reading of this novel in particular makes crew, rather than passive passengers, of us all. Working on board a whaler, like participating in this reading, drives off the maladies attendant to the passenger's role as passive consumer, fussy and inconsolable, prone "to be over conscious of my lungs," like so many intolerant travelers who become "sea-sick—grow quarrelsome—don't sleep of nights—do not enjoy themselves much, as a general thing."[10] Marathon readers and audience are not a fastidious or needy group, for we are in hot pursuit of a fast fish, and like the lookout aloft on the masthead, must have our powers of perception on the alert. The novel's most profound moments we must catch; its elusiveness demands that we must actively, if not doggedly, pursue its riches. Like the modernist literature of the 1920s, whose authors revived interest in Melville, *Moby-Dick*'s meanings are difficult to grasp, but with focus and intensity, they can be spotted in all their serene subtlety, their patterns emerging gracefully like the course of the whale himself.

For Melville, going to sea was an imperiled situation that drew him closer to death so that, like Ahab, he could better feel the life in him. We marathon readers similarly read all night—go through the dead predawn hours, the graveyard of human consciousness—for the very sake of vitality. Shipping out with this marathon reading is decidedly unreasonable and romantic by nature, a mystical prospect of the sort that echoes Queequeg insisting Yojo, "his little black god," select the ship for him and Ishmael. We "set about this business with a determined rushing sort of energy and vigor," like Queequeg and Ishmael.[11] What fueled Melville's own "rushing sort of energy and vigor" to ship out with the *Acushnet* were his romantic dreams of life at sea. He had likely heard of or read reviews or portions of Richard Henry Dana Jr.'s *Two Years Before the Mast*, a book that had been receiving a great deal of notoriety at the time. Melville would later write to Dana on May 1, 1850, that "those strange congenial feelings with which after my first voyage, I for the first time read 'Two Years Before the Mast,' and while so engaged was, as it were, tied & welded to you by a sort of Siamese link of affectionate sympathy."[12] This was the perfect venture for a "wild dreamer" drawn to the glory of whaling and even to the macho swagger and sexual charisma the culture had attached to whalemen at the time, whose work, though dangerous and dirty, was to hunt nothing less than the largest mammal on earth, traveling to unknown reaches of the globe to do so.[13]

The romance of whaling transformed whalemen into "a species of culture hero."[14] Bravery, honor, and glory, much like those attached to soldiers at war, were associated with the dangerous whale-hunting methods that had become well known in the culture. This was a sort of hand-to-hand combat in which chase boats accosted whales and harpooners, like Queequeg, would hurl their weapons with great accuracy into the beast to subdue it while the others attacked with their lances. If they were successful, the whale would bleed to death and be drawn to the main ship for "cutting in." The close, hostile encounter with an animal over sixty feet long weighing over sixty tons, along with the adventure of sailing to unknown seas and barbarous coasts, made whalemen celebrities. Ahab's final three-day confrontation with the White Whale has him physically wrestling the beast, his whalebone peg leg shattered in the melee, "half smothered in the foam of the whale's insolent tail, and too much of a cripple to swim—though he could still keep afloat, even in the heart of such a whirlpool that; helpless Ahab's head was seen, like a tossed bubble which the least chance shock might burst."[15] The two grapple face to face in their final conflict, as Ahab deliriously howls, "I stab at thee; for hate's sake I spit my last breath at thee."[16] By the 1850s, such epic battles with whales had become theatre, especially in E. C. Williams's traveling lectures, which enacted the whale hunt on stage, complete with painted ocean vista backdrops, a fully rigged whaleboat, and musical accompaniment.[17] As the industry was fading after its heyday the previous decade, it had officially entered the world of camp, not unlike the comic books of the 1950s that valorized World War II combat scenes in stylized melodramatic narratives.

The whaleman's charisma was built upon the mortal risk inherent in the business of engaging a creature of stunning proportions in highly dangerous conflict. Equally charismatic, the sperm whale is appealing as an object of natural wonder, as it boasts a dizzying array of superlatives. No other type of whale is known to have deliberately sunk ships; it has the largest skull of all whales, as Ishmael considers in his comparison of "The Sperm Whale's Head" and "The Right Whale's Head" in chapters 74 and 75; it reaches depths beyond those of any other whale (over a mile), and thus has the distinction of having the largest lung capacity, the key to his "surplus stock of vitality," as Ishmael calls it, which enables him to stay under water over ninety minutes — far longer than any other kind of whale.[18] As noted in the chapter "The Blanket," the sperm whale has the thickest skin of all mammals, up to fourteen inches. In proportion to its body, its tail is the longest of any species of leviathan, a stunningly sublime work of art as it arches out of the water in all its beauty and strength, a powerful tool of propulsion for the animal, and a weapon known to destroy men and whaleboats in a single blow. The sperm whale was the most profitable to catch as it yielded as much as three tons, or twenty-three barrels, of spermaceti, an extremely valuable source of clean-burning oil for illumination. The biggest cash prize of the whaling industry is fittingly hard won, as it possesses tremendous speed, elusiveness, and a willingness to fight back fiercely when attacked. Unlike any other whale, the sperm whale fights rather than feeds with his teeth, as the jaws, once fully extended, are big enough to accommodate several full-grown men.[19] Its tail and head, however, claimed the most lives of antebellum whalemen, as it frequently rammed ship hulls at speeds of up to twenty knots, buffering the impact, ironically, with the treasure trove of spermaceti encased in its head, the very object of the hunters' desire.

Whereas the whaling industry certainly made New Bedford wealthy in the 1840s, as evidenced by the chapter "The Street," Melville never went to sea to make his fortune and thus never saw the whale as merely swimming capital. Melville already had sought his fortune out west and was now on an adventure, shipping out in a spirit more like Ishmael's than that of the antebellum entrepreneur and trapper John Jacob Astor. Melville's sense of the whale certainly included its status as capital, an apt symbol for his market culture's increasingly frenetic chase of money, but it encompassed much more. His broad understanding of the whale bespoke his broad understanding of the world, which stood in sharp contrast to the materialistic farmers Henry David Thoreau assails in *Walden* for seeing the leaves of their crops as so many dollars waving in the wind. Indeed, the other allure of the whale is that he lives beyond our reach, seemingly in another world. The whale dives too deep for us to fathom; scientists still are at a loss for explaining how sperm whales catch their prey, since no pictures or film exist of them eating 3,000 feet beneath the surface in the darkest depths of the ocean.[20] Leviathan remains a mystery.

The mystification of the whale, particularly his legendary status, compounded both his position as the object of capitalist pursuit and the attendant dangers of physically confronting him, setting the imagination of the young Melville on fire. For Melville, the lure of shipping out with a whaler was fueled by a well-circulated story, first told in *Knickerbocker* magazine in May 1839, of a white sperm whale named Mocha Dick. Melville's uncle in Albany, Peter Gansevoort, had a subscription to the magazine, and it was readily available across the nation. More important, Melville had likely heard the story of this real whale at gams or aboard the *Acushnet*. For here was a legend that came of fact: Mocha Dick was "an old bull whale of prodigious size and strength," *"white as wool,"* about whom whalemen would frequently ask, "Any news from Mocha Dick?"[21] The whale was battle scarred, much like Moby Dick, with "not less than twenty harpoons" in his back, "rusted momentos of many a desperate encounter."[22] The story was widely circulated at sea among whalemen, and thus rumors of his reappearance after death surfaced.[23] Melville would seize upon this in the novel by emphasizing Moby Dick's ubiquitous immortality.

In *Moby-Dick*, "Chief among [Ishmael's] motives was the overwhelming idea of the whale himself. Such a portentous and mysterious monster roused all my curiosity. Then the wild and distant seas where he rolled his island bulk; the undeliverable, nameless perils of the whale."[24] Such perils were inspired by Melville's own fascination with tales of Mocha Dick ramming and sinking ships, as well as the grisly tale of the *Essex*, a whaler sunk by a sperm whale,[25] whose surviving crew resorted to cannibalism aboard a chase boat in the weeks following. Melville had heard this tale from William Henry Chase, the teenage son of *Essex* captain Owen Chase, at a July 23, 1841, gam with the *Lima* seven months into the *Acushnet*'s voyage. All of these factors, Ishmael (and by extension, Melville) confesses, "helped to sway me to my wish,"[26] as Melville recollected his own youthful motives from Arrowhead, his Pittsfield farmhouse, one decade later. His room, significantly, looked out on Mount Greylock, his stand-in whale: "one grand hooded phantom, like a snow hill in the air."[27]

Melville's family was likely oblivious to the romantic imagination the wayward twenty-one-year-old was cultivating. They were mainly concerned for his safety, and their careful appraisal of the situation led them to conclude that, while dangerous, shipping out with the *Acushnet*, especially on Gansevoort's good word, was right for him at this time in his life. They were by no means averse to such a low-paying position as a green hand on a whaler (skilled harpooners like Queequeg earned slightly more than one percent of profits, while unskilled rookies like Ishmael could only garner three tenths of a percent, or the "three-hundredth lay") since his Melvill and Gansevoort cousins had already made whaling voyages themselves and heartily encouraged the young lad to do the same. Now the question, as it confronts Ishmael in *Moby-Dick*, remained: which one to ship with? Only Yojo knows—or does he?

Shipping out with a whaler in 1841, like attending a marathon reading of *Moby-Dick* in 2009, presented a range of options and ports. For Melville, Nantucket offered a fraction of the vessels available at New Bedford. Nantucket was slowly giving way to New Bedford in its reign over the industry, just as Mystic Seaport has handed over the title as the most celebrated marathon reading venue to the New Bedford Whaling Museum. Nantucket, Ishmael proclaims, is now barren, choked with sand, so devoid of life that the weeds there are rumored to be imported, totally isolated, "shut up, belted about, enclosed, surrounded."[28] But the choice is not obvious for the marathon reader, just as it was not obvious for Melville, or Ishmael by extension, whose final selection of the *Pequod* has more to do with the romance of antiquity and an instinct for the boat's storied past than any reasonable judgment. For the marathon reader, is it Mystic or New Bedford? Summer or winter? Cake or grog? An antebellum whaleship or the Seamen's Bethel? A significant decision indeed, but one fraught with the dizzy hand of fate which points toward unintended consequences, voiced emphatically by Ishmael and Queequeg choosing nothing less than Ahab's ship, a vessel bound for the White Whale with a captain willing first to exploit and then to sacrifice his entire crew in the process.

Leaving Queequeg in his room to his Ramadan, Ishmael "sallied out among the shipping" to find three whalers to choose from: the *Devil-Dam*, the *Tit-bit*, and the *Pequod*.[29] The *Pequod* strikes him as "the very ship for us" initially because of the musty allure of history in its wood, the shadowy grandeur of the past, as Washington Irving called it. Not unlike Geoffrey Crayon, the narrative persona of Irving's famous *Sketch Book* (1819–1820) that deeply influenced Melville, Ishmael is taken by the "old fashioned claw-footed" antiquity of the ship, "long seasoned and weather-stained in the typhoons and calms of all four oceans . . . her ancient decks were worn and wrinkled."[30] Most marathon readers are attracted to the event for its historical significance, its promise to transport us back through the antebellum streets of New Bedford and onto the *Acushnet* with Melville on that frosty January morning in 1841. The whaling museum provides the perfect chronological portal to send us back through time, with the trappings of the trade in all its grandeur spread before us, the ghosts of Melville himself and Gansevoort treading down the aisle and into a pew in the Seamen's Bethel across the street. Indeed, the *Pequod* attracts Ishmael by the marks of its storied past, a veteran of wars with whales, like its captain, "her old hull's complexion was darkened like a French grenadier's, who has alike fought in Egypt and Siberia."[31]

In December of 1840, Melville sauntered beneath a canopy of placards upon landing in New Bedford from New York, likely by steamship, with Gansevoort. The signs above the small offices, the antebellum equivalent of today's military recruiting offices in suburban strip malls, beckoned whalers to enter and sign on. One early account of the whaling industry depicts such recruiting venues as traps for young men naïve to the risks and peril of the trade. In shipping offices, as one analyst of the industry from the era observed, "the runaway young man from the country is entrapped; stories are told him, which he, from his want of knowledge readily believes, and thus becomes an easy victim to the wiles of those heartless men who get their living by selling men for a term of years, uncertain in their number, at five dollars a head."[32] Disturbingly, the language alludes in some ways to the slave trade, as well as to the worst of the northern market's guile and treachery, to the buying and selling of human stock for industry. But Melville was less naïve, as his own romantic dreams were readily disabused of the notion that he would be on a pleasure cruise free from real work rooted in the exigencies of the world of trade. He knew a whale ship was, in part, a floating factory, "the Pacific as sweatshop,"[33] and indeed knew his place on it as a lowly worker, for "who ain't a slave?" Melville asks through Ishmael, fully recognizing that his adventure is defined in part by labor and profit.[34]

When they approached the harbor on the Acushnet River, Melville was likely struck by the neatness and organization of the industry before him, with some of the largest and newest vessels in the world docked before giant granite warehouses. The whaling business, at this point, impressed him as efficient and orderly, and setting foot on the *Acushnet*, built at Mattapoisett and announced as sailing from Fairhaven on its maiden voyage, provided a feast for his imagination. The ship pointed toward the industrial future as emphatically as Ishmael's *Pequod* testified to its grizzled veteran antiquity. For here, aboard the *Acushnet*, was evidence of the human community of specialized market production, with the instruments of the trades of sail-maker, blacksmith, carpenter, harpooner, and cook all assembled around the tryworks, epicenter of the main deck and the roiling generators of profit, giant pots designed to boil down whale blubber and spermaceti (from the sperm whale's head) into profitable oil and fine wax. "The Doubloon," which depicts Ahab's ingenious transfiguration of his personal psychological obsession for revenge into the worship of capital, is the symbolic expression of the tryworks. Herein lies the final step of transforming whales into the raw materials for corsets, hairbrushes, brooms, perfume, and lamp oil, an expression of its bold, energetic, ingenious industry that made New Bedford rich.

Once in the cabin of the *Acushnet*, Melville observed an immaculate and tidy image of his quarters aboard the ship. Totally unused, the bedding was spotless and new; he could even stand fully upright given the six-foot ceiling in the forecastle of this brand new vessel. With Gansevoort still as Melville's companion and urbane foil (paradoxically inspiring the fictional foil for Ishmael's cannibal companion Queequeg in *Moby-Dick*), Melville would sign on for "1/175th" of the profits on Christmas Day of 1840. Two days later, he and Gansevoort would make a pilgrimage to the Seamen's Bethel atop Johnny Cake Hill. The chapel is a virtual shrine and monument to those who lost their lives in pursuit of leviathan, with artwork and inscriptions commemorating the dead whalemen. In some ways it is as moving a place as the Viet Nam War Veterans' Memorial Wall in Washington, D.C. Melville confronted his own mortality that day, as he and Gansevoort listened to a sermon by Enoch Mudge, a minister preaching a maritime gospel seasoned by his own years at sea.

"I knew not; but so many are the unrecorded accidents in the fishery," Ishmael observes in the "Whaleman's Chapel" where Father Mapple preaches. Memorials surround him, one in "the sacred memory of . . . one of the boats' crews of the ship *Eliza* who were towed out of sight by a whale, on the off-shore ground in the Pacific," and another dedicated to a captain, "who in the bows of his boat was killed by a sperm whale on the coast of Japan," a foreshadowing of Ahab's own demise.[35] The intangible quality of a death at sea, its "bitter blanks in those black-bordered marbles which cover no ashes," bespeaks a disappearance of body and soul into the black void, "a speechlessly quick chaotic bundling of a man into Eternity."[36] Death here is silent and invisible, a blankness Ishmael also sees in the brow, the indefinable face, and mostly in the whiteness of the whale.

In the days following his signing on, Melville wrote his mother to bid her farewell. Although the letter is not extant, one can distill the essence of Melville's spirit upon shipping out with the *Acushnet*. Maria reports that

> Last week I received a long letter from Herman, who has embarked for a long voyage to the Pacific, under the most favorable auspices, and feeling perfectly happy, Gansevoort was with him to the very last and assisted with his more mature judgment in supplying him with every comfort, Gansevoort says he never saw him so completely happy, as when he had determined upon a situation and all was settled, he sends much love and affectionate embrace to his Sisters.[37]

Now "completely happy," even "perfectly happy," Melville could taste his future, as "the floodgates of the wonder world swung open," as Ishmael says, since this voyage promised him access to "forbidden seas" and "barbarous coasts" giving vent to his "wild conceits."[38] Maria has a mother's concern in the letter, finding solace in Gansevoort's paternal guidance, his "more mature judgment" giving her peace of mind that Melville's own twenty-one-year-old judgment could not provide. From her point of view, like Gansevoort's, the concerns were to keep him comfortable, happy, and loved. He assured them in a letter written from Peru sometime between June 23 and July 2, 1841, according to Gansevoort, that "He was then in perfect health, and not dissatisfied with his lot—the fact of his being one of crew so much superior in morals and early advantages to the ordinary run of whaling crews affords him with constant gratification."[39] But such gratification was not enough to keep him on board, since he jumped ship with Richard Tobias Greene in Nuku Hiva in the Marquesas eighteen months into the voyage on July 9, 1842. The episodes with cannibals and beautiful native women fictionalized in *Typee* originally took place here. (The *Acushnet* would eventually return on May 13, 1845, after a journey of four years and four months.) By all accounts, Captain Valentine Pease maintained a well-run ship. Despotic sea captains would emerge later when Melville served on the *Lucy Ann*, an Australian whaler wracked with such controversy that crew refused to work given the ill health of one of its mates, Henry Smyth, in August 1842.

Melville shipped out with the opposite mindset of the "insulated Quakerish Nantucketer," Captain Peleg, with whom Ishmael would sign his contract.[40] Full of "insular prejudices, and rather distrustful of all aliens," Peleg strikingly contrasts with the open-minded, questing Ishmael, who proclaims earlier that "I am quick to perceive a horror but could still be social with it"[41] and later takes Queequeg, a cannibal, for a "friend, thought I, since Christian kindness has proved but hollow courtesy."[42] Like those in attendance at the reading, Ishmael's perspective is broad. The chief reason he gives Peleg for wanting to ship out with a whaler is to see nothing less than the entire world itself. *Moby-Dick* itself engages the practical quotidian tasks of whaling to access the wider world in the spirit of Ishmael's reply: "Well, sir, I want to see what whaling is. I want to see the world."[43] It is a wonderfully simple statement syntactically, yet it bespeaks his expansive scope of vision, and tireless intellectual and spiritual searching. Peleg suggests that he rest content with the narrow vision of the world that is right in front of him, rather than suffer the monotony of "nothing but water" and risk squalls around Cape Horn. "Can't ye see the world where you stand?" he asks a refusing Ishmael, determined to "go a-whaling" since "the *Pequod* was as good a ship as any" yet troubled with a mysteriously disturbed captain lurking below deck, seething in his madness.[44]

So this departure becomes a stepping forth in time and place, a broadening of life's narrow perspectives. Such is the situation with the reading as well, for it is a commitment, a leap onto a ship that will drift away from one's prior life: this reading will take us on a familiar voyage, but we will experience its course anew. Monotony lurks in a nonstop reading of this length, just as the thought of "nothing but water" on a global voyage threatens to shake Ishmael of his romantic vision. Squalls around Cape Horn are like the moments when mind and body revolt at the duration and dips in the event, the inevitable "rough patches," as the English euphemistically describe the most harrowing moments of the athletic marathon. But go a-whaling we must, as we ship out for the New Bedford Whaling Museum in January of 2009, chasing our futures through a vision 168 years in the past.

The Allure of the Moby-Dick Marathon Reading

THE DIVE INTO the past, and all the risks and romance that entails, unites all in attendance at the *Moby-Dick* Marathon reading. It is easy to underestimate why people attend the event, whether they read, listen, or both, since so many attendees describe their motives in terms frequently bluntly simplistic, implying either an unwillingness to unpack the metaphysical fine tunings of their motives or in some cases acknowledging the futility of providing a reasonable explanation to the uninitiated. A scene from the 2008 reading depicts actions that speak of a stalwart determination behind words more politely superficial than indicative of the depth of the spectators' commitment. Asked what concoction she was mixing up during the reading, a young woman said it was a drink to keep her and her friend awake. They planned to stay for the entire marathon, and when asked why they came, the young woman replied with a smile, "We just like *Moby-Dick*," adjusting their nest of blankets and pillows arranged under the stairs.[45] Her answer is something like the elliptical, even glib response mountain climbers have given to explain their harrowing Himalayan ascents: we climb it because it's there. *Moby-Dick*'s presence is mountainous; we climb it in a day because, in all the fraught, jarring, absurd, sublime, and transcendent complexity it holds, it's there and we just like it.

It is particularly appealing that not just Americans but an international mix of wandering individualistic Melvillians — a "people of Ishmaels" — share the usually solitary pleasures of reading *Moby-Dick* in this unique event.[46] We are not alone as readers in our enthusiasm; we can hear it in the voices of the readers who dramatize the first exciting chase scene and chuckle at its absurd conclusion, laughing with Ishmael at his excessive presentiment and romantic anticipation in the chapter "The Hyena." The normally individual, piecemeal reading of this gargantuan novel is now communal and unceasing; we ebb with the rhythms of the prose and sea aboard the same ship, yet all experience the novel's nuances differently, often radically so, as do the crew in their vastly disparate readings of the Spanish coin nailed to the mast in "The Doubloon." The bark *Lagoda* housed in an adjacent room and a giant whale skeleton hanging overhead provide common objects of visual meditation to accompany the verbal feast before us. The uninitiated reader enters the museum like a child attending a first big-league ball game, the field impossibly bright and green, white lines crisp and straight, infield dirt meticulously smooth, in all its pastoral purity. For Melvillians, this is our field of dreams, "an experience of SPACE, its power and price" as Charles Olson says, with "the Pacific as part of our geography, another West, prefigured in the Plains"[47] — a Pacific Ocean not unlike the heart of Iowa, as brit, the yellow substance that right whales feed upon, becomes the stuff of meadows, "boundless fields of ripe and golden wheat."[48]

If you build it, they will come; Melville built it, and the New Bedford Whaling Museum and others have choreographed its reading, so that we will move toward the event, as if drawn toward the water to which all paths lead: "Take any path you please, and ten to one it carries you down in a dale, and leaves you there by a pool in the stream. . . . There is magic in it. Let the most absent-minded of men be plunged in the deepest reveries . . . meditation and water are forever wedded."[49] Set the feet of any Melvillian going in early January, and they will inevitably lead to New Bedford. As word spreads of the magic of this event, of the allure of "the deepest reveries" to be plunged into at this harbor town, more neophytes like Ishmael himself attend. Though most evade such an Ishmaelesque confession of their romantic urges—the New England upper lip remains forever stiff—otherwise flatly utilitarian understandings of the purpose of the event betray a deeper passion. Its function is to "galvanize interest in Melville, and in the book, and perhaps, most important, the museum," according to Raymond Veary, a former assistant district attorney costumed as Ishmael and honored with the privilege of reading the first lines of the novel.[50] "It's a humbling experience," former New Bedford Whaling Museum Director Anne B. Brengle said of the 2000 reading. "Every year we get a lot of new people, and it's just delightful."[51] James Russell would take over her position in 2009 and thus inherit an embarrassment of riches in the success of the reading. Social and civic benefits aside, the former D.A. wears his enthusiasm in his costume, and the former director of the museum reveals hers in her astonishment at the event's renewing and building vitality seen in the parade of new faces that enters her door annually, flattering her professionally, yet humbling her with the truth that the event has developed an evolving life of its own.

The promotion of reading in general and the plight of the whaling museum in particular bears with it a civic and social balm, a panacea for the liabilities of life among technology and its attendant postmodern ills in a charmingly retro event. Ricardo Pitts-Wiley maintains that it is "good for us," like medicine we might take to cleanse our souls, to take in *Moby-Dick*. "It's simple," the performance artist, educator, and youth advocate said. "We're saying, if you read *Moby-Dick*, you will be better." He is referring to people in prisons and gangs, in streets and in schools in Pawtucket, Rhode Island, where he and his wife Bernadet are founders and directors of Mixed Magic Theatre. He encourages youth who do not read much, whose parents also do not read much, to read *Moby-Dick*, despite resistance ("Rick, man, this is *hard*," they protest) and to "produce a theatrical performance, an adaptation of the novel in their own idiom. But they have to read the book; absorb it entirely." His aim is for ten thousand people—kids, neighbors, students—in Pawtucket to read the novel to build community and pride.[52]

Readers who bring small children to the event take a similar pedagogical approach, saying it will teach their children to value the literary world. The promotion of reading in general has been cited as one of the virtues of the event; a ten-year-old boy read from the podium at the 2008 event and a five-year-old boy was in attendance reading along with his children's edition of *Moby-Dick*. The reading indeed has the allure of being low tech, like the nineteenth century itself, and thus resuscitates the lost art of novel reading in general and of spoken readings, a vestige of the antebellum lyceum circuit, in particular. Author readings today are related to this event, yet they are always commercially driven, with book signings taking place under the assumption that listeners, or at least the majority of them, will purchase a copy of the author's book, often as a form of gratuity. Other public speaking events tend to be predominantly political and thus also driven by self-promotion. Even academic talks without the scholar hawking the latest book are rare. The service to community that the *Moby-Dick* Marathon provides is thus especially rare in our culture and needs to be treasured all the more.

The function of the novel as a social corrective and even as a pedagogical tool brings Melville into the same circle as Shakespeare, whose plays were used to improve the moral fabric of society, through urban projects like Pitts-Wiley's. Reaching the masses with the arts is a noble purpose attached to the marathon. Yet if such objectives to nourish the culture and provide a corrective emotional response to individuals become too self-sacrificial or replete with duty—national, civic, parental, social—one wonders where the wonder has gone in the novel itself, where the obsessive magnetism of the novel itself fits in. Like Shakespeare's plays, *Moby-Dick* is not, even according to its coarsest interpretations, a didactic novel. It is a novel written in the name of the devil, as Melville confided to Hawthorne, a novel broiled in hellfire: "I have written a wicked book, and feel spotless as the lamb."[53] However appropriated as an ambassador of the wholesome and healing qualities of the literary classics, *Moby-Dick*, make no mistake, is at times a Dante-esque trip through hell culminating in a swirling vortex pulling the *Pequod* straight to perdition. If such darkness were not leavened by Ishmael's sunnier and more exultant musings, the book may not have been viewed as pedagogically worthy, just as Shakespeare's bloodiest play, *Titus Andronicus*, is never considered the ideal choice for youth mentoring and urban outreach projects.

The darkness of the novel is as much a draw for readers as its socially and psychologically corrective powers. The whale himself, the danger of the hunt, and the lures of the sea and an all-night reading complement perfectly an insomniac, compulsive captain incapable of rest or sleep. "Ah, God!" Ishmael exclaims, "what trances of torments does that man endure who is consumed with one unachieved revengeful desire. He sleeps with clenched hands; and wakes with his own bloody nails in his palms."[54] With plagued sleep he is no different than Kafka's Gregor Samsa in *The Metamorphosis*, or even Scorsese's Travis Bickle in *Taxi Driver*, also obsessive characters suffering from tormented souls that will not allow them to sleep, a symptom and metaphor for their profound psychological imbalance and aching inner disease. Ahab's insanity is searingly painful and visceral, down to his own whalebone prosthetic that castrates him, robbing him of his manhood. He pours over his frenzied charts by night in a monomania that renders useless the calming effect of his pipe, which, in his frustration, he hurls overboard. "What business have I with a pipe," he fumes. "This thing that is meant for sereneness, to send up mild white vapors among mild white hairs, not among torn iron-grey locks like mine."[55] His story is hardly hopeful, as his wracked soul only worsens as the novel progresses; in many ways we share in his dark desire, for reading *Moby-Dick* nonstop is our "delirious but still methodical scheme," as Ishmael describes the crackpot science of Ahab's geometry of whale chasing.[56] This allure of the novel lurks beneath the surface of such sunny pat assurances as "We just like *Moby-Dick*" and paradoxically coexists with Pitts-Wiley's youth outreach project by bringing the frequently desperate lives of his clientele in touch with the desperation and imbalance of life aboard the *Pequod*, so that they, like the marathon readers, might confront their own demons and give them creative vent to make true the maxim, "If you read *Moby-Dick*, you will be better." We all-night readers, like Ahab, will not stop, will not be better, until we reach the whale.

168 Years Hence: January 3, 2009

WHY ATTEND the *Moby-Dick* Marathon? Was it a desire to connect with whaling's past and Melville's voyage on the *Acushnet*? Did the whale himself attract you? Or was it the voice and vision of Melville that drew you here? Is *Moby-Dick* good for what ails you and society? Or is it more that this novel will not so much function medicinally to correct a deficiency of character already present but that it will make you better in the sense of self-improvement: intellectually, spiritually, and thus psychosocially? On January 3, 2009, I asked the attendees of the *Moby-Dick* Marathon reading such questions. But first, I had to ship out with them myself.

On November 15, 2008, at the stroke of noon, the automated toll-free phone line for the thirteenth annual *Moby-Dick* Marathon reading reservations opened. Naïvely, I underestimated the interest in the event and blithely called late that evening to reserve a reading slot, certainly not a requirement of all who attend the event, but an honor and a level of participation that befits the zeal of one who has committed to staying through the entire event. Over a month later, I discovered that among the 148 reading slots scheduled, each roughly eight to ten minutes long, I was shut out along with a host of other Melvillians. Dazed at the masthead, we who missed the equivalent of the first whale sighting, mostly green hands like Ishmael, did not call at precisely 12:00:01 on November 15. Athletic marathons are also filling up at alarming rates, with many now requiring registration months in advance, some even instituting lottery systems. If the 2009 reading is any indication of the future of the event, a lottery system will likely become a necessity. The New Bedford Whaling Museum's phone registration system clearly indicates the skyrocketing popularity of the event, which in 2009 promised even larger crowds than ever, since January 3 fell on a Saturday that year. Expectations were exceeded, as attendance was the highest ever for the event with a record 170 readers (59 of them women, a confirmation that the novel's gender politics are more inclusive and progressive than once assumed) and 1,300 visitors shipping out. The number of all-night marathoners also promised correspondingly to climb to unprecedented heights, as the weekend hours in 2009 did not interfere with most work schedules. But the hard-core nature of that experience kept the number of all-nighters for 2009 to twenty-two, well within the average for the past twelve years. Like the Boston Marathon to the north, New Bedford's reading marathon will continue to be held on the same calendar day, regardless of where in the week it lands, and like that legendary athletic event, it promises to draw ever greater numbers. What bodes well for the timing is that most academics at all levels enjoy the first week of January free of work-related commitments. Like the young Melville in 1841, shipping out is an option that is particularly appealing to those with unstructured time, during a season saturated with religious ritual (perhaps not coincidentally) from late December to early January.

Undaunted by my first misstep, I set out on a frosty Friday in January for Boston, planning to garner a reading slot by placing my name on the "stand by" list. The gesture was not entirely in vain, or so I was promised by museum staff, given bad weather and the current economic recession. These calamities they attempted to cheer me with, since stand-by volunteers would account for many more openings than could be filled. The Wall Street crash, as we have been told, has its winners, but I was nonetheless not reassured so much as inwardly smiling at the charade of supply and demand that was playing out, which Melville himself would have adored satirizing. Indeed, the thought of Queequeg's rejection of Ishmael's attempts to ship him aboard the *Pequod* came to mind. Where's my grease spot? I can *prove* myself onto this ship, like Queequeg, I thought, not a little ridiculously, in an absurdly postmodern moment reminiscent of James Thurber's fantasy-prone yet palsied Walter Mitty. My moment to pounce, I was told, to put my name on this waiting list, was at 10:30 AM, the time of the lecture by Wyn Kelley on "Crossing the Line and Exploring the Equator in *Moby-Dick*" prior to the noon commencement of the reading. If this doesn't work, I thought, maybe I'll flash a twenty at some bleary-eyed soul set to read at 4 AM in a sick profaning of this decidedly anticommercial ritual. Why not just buy my piece of the whale? Organizations sell tickets to see the Pope, so how blasphemous could that be? No such bizarre and erratic measures were required, however, as Pam, the staffer who counseled me through this awkward two-step guaranteed a spot with such confidence that my inane thoughts fled. Her word proved true, as I eventually received notice by phone that I was scheduled to read at 9:30 AM Sunday, the calm before the storm of the raucous finish that would take place hours later at the approach of midday.

I was spared reading during the desolate wasteland of the event that extends from 2 to 6 AM, hours when some of the most engaging chapters of the novel—"The Monkey-rope," "The Blanket"—fall on somnolently unconscious, if not deaf, ears, as the upper portion of the museum draws sleepy Melvillians to its carpet and relative warmth. The scene looks like the waiting areas of O'Hare airport after mass flight cancellations during the holidays, yet with a difference. Melvillians sleep in public by choice, many of them well equipped to pass the evening meaningfully, if not comfortably. Some have come prepared with sleeping bags, pillows, and blankets, one forming a nest under the protruding fin of what now appears to be a caring whale covering an entire museum wall in relief and to scale. A giant skeleton of a mother right whale and baby hover ethereally from the ceiling nearby completing the sweet serenity of the whale dream, the steady stream of Melville's words read from the podium below flowing through and connecting all. Though not under the protective maternal fin—sleep demands such safety—my head also rested with the crew, just as Ishmael's voice went up with the rest, as I reclined on the carpet of the museum's upper level along with these the most obsessed of Melvillians.

Milton was right: they also serve those who stand and wait. And wait I did, twenty-two hours, to read "The Gilder" and "The *Pequod* Meets the *Rose Bud*." It was not so much a wait to read but a fascinating journey, a kind of quest in its own right that, once achieved, was positively exhilarating. (I describe that experience in the final section of chapter 6, "The Breach.") The quality of the hours of the event, of course, are determined by the quality of one's frame of mind; I found that marking time was the kiss of death for me, which in a larger sense has always been a sign that my outlook on life was suffering. Suffering, of course, is optional in any pursuit, particularly voluntary ones, and marking time—wishing away the hours—is a bad sign, for this is what prisoners do. Robinson Crusoe's first gesture may be to track time, for example, but not to wish it away so much as to find his coordinates in time and space and proceed in his project of naming to make meaning on the unknown island on which he finds himself. The hours of 2 to 6 AM during the reading are not stimulating so much as they are soothing; the readings themselves sound like bedtime stories, as stridently animated or nervous voices are seldom heard from the podium at this time. Empty chairs outnumber occupied ones on the spectator side, and the stable of waiting readers, numbered on their upper left arms like so many triathletes corralled and waiting for the gun, is decidedly thinner than in the prime time of the first and last three hours of the reading. The preponderance of no-shows occurs during this time as well; I realize in these wee hours that I am privileged to be reading at 9:30 AM Sunday, when the crowd grows again to its original size.

With a fortuitous reading spot secured, I arrived on Johnny Cake Hill for the stimulating pre-reading lecture by Wyn Kelley on *Moby-Dick* and the equator, a controlling image in the novel linked to Melville's obsession for lines, weaving, and tapestry, as well as the transgression of social, political, and ideological borders. Like Melville, her words rang with the truth of an eyewitness fresh from firsthand experience at sea. Hers was an exploration of the equator via the Galapagos, a region that entranced Melville. Kelley had us gaze into the eyes of ageless primeval giant tortoises that seemed to stare back at us with the indifference and self-sufficiency of nature itself, a timeless sweep entirely indifferent to human intervention. She spoke to us as a veteran voyager of the open sea and intellectual diver with the precision of science and inquiry and the wonder of the unknowable, habits of mind anticipating those of our next narrator, Ishmael. Peter Whittemore, the great-great-grandson of Herman Melville, made the most rich and subtle comment during the question period following the lecture. Pony-tailed and intense, the sea green stare of Melville in his eyes, his mind also worked like his famous relative's, subtle, alert, and fraught with the struggle to reconcile the inconsistencies of the world. He noted that the line that separates so much of the world into discrete binaries is shattered in *Moby-Dick* through Ishmael's open-minded, pluralistic tolerance. Kelley and Whittemore had inspired us—our senses heightened and our hearts believing—in a bibliophile's secular/sacred ritual worthy of "The Quarter-Deck" itself.

Emerging from the auditorium and into the lobby before entering the reading area, we encountered impeccably dressed local officials, the equivalent of antebellum New England dandies, including Scott Lang, Mayor of New Bedford. On this day, Lang was in his glory, as he should have been, relishing the celebration of his city's rich whaling past and happy, in his words, "to make fireworks of our own today" to make up for the cancellation of an actual fireworks display on another date due to weather. "All astir" in the minutes before the start, the museum's president, James Russell, delivered a fitting introduction linking *Moby-Dick* to the current economic crisis via the "Ahabs of Wall Street," a stunning reminder of obsession's dark consequences when placed within the broader economic context. Shortly after the momentous opening line was read—the journey of a thousand miles begins with one step, according to Buddhist wisdom—Congressman Barney Frank approached the podium, soon followed by a memorable reading of Father Mapple's sermon in the Seamen's Bethel chapel by the Reverend Edward Dufresne, with Raymond Veary playing the narrative role of Ishmael. The carnival atmosphere was buoyant and joyous; no dark words could be heard about those deathly wee hours of the morning. Few, if any, were discussing the event as a twenty-five-hour commitment, as the vast majority departed after the Mapple sermon.

Those with whom I raised the issue of staying for the duration politely deferred comment, one person going so far as to denounce such a charade.

The hard-core element of the affair, those twenty-two of which I myself was a part in 2009, may seem inexplicable to most, yet it is they who have provided the dimension that has drawn such a close following and increasing global attention. It is not an abridged reading; to truly experience the event, I realized, one must stay all night. John O'Connor, who was covering the 2009 reading for the *London Financial Times*, for example, took a keen interest in the all-night dimension of the event. A hearty soul, he turned up at precisely 3 AM to gage the morale of the crowd (since he left the building intermittently, he was not counted among the twenty-two survivors) and found me in a daze, crouched beneath a small Christmas tree, bodies strewn around me in various stages of repose. I must have looked something like the crazed and disheveled Dennis Hopper character in *Apocalypse Now*, Francis Ford Coppola's refiguring of Joseph Conrad's Russian Harlequin in *The Heart of Darkness*, when he greets the boat that arrives in search of Kurtz. "*Me?* I'm a *small* man," he says with insane zeal; "*Him?* He's a *great* man," his voice strung out and ragged yet vibrating with wild belief. I was only half coherent, babbling into my recorder at that point, dazed yet wide-eyed, simultaneously conscious and unconscious. O'Connor and I represented the myriad of media coverage that included local newspapers and television. His presence in particular lent an air of importance in the exciting minutes leading up to Ray Veary's intonation of the famous first line, "Call me Ishmael."

The spectators I spoke with gave a variety of reasons for being there, mainly gravitating around a love of the novel for its own sake, especially the beauty of the language and its humor, particularly impressive when read aloud. Mayor Scott Lang gave the most comprehensive view of the reading's purpose and greater significance, citing civic historical pride directly connected to national memory. He expanded on the sense of community and shared social capital building in an era of individual cell phones, lap tops, and Ipods; the pretechnological tenor ("You won't hear or see a cell phone," Lang assured me, with words that amazingly proved correct.) He then praised the flair and panache, if not obsession, of the twenty-five-hour nonstop dimension of the reading. Testing his mettle prior to the event to see if there was substance behind his impeccable and polished rhetoric, I asked if he himself would stay for the duration. "Only as a civilian," he said without hesitation. Once through with his mayoral duties, he assured me, he would read all night. Lang fully recognizes and appreciates the special status that accrues to the reading from its marathon aspect. This mayor is no stuffed shirt; raised in New Bedford and elected by its 100,000 citizens, he has the democratic grit to send his voice up with the rest and ship out in the forecastle for the entire voyage, in an acknowledgment of the reading's status as the truest expression of the town's spirit, functioning as its most important source of respect, recognition, and revenue.

Most readers cited the status of *Moby-Dick* as world-class literature as a chief reason for attending the reading, some proclaiming it the great American novel. Keith Hilles-Pilant, Melville aficionado and former Harvard professor of mathematics, said *Moby-Dick* ranked with *Walden* as the "top two books" of all time, lauding their distinctive American flair, notable in Melville through the spirit of independence of Ishmael's break from the conventional life on land to go a-whaling on the open ocean. Bearded, bespectacled, and diminutive, the affable Hilles-Pilant was brimming with vitality near midnight, speaking candidly in the lobby area about what made those works uniquely American. "*Moby-Dick* and *Walden* are quintessentially American because they're about self-reinvention," he mused, observing how "our culture understands the urge to move away and start over." His comment calls to mind such a moment in Tobias Wolff's memoir, *This Boy's Life*, in which Wolff's mother points to a random city on the map after missing their first bus at the Greyhound station and says, "Ok, Toby, Seattle, that's where we're going." *Walden*, according to Hilles-Pilant, does the same thing. "Go to the pond; leave Concord. Europeans," he said, "do not accept those sorts of declarations of independence as readily—those wholesale reinventions of professional and personal identity—as Americans do. In fact," he continued, "we not only tolerate such behavior, we admire it, and say, 'good for you,' whereas in Europe it would be viewed as a problem." We both agreed that what Americans see as heroically individualistic is often considered deviant and disruptive in the more engrained class-driven society of Europe—we had England in mind here more so than, say, Holland—marked by more rigid expectations for one's life work. "People don't just hop into a VW van and venture forth there like they do here," he urged, revealing his 1960s countercultural roots, eyebrows arched and eyes flashing with radical visions of freedom. Eleven hours earlier, just following Wyn Kelley's lecture, Chris Sten mentioned the allure of breaking not only societal but self-imposed boundaries inherent in the marathon format. The romantic questing spirit of doing the impossible, achieving the unthinkable, according to the George Washington University professor and member of the Melville Society, "is like the running marathon. You think you can't do it, but it can be done."

We might assume our lives unchangeable or a tome like *Moby-Dick* unreadable in a day, if at all, yet the reading affirms we can do both by shipping out with Ishmael on a quest for knowledge of self and world. The mayor has a very convincing list of why this event takes place and its greater significance. But it is that quest the Harvard professor admires so much, that encounter with the unknown connected with an exploration of self and world—not the fanfare and the chamber of commerce tie-ins—that take over after the first line is read. As the journey itself begins, expectations, as in athletic marathons and childbirth, must be thrown aside as we encounter meaning anew and grapple to find meaning in something this large, powerful, unwieldy, and like the whale, often inscrutable.

Once aboard and on the open sea of the reading, *Moby-Dick*'s epistemological quandaries, as in "Cetology," and its epic ambiguities, as in "The Whiteness of the Whale," actively resist the superficiality of didacticism. Political promise cannot be construed from the wreckage of the *Pequod*; the novel raises more questions—and famously so—than it answers. It is not so much interested in cementing conclusive laws about truth as it is in preparing us for the open-minded quest for it. The novel enables us to rehumanize ourselves by glimpsing the ordinary from the drastically altered, potentially disorienting perspective of the sea. It is to the novel's challenge to "read it if you can" and to readers' methods of grappling with inscrutability and ambiguity in the novel that we now turn. The consequence of shipping out into the great unknown is the confrontation with the "other" in its myriad forms, including a foreign natural world, political structure, and set of religious beliefs. The initial idealistic inclination for shipping out is that "there is magic in it"; the reality is that Ishmael's and the reader's world views are challenged, sometimes abruptly and violently, sometimes pleasantly, but usually in such a way that demands an open-minded investigation into enigmas totally foreign to our own world. Queequeg's byzantine network of tattoos, his ink, that covers his entire body speak to this ethnic and religious other world that draws us closer, luring us into the challenge of reading it if we can, for nothing less than an entire theory of the cosmos is inscribed therein.

Portrait of Tupai Cupa, from *The New Zealanders* by George L. Craik (London 1830).
Courtesy Macmillan Brown Library, University of Canterbury, New Zealand.

·2·

Queequeg's Ink
The Dilemma of Reading the Inscrutable

$\mathcal{S}$ HIPPING OUT WITH Ishmael means hearing two of his voices. One expresses the hard facts, the sober schoolteacher's testimony of the disaster he witnesses, and the other the fabulous, even sensationalistic "exaggerated yarn of incredible adventures and unbelievable monsters," as Eyal Peretz explains.[1] The duality raises a crisis of interpretation: "If the one has to do with invention, imagination, and even with lying, the other has to do with historical truth" of the sort that forms the prime objective of the New Bedford Whaling Museum and the New Bedford Whaling National Historical Park.[2] The museum and park are less interested in showcasing the artistry of *Moby-Dick* than its documentation of the town's history. Melville's narrative strategies, formal experimentation with the novel as a literary genre, and use of tall-tale conventions all constitute the side of *Moby-Dick* that is indeed an exaggerated yarn, and thus not the primary concern of these institutions.

New Bedford does not foreground the reading as a literary pilgrimage—for Arrowhead, Melville's home in Pittsfield, Massachusetts, already provides that role—so much as a shrine to its past, a primary source document testifying to the history of whaling. Although these two attributes demonstrate the impulse to separate them that has produced nearly a century of interest in the division between the novel's literary and historical significance, the two voices remain ever present in *Moby-Dick*, and thus ambiguity reigns. Readers have noticed how "the novel itself is acutely aware of this fundamental ambiguity of its language and constantly raises the issue of this ambiguity, and from many perspectives."[3] The vacillation between sober truth and superlative sensationalism that I explore in this chapter involves alien worlds, particularly those of Queequeg and Moby-Dick, that confront Ishmael and the marathon reader shortly after shipping out, once that "everlasting itch" for things remote has worn off, the lee shore has vanished, and the great broad sea that summoned now surrounds.

Reading Queequeg: "A Wondrous Work in One Volume"

NEWCOMERS TO New Bedford in 1841, like Melville himself, were as stunned by the displays of wealth among the whaling industry's nouveaux riches as they were appalled by the appearance of tattooed cannibals on virtually every street corner. (The two, of course, are intimately connected, as global trade brings cultural hybridization, which I discuss later.) Ishmael's initial shock (and Melville's by extension) is only assuaged after careful consideration: "If I had been astonished at first catching a glimpse of so outlandish an individual as Queequeg circulating among the polite society of a civilized town, that astonishment soon departed upon taking my first daylight stroll through the streets of New Bedford."[4] The play of evening lights enhances the mystery of Ishmael's astonishing tale, while broad daylight hours cast it in controlled, even scientific, accuracy as he dons the roles of anthropologist, cetologist, attorney, and natural scientist. Incredible adventure begins with the carnivalesque introduction of Queequeg in all his pipe-smoking, tomahawk-wielding, embalmed-head-peddling glory. The most frightening aspect of Queequeg upon Ishmael's first sight of him is his facial tattoo, an intricate set of symbols reflecting his own culture's theory of the cosmos, fate, destiny, and the afterlife. His introduction, however, moves away from such detail that might inspire a culturally sensitive investigation of his identity and values, and instead is a Poe-esque unveiling of the monster reminiscent of the door swinging open at the end of "The Fall of the House of Usher" to reveal the undead twin sister of Roderick Usher. The effect occurs as "he turned around—when, good heavens! What a sight! Such a face!"[5] Ishmael's otherwise eloquent syntax is reduced to a series of breathless monosyllabic shrieks as controlled analysis gives way to pandemonium.

After the initial shock, he awkwardly grapples with the ambiguity of Queequeg's identity, fumbling through a series of mistaken assumptions. He first takes the "blackish looking squares" to mean that he had been in a fight; then he jumps to the conclusion that this was a white man, who "falling among the cannibals, had been tattooed by them."[6] What begins as an interpretive dilemma that functions as a vehicle for comic high jinks later transforms into a fascinating meditation on xenophobia. The fear of the ethnic other is visible in Captain Peleg, the "insulated Quakerish Nantucketer, [who] was full of his insular prejudices and rather distrustful of all aliens,"[7] and in the strangers who stare at Ishmael and Queequeg heading toward the docks together, shocked at "seeing him and me on such confidential terms."[8]

What initially defines the partnership between Queequeg and Ishmael is their mutual interest in whaling. As such, they are business partners, and in the emergent antebellum capitalist culture, nothing could be more natural than two men heading to the docks together to sign papers committing themselves to the business of a whaling voyage. The staring strangers might sympathize if they understood Queequeg in this light. His humanity emerges when he saves a bumpkin from drowning, a feat that prompts Ishmael to vow permanent loyalty to his friend, since at that moment the native represents to him "man in the ideal."[9] Ishmael describes Queequeg's humanitarian heart in economic terms, maintaining that the "mutual, joint-stock world, in all meridians" motivated Queequeg to uphold the principle that "We cannibals must help these Christians."[10] Indeed, when they are engaged in the work of their trade, whether rocking to the rhythmic motions of mat-making or cutting into a whale carcass while attached at both ends of the monkey rope, their economic productivity, if not their physical safety and mortality itself, lies in each others' hands. In the chapter "The Monkey-rope," if Ishmael were to mismanage his end of the rope, Queequeg would become liable to being crushed between the whale and the ship's hull; if he drops him in the water, he will be greeted by the already swarming host of sharks attracted to the whale's blood and scraps of flesh floating around the boat. This is truly a joint-stock company of two, as mutual interests, even capital ones — especially being well-coordinated and reciprocally sensitive to the other's needs, movements, and vulnerabilities — can eventuate in love, and not just any love, but the kind that can save your life.[11]

Melville himself was acutely aware of his tie, his monkey rope, to the lives of the ship's crew representing "all meridians" one evening aboard the *Acushnet* while assigned to steer the ship from 9 PM until dawn. As the *Acushnet* approached Rio de Janeiro in March of 1841, Melville had a harrowing experience that would enlighten him to the responsibilities of his duty and the crew's dependency upon his competence. As "long hours silently glided away . . . I began to yield to that unaccountable drowsiness," not unlike the dreamy reveries to which the sailor aloft in the masthead is prone. Though it "ever would come over me at a midnight helm," he wrote in his journal:

that night, in particular, a strange (and ever since inexplicable) thing occurred to me. Starting from a brief standing sleep, I was horribly conscious of something fatally Wrong . . . I could not see the compass before me to steer by, though it seemed but a minute since I had been watching the card . . . Uppermost was the impression, that whatever swift, rushing thing I stood on was not so much bound to any haven ahead as rushing from all havens astern. A stark, bewildered feeling, as of death, came over me. Convulsively my hands grasped the tiller, but with the crazy conceit that the tiller was, somehow, in some enchanted way, inverted.[12]

Realizing that "in my brief sleep I had turned myself about" (probably to put his back to the wind) and thus was "fronting the ship's stern with my back to the prow and the compass. In an instant I faced back and just in time to prevent the vessel from flying up into the wind, and very probably capsizing her."[13] The joint-stock company was in peril and Melville knew it. He therefore forced himself awake as much out of fear for his own life as for the lives of the oblivious crew sleeping in their bunks below deck.

The tension here is between the dream world and the real world, a confrontation with a deceiving vision—the inverted tiller, the disorientation of facing backward, with senses signaling the rushing sea leaving rather than approaching—that if yielded to results in destruction. Ishmael's first confrontation with Queequeg himself also occurs in a deceptive, dreamlike state of half-consciousness, darkness, and sleep. Ishmael emerges out of a fitful slumber, propping himself up in bed, squinting to see if the real man has met the wild expectations of his imagination. In a surreal near-hysterical hallucination, depicted as far funnier than frightening in contrast to Melville's description of the midnight helm, Queequeg's tattoos make him appear profoundly threatening. Long after the incident, Ishmael considers them as art and religion, a symbolic system to be decoded, since they are detailed with penetrating insight into the values held sacred by Queequeg's culture. As such, the tattoos first frighten then allure Ishmael as well as the reader into the interpretive challenge of decoding its fascinatingly mysterious meanings, not unlike the magnetic effect of the novel itself.

Like Melville, Ishmael's ceaseless pursuit of meaning has him not only grappling with the befuddling iconography of Queequeg's ink but also staring bewildered at the painting in the Spouter Inn. The painting lures in Ishmael, who opens doors to throw new light on it in search of its essential meaning. He fumbles toward its meaning the same way he does upon Queequeg's introduction with a series of stabs in the dark ("It's the Black Sea in a midnight gale—It's the unnatural combat of the four primal elements—It's a blasted heath—It's a Hyperborean winter scene—It's the breaking up of the ice-bound stream of Time")[14] that attempt to reconcile testimony with exaggeration, fiction with fact. "In *fact*, the artist's design seemed this: a final theory of my own, partly based on the aggregated *opinions*," that is, orally transmitted legend prone to exaggeration, "with whom I conversed upon the subject."[15] Could this have really happened? Ishmael wonders as he moves in closer to make out the image of a sinking ship and a whale "purposing to spring clean over the craft, [who] is in the enormous act of impaling himself upon the three mast heads."[16]

The painting foreshadows Ishmael's struggle to decipher the whale himself, which he focuses his full attention on in the middle portion of the novel after he has made sense of Queequeg's behavior and identity. Coming to a clear understanding of who Queequeg is necessitates a reconsideration of his own values, thus making up the first epistemological crisis of the novel. Ishmael's measured examination of his own prejudices and the deliberations he goes through to open his mind are grossly, and often comically, at odds with his capacity for hyperbole. He in fact is frightened out of his wits and overreacts to what seasoned sailors otherwise have come to know about Pacific Islanders such as Queequeg from regularly sharing intimate space with them and witnessing their rituals, such as the Ramadan. (The pattern of Ishmael's exaggerated expectations undermined by common occurrences at sea continues throughout the novel; the glorious adventure promised by the first lowering, for example, results in the crew being knocked out of the boat and anticlimactically losing their whale.) Ishmael himself is all too aware of the folly of his struggles to maintain the bearing of the sober witness and repress the jumpy green hand in him. He notes "the grinning landlord, as well as the boarders, seemed amazingly tickled at the sudden friendship which had sprung up between me and Queequeg—especially as Peter Coffin's cock-and-bull stories about him had previously so much alarmed me concerning the very person whom I now companied with."[17] Like Washington Irving's Ichabod Crane, his gullible superstition,[18] overactive imagination, and proclivity to color reality with "fancy" lead to his wild misreadings of situations, which are often humorously exposed.

"The Ramadan" humorously dramatizes precisely the ambiguity of reading the cultural other. For as much progress as Ishmael has made in accepting the foibles of Queequeg's daily life from his outlandish table manners in "Chowder," for which he does not apologize, to his bizarre dressing and shaving rituals (the tomahawk blade works surprisingly well), as well as showing profound respect for his life story in the chapter "Biographical," he regresses dreadfully in "The Ramadan." In his derision of Queequeg's attempt to fast motionless in an enclosed room for twenty-four hours, he righteously assumes cultural superiority. "I told him too, that being in other things such an extremely sensible and sagacious savage," Ishmael intones in a ridiculously contradictory phrase delivered in an all-knowing condescending voice, "it pained me . . . to see him so deplorably foolish about this ridiculous Ramadan of his."[19] But what rescues Ishmael is his indictment not just of Queequeg's ritual but also of "all these Lents, Ramadans, and prolonged ham-squattings in the cold."[20] To Ishmael's credit, he includes a Christian ritual, Lent, in his antireligious rant, taking some, but not all, of the sting out of his paternalistic diatribe which, at the very least, does not fall into missionary rhetoric that seeks to supplant paganism with Christianity.

As *Moby-Dick* Marathon readers, are we engaging in such foolish self-denial? Is our ritual equally as empty? Indeed, it can appear that way from an outsider's point of view, as spouses and friends have been known to tear audience members away from the event, though not with the dramatic flourish of Ishmael banging down the door. What rivets many to the marathon reading is precisely what draws Ishmael toward Queequeg and the Spouter Inn painting: this is a shocking, revolting tale that forces us to reconsider our own prejudices and assumptions toward the world, and specifically toward other cultures. And Melville, especially early in the novel, appreciates the humor of that situation.

Ishmael learns and grows by reflecting on Queequeg as an ethnic other. Then when confronted with the isolation and withdrawal of Queequeg's real religious practice, the Ramadan, he comically regresses into a xenophobic panic, forming a keynote for Melville's satire on race relations. Readers have noted that Melville appears to have drawn from Chaucer's "The Miller's Tale" for the scene's comic situation. In both, a panicked observer, fearing for the safety of his loved one, comes to the rescue by breaking down a door. But unlike Chaucer, Melville satirizes instability in the face of an ambiguous ethnic other. "After watching Queequeg unveil his tattooed body, worship Yojo, smoke from a tomahawk-pipe, and display a shrunken head,"[21] for example, Ishmael is beside himself with fear: "Landlord! Watch! Coffin! Angels! Save me!"[22]

In this confrontation of an ambiguous alien world, Melville pokes fun at the baptism by fire of neophyte Ishmael, much as he does the title character of *Redburn*, whose first sea voyage harshly chafes his tender soul. This trope shows up again in Melville's 1852 novel, *Pierre*, when the main character idealistically ventures to New York City with writing desk and painfully naïve plans in tow to set the literary world afire with his writing. He, of course, is a lamb going to the slaughter. In yet another tale of harsh initiation, the protagonist of *Billy Budd, Sailor* is introduced to life aboard a navy ship by witnessing at close range his first flogging of a shipmate for a petty offense. The screams and blood effectively throw innocent "Baby Budd" headlong into the fallen world of experience and the barbaric system of military justice.

The initiation is difficult for Ishmael, just as it is difficult for the reader of *Moby-Dick*, because his dealings with Queequeg raise the issue of the arbitrariness of cultural preference. He comes to the conclusion not that the Ramadan is worthy of his own willing embrace and participation but that he should grant Queequeg his space and respect his desire for distance, because, "All our arguing with him would not avail; let him be, I say."[23] The solution prompts self-examination, specifically a reconsideration of his own Presbyterianism. "Heaven have mercy on us all," he concludes, "for we are all somehow dreadfully cracked about the head, and sadly need mending."[24] This moment, like that in *Typee* with respect to missionary work in the Marquesas, "appears designed to force Western readers to doubt their glorified self-opinions regarding civilized and/or virtuous behavior and to re-examine religious, scientific, and other colonial procedures and goals in the South Seas."[25] Ishmael is not out to reform or civilize Queequeg. For Melville, the notion of civilized Western man standing for all of humanity crumbled when he wrote *Typee* in the 1840s, and the deconstruction continued through the writing of *Moby-Dick* in 1850 and 1851.

In creating Queequeg, Melville drew from a cannibal character in London novelist George Lillie Craik's *The New Zealanders* (1830). But in doing so, he aggressively reversed Craik's imperialist propaganda based on the assumption that the concept of the human could be fully encompassed by the category of Western civilized man. Te Pehi Kupe of *The New Zealanders* is presented as less than human although eagerly learning how to become one: an apprentice human, as it were, whom Craik praises for successfully imitating the white man. Craik's character inspired Melville to forge Queequeg with more respect for his values, traditions, religion, and his very humanity, thus working against imperialistic arrogance in his characterization. But *The New Zealanders* was not just an anti-model for Melville's method of ethnic characterization. Craik's novel revealed to Melville the possibility of a warm, interracial friendship, which, prior to *Moby-Dick*, he had never considered. Geoffrey Sanborn has astutely recognized that at least two of the novels before *Moby-Dick*, particularly *Typee* (1846) and *Omoo* (1847), "represented Pacific island men as attractive but out of reach, natives to places where he was a stranger and strangers to places where he was a native."[26]

So in 1845, while researching travel literature on the Pacific islands for *Typee*, Melville discovered a reciprocal relationship in *The New Zealanders* that prefigured the egalitarian interracial friendship of Queequeg and Ishmael. Standing in the way of interracial relationships in his first two novels is a mercenary insincerity among natives. The magnanimous larger-than-life character of Queequeg in *Moby-Dick* shatters that mold. The composite ethnic other and bosom friend of Ishmael is anything but narrowly self-interested— especially when he dives in after the bumpkin to save his life early in the novel—or inauthentic, as when he wills himself back to health after suffering a near-fatal disease. However curative of the civilized hypocrisies and bland deceits plaguing Ishmael's life on land, Queequeg still remains inscrutable, leaving open the capacity for mercenary duplicity within the ethnic other. He cannot, finally, be controlled nor thus colonized, as Ishmael discovers of the Ramadan. It is telling, in this sense, that Queequeg's tattoos defy meaning, not just to Ishmael but to Queequeg as well. He is untamable, yet hardly idealized, because he is just as vulnerable to interpretive blindness as Ishmael.

Te Pehi Kupe of *The New Zealanders* memorizes his own tattoos and can reproduce them on paper, yet unlike Queequeg, he is fully aware of their meaning and his own identity in relation to them. The tattoo was to Te Pehi Kupe not a theory of the cosmos, but more narrowly, "the distinctive mark of the individual." He referred to "the mark just over the upper part of his nose" as his name, commenting that "'Europee man write with pen his name,— Tupai's name is here,' pointing to his forehead."[27] The mutual learning and exchange of cultural practice flattens out cultural difference here, homogenizing the European written name on paper with the tattooed name on the Pacific Islander's face through an em-dash ("'Europee man write with pen his name,—Tupai's name is here'") that logically functions as an equals sign.

Further, the inscriptions themselves are totally unambiguous, with the signifier of name bluntly and unproblematically pointing to the man it signifies. In *Moby-Dick*, identity, and the tattoos that correspond with them, could not be further from this depiction, as they are infinitely associative and relational, resisting reification into flat, one-dimensional meaning. The notion of identity, like most realities in *Moby-Dick*, becomes more complicated the closer we get to it. In Craik's version, they clear up into apple-pie order.

Conversely, Queequeg's ink is in anything but apple-pie order. It is Maori tattooing, which Melville describes in *Israel Potter* as "blue, elaborate, labyrinthine, cabalistic [with] large intertwisted cyphers"[28] and in *Moby-Dick* as "an interminable Cretan labyrinth of a figure."[29] Stubb compares Queequeg's markings to "the cabalistics" on the doubloon, which represent the signs of the zodiac.[30] While Queequeg copies his tattoos into his coffin, Ishmael describes them as "twisted . . . in all manner of grotesque figures and drawings."[31] What initially struck Ishmael as "large, blackish looking squares" upon his first sight of Queequeg is really a rococo, even byzantine, curvature pattern of interlacing lines. Deciphering their very shape even proved difficult in Ishmael's first encounter with Queequeg, as he could not quite grasp the shape of his roommate's character (Melville's pun on letter and identity), proving identity and its interpretation a slippery dynamic at best.

In the chapter "Queequeg in his Coffin," Melville draws a particularly shrewd metaphor for literary pursuits, in both reading and writing, which we continue to pursue, though we may never reach a definitive answer. Like Melville's own unceasing spiritual quest that Hawthorne so admired, Queequeg holds fast to his own culture's higher truths with the same tenacity that he clings to the ring bolts of the *Pequod* early in the novel. He clings to them yet cannot decipher them. The significance of the tattoos is unquestionable, for they "had been the work of a departed prophet and seer of his island, who, by those hieroglyphic marks, had written out on his body a complete theory of the heavens and the earth, and a mystical treatise on the art of attaining truth; so that Queequeg in his own proper person was a riddle to unfold."[32] Copying the cosmic belief system's icons will not prevent them from decaying, as they "were destined in the end to moulder away with the living parchment whereon they were inscribed, and so be unsolved to the last."[33] But work he must, emptying his energy and "his canvas bag of clothes" into the coffin transforming it into a sea chest since, in fact, his illness had dissipated and he could sense that he would not die any time soon. And work he does, as "many spare hours he spent," and indeed, not unlike Melville at his writing desk composing *Moby-Dick*, "he was striving" "with a wild whimsiness" at his outlandish inscriptions, racing against decay, defeating death for the time being, and reaching for the immortality such a "mystical treatise" bears. Not reaching it, "though his own heart beat against them," nonetheless does not inhibit his faith, nor Melville's by extension, in its presence and promise. At the marathon reading, the hieroglyph that is *Moby-Dick* will be nobody's to unlock and take home; not even Hershel Parker, John Bryant, Carolyn Karcher, or others among the greatest minds in Melville scholarship. But read it we must, copy it into our minds and souls yet again, for we trust its truths to be sacred. The cultural performance and products *Moby-Dick* inspires — reading it for twenty-five hours straight, re-inscribing it in poems, paintings, plays, and pop-up books to name a few — bear a certain vitality in the face of death, a growing entity, a true *culture* that resonates with the unstoppable vitality of Queequeg's conscious decision to choose life and will himself out of sickness. The living culture of this novel shares the spirit of Queequeg's sense that "whether to live or die was a matter of his own sovereign will and pleasure...if a man made up his mind to live, mere sickness could not kill him: nothing but a whale, or a gale, or some unintelligent destroyer of that sort."[34] Maybe *Moby-Dick* is not quite inscribed on any of the Melvillians' coffins (although it is possible, given our zeal), but we are happy to make sea chests of all sorts out of it, the marathon reading and this very book being but two of them.

Just as Queequeg trusts that the inscriptions on his body are sacred, we readers also invest our faith in the deeper secrets of *Moby-Dick* just out of the range of Ishmael's and our own vision. But what if there are no secrets? Then the joke is on us, as all struggles for meaning become pointless. Melville considers just that in a letter to Hawthorne when he half-jokingly expostulates that "perhaps, after all, there is *no* secret . . . We incline to think that God cannot explain His own secrets, and that He would like a little information upon certain points Himself. We mortals astonish Him as much as He us."[35] He considers in the next line that under such circumstances, we would do well to eradicate the concept of God altogether. Yet Melville indeed sought out, if not a singular spiritual secret to the universe, a form of the divine, in his trip to the Middle East to visit the Holy Land. Hawthorne perceptively described Melville's "wandering to-and-fro over these deserts, as dismal and monotonous as the sand hills" in search of meaning fuelled by his powerful and incessant intellectual restlessness as equal parts gift and curse. His lack of inner peace echoes Ahab's aborted attempt at meditation in the chapter "The Pipe." Like Emily Dickinson, Melville negotiated for his soul's destiny with a "Mighty Merchant" whose offers he never invested in, instead preferring "this smart Misery" to a life "Merry, and Nought, and gay, and numb," as Dickinson phrased it in 1862.[36] In Hawthorne's words, "he can neither believe, nor be comfortable in his unbelief; and he is too honest and courageous not to try to do one or the other." This is not for lack of spirituality, as Hawthorne makes certain not to confuse him with a dry, bloodless skeptic who has placed all his faith in science (as the "Cetology" chapter ringingly testifies): "If he were a religious man, he would be one of the most truly religious and reverential; he has a very high and noble nature, and better worth immortality than the rest of us."[37] This was Hawthorne's return of an earlier compliment Melville had given him in an astonishing transposition of biblical and interpersonal faith. "Knowing you," he wrote, "persuades me more than the Bible of our immortality."[38]

In *Moby-Dick*, the relentless pursuit of spiritual meaning courses through the diverse and unexpected channels of cultural hybridization attendant to the global trade of whaling.[39] A whole new range of possibilities for spiritual questing emerges in the global context of the whale trade, which brings Queequeg and Ishmael together in the first place. Whereas *Moby-Dick* respects the ambiguity and global reach of foreign cultures, *The New Zealanders* approaches it as something to be simplified and domesticated. Melville does not treat the challenge of culturally interpreting the ethnic other as a "facile celebration" of the interracial buddy narrative.[40] Instead he emphasizes separation and equilibrium that honors distance and space, precisely the kind Ishmael first violates and then grants in the Ramadan scene. The love between Queequeg and Ishmael, however idealized, still avoids a "romantic or sentimental feeling of love," as Sanborn notes,[41] and thus moves away from a colonial union that threatens to hammer out the "irregularities" of the native culture to propagate a fantasy of equality that never existed. Melville, on the contrary, does not "relax the tensions of globalization in a warm bath of good feeling," as Sanborn says, like most interracial buddy narratives.[42] Instead, he lets Ishmael's fits of condescension out into the open, yet has him recant his views later, in a kind of deliberative open forum of thought on race relations. Ishmael's language is frequently philosophical at these moments, as he searches for reasonable solutions to the cultural clashes he encounters. *Moby-Dick* marks progress for Melville in his fictional treatment of race relations, since little open deliberation for solutions, if any, is included in his acrid denunciation of Pacific and South Sea missionaries in *Typee*, while *Mardi* and *Omoo* reveal him beginning at least to search for answers.

Queequeg and Ishmael's relationship is the very fruit of global trade itself, the proud offspring of cultural hybridization. Melville goes far in *Moby-Dick* to celebrate the exploration of unknown land in uncharted waters for wealth and cultural exchange such as this. Significantly, one of Ishmael's most profound spiritual insights comes at a foreign port where, like Queequeg copying the spiritually significant hieroglyphics[43] into his coffin, he inscribes a sacred whale skeleton on his own skin. Appearing at first as scientific notation, the pattern of the whale skeleton on his skin takes on the status of a sacred hieroglyph. This all happens at a remote island as depicted in the chapter "A Bower in the Arsicades," exemplifying the higher spiritual benefits that accrue from trade in remote lands. The wealth that it brings, also, should not always be attached to cultural domination. For example, Queequeg happily sells his shrunken heads about town out of his own free will as an independent entrepreneur. The capital they command does not profane their sacred status but reinvents them in the capitalist context so that the dead body parts now take on new life. The sacred heads' power is actually enhanced in the market, just as Queequeg's spear-throwing skill becomes a point of personal pride precisely by the essential role it secures him on whaling ships. Thus Queequeg ships out with his own harpoons, as the trade and his job in it have become connected to his identity. He takes his skill seriously. True craftsmen own their own tools, just as "many inland reapers and mowers," Ishmael reminds us, "go into farmers' meadows armed with their own scythes—though in no wise obliged to furnish them—even so, Queequeg, for his own private reasons, preferred his own harpoon."[44] Chief among those reasons was the success he enjoyed with those particular irons, made "of assured stuff, well tried in many a mortal combat, and deeply intimate with the hearts of whales."[45] He is neither alienated from, nor forced into, his labor as a whale man, but indeed is so "deeply intimate" with it as to prefer his own tool of the trade.

Reading the Whale

MELVILLE'S DICTION in his description of why Queequeg carries his own harpoons is not so much the language of a hunter as it is that of a lover. For to be "deeply intimate" with anything, especially a living creature, implies a closeness and tenderness evoked by the phrase "hearts of whales."[46] The irony is as iron as the harpoon itself, which of course is anything but tender and is designed precisely to pierce such hearts to death. This brutal reality is leavened with Queequeg's respect and reverence toward the animal he hunts, given its power to enrich him. As an object of scientific and aesthetic wonder, Ishmael holds the whale in such sacred esteem. But his stance is complicated by the blood oath he pledges in "The Quarter-Deck," along with the rest of the crew, his voice rising among those of his shipmates crying out "Death to *Moby-Dick!*" and later by his arguing convincingly in the chapter "Moby Dick," on behalf of Ahab, that the White Whale is willfully malevolent.[47] The paradox is emphatic, as Moby-Dick appears to be the embodiment of all good and evil, transcending like its very whiteness both categories all together, just as Ishmael discovers of Queequeg and his pagan culture.

At the heart of this ambiguity, as with deciphering Queequeg's identity, are the two voices Melville employs throughout the novel. The sensationalistic, pitched rhetoric of Ahab in "The Quarter-Deck," along with his black magic ritual consecration of the harpoons for his murderous obsession, stand in sharp contrast to the tone of Ishmael's legalistic, methodical argumentation of the chapter "Moby Dick." The ambiguity regarding the whale's inherent goodness or evil emerges from these two discourses, as they did of Queequeg's hysterical introduction followed by the sober, nearly documentary history of his life and culture in the chapter "Biographical." The controlled, scientific testimony about the whale famously breaks down in "Cetology," as Ishmael suspects his mix of old and new facts to be "mere sounds, full of Leviathanism, but signifying nothing."[48] Later chapters such as "The Fountain" ("As for this whale spout, you might almost stand in it, and yet be undecided as to what it is precisely"[49]) and "The Tail" ("Dissect him how I may, then, I but go skin deep; I know him not"[50]) attest to the same pattern. Should we approach him with religious awe, or as a scientific specimen, or even a swimming treasure chest, replete with capital? Ahab's quest, as well as his influence over the crew, throws all of these perspectives into doubt, for he has transformed the beast into a mythological monster transcending these categories. The whale escapes these definitions, just as it escapes the *Pequod.* Ishmael at his best tolerates the ambiguity with an uncanny balance regarding "doubts of all things earthly, and intuitions of some things heavenly; this combination makes neither believer nor infidel, but makes a man who regards both with equal eye."[51]

Ishmael views the whale precisely through such an equal eye in "A Bower in the Arsicades," as he is part religious pilgrim and part scientist, wearing the hats equally of anthropologist and cetologist in his analysis of the whale's skeleton, the deepest part of the animal's anatomy. Ishmael refers to himself in the third person, as Melville seems to call the plausibility of his own narrative technique into question. Note the effort to ward off any suspicion of exaggeration in his narrative through an appeal to Ishmael's reliability as a witness: "A veritable witness have you hitherto been, Ishmael; but have a care how you seize the privilege of Jonah alone; the privilege of discoursing on the joists and beams; the rafters . . . making up the framework of Leviathan."[52] A whaling voyage would not have plausibly offered an occasion for the analysis of the whale's skeleton, due to its primary concern for fragmenting and processing the whale for its oil and spermaceti. It is unlikely that the unlearned shipmates like Stubb who populated most whalers would have been capable of providing him with scientific data on the fine points of the whale's skeleton. Thus some other occasion must have provided Ishmael with his information. Significantly, what brings him his authority is global trade, as "years ago, when attached to the *trading-ship Dey of Algiers*, I was invited to spend part of the Arsacidian holidays with the lord of Tranque . . . at Pupella; a seaside glen not very far distant from what our sailors called Bamboo-Town, his capital."[53] It makes sense that Ishmael would discover the rich significance of the whale skeleton in a foreign port, since global trade breaks down national borders and encourages such wide-ranging exploration. When Ishmael examines the other parts of the whale, he is not in U.S. territory but instead is on the open sea. As such, the whale's ambiguities appear as an extension of those of the foreign cultures he encounters. The whale thus becomes an emblem of the alien world of the sea, nonetheless speaking to the human folly and dignity that runs throughout the narrative.

Once there, Ishmael takes us inside his workshop, as it were, in which he finds language and God, but not in any fixed or finite sense, for his purpose continues to be to revert narrow views of the world to the open-minded quest for it. After discovering a beached sperm whale, the Arsacidians carefully transported the whale from the beach "up the Pupella glen, where a grand temple of lordly palms now shelter it."[54] The whale skeleton is an object of religious worship to the natives, as "the ribs were hung with trophies; the vertebrae were carved with Arsacidean annals, in strange hieroglyphics; in the skull, the priests kept up an unextinguished aromatic flame, so that the mystic head again sent forth its vapory spout."[55] In this wholly organic context blending death (the whale bones) with life ("the wood was green as mosses of the Icy Glen; the trees stood high and haughty, feeling their living sap"),[56] the teeming vitality of the verdure inspires Ishmael to abandon issues of plausibility and science for a mystical rumination on the origins of life. When he considers that the "industrious earth beneath was a weaver's loom," he veers toward an exalted state where he directly addresses God, the origin of all organic life, pleading for answers. "Oh, busy weaver! Unseen weaver!—pause!—one word!—whither flows the fabric? What palace may it deck? Wherefore all these ceaseless toilings?"[57] Confronted with a silence that prompted Melville's contemporary, Emily Dickinson, to write, "Of Course—I prayed— / And did God Care?"[58] Ishmael scrambles for an explanation. It is not that the weaver, to Ishmael, is uncaring or indifferent but that he simply cannot hear the questions. "The weaver-god, he weaves; and by that weaving is he deafened, that he hears no mortal voice; and by that humming, we, too, who look on the loom are deafened," such that only in death are the sounds audible, because "only when we escape it shall we hear the thousand voices that speak through it."[59]

Ishmael moves deeper into the scene, no longer content to justify the weaver's silence with a disembodied rationale but instead finding the weaver before him in the form of the whale skeleton. Ishmael ironically calls the skeleton "the mighty idler" immediately after establishing an extended metaphor of the weaver as industrious, busily working amid the deafening humming of "material factories" and "flying spindles."[60] He does so to set up his other, more important paradox of "Life folded Death; Death trellised Life," as he lies motionless around the teeming vitality that immerses him: "Yet as the ever-woven verdant warp and woof intermixed and hummed around him, the mighty idler seemed the cunning weaver; himself all woven over with vines, every month assuming greener, fresher verdure."[61]

The ambiguity in the wake of Ishmael's unanswered questions of the weaver-god only opens him up to higher and greater spiritual vision. Indeed, his zeal exceeds that of the native priests and King Tranquo, as he "marveled that the priests should swear the smoky jet" at the whale-skull altar "was genuine," and that the king should "regard the chapel as an object of virtue."[62] The latter suggestion inspires laughter from the king. Ishmael then turns to the jungle on a pathless ramble unwinding a "ball of Arsacidean twine" as he plunges ever deeper into the "winding, shaded collonades and arbors."[63]

Then the signal comes that his mystical meditation and profound worship of the whale skeleton as weaver-god has ended: "But soon my line was out; and following it back, I emerged from the opening where I entered."[64]

The intuitive trajectory of his course into the jungle is now reversed, as Ishmael rationally and dutifully follows the line back. Ishmael's full immersion into mysticism, his willingness to commit his faith in this whale and explore the jungle of his weavings, now reverses itself into a directed scientific pursuit of measurement and recording. His path through the woods is no longer intuitive and improvisational but follows a specific line. Significantly, he tattoos the skeleton dimensions on his own right arm and copies from it to write the next chapter, "Measurement of the Whale's Skeleton." Ishmael's argument to assuage skepticism in his testimony is so hyperbolic and overdetermined—an exaggerated tall tale in itself—that it leans toward satire.[65] For who could question a firsthand eyewitness to the whale skeleton whose data is emblazoned on his right arm? Why would Ishmael tattoo himself for the sake of note-taking alone—like the memory-impaired protagonist of the film *Memento* (2000)—as a kind of record-keeping strategy? His joke that follows is that the whale-skeleton tattoo did not take up too much space, which was good, because he "wished the other parts of my body to remain a blank page for a poem I was then composing."[66]

The function of the tattoo as permanent, and thus presumably irrefutable evidence of a white adventurer's interface with native culture, was in wide circulation five years prior to Melville's boarding of the *Acushnet* in January of 1841. Melville likely knew of, and perhaps had read, a wildly popular biography called *A narrative of the shipwreck, captivity, and suffering of Horace Holden and Benjamin H. Nute* that went through several editions from 1836 to 1841.[67] In it, Horace Holden describes a harrowing incident in which he and his mates were captured by savages and tattooed from head to toe. His comrades did not survive the ordeal, while Holden did and was lucky enough to have been spared the torture of forcible facial tattooing. James F. O'Connell, an Irishman who had lived on the Micronesian island of Ponape, was the first tattooed man to tour America as a freak-show exhibit. He had been living on the tiny island for years before an American ship, likely a whaler, returned him to New York in 1835. He helped popularize exhibits of tattooed persons at sideshows, circuses, and museums, especially as presented by P. T. Barnum from the 1850s on through the end of the century. O'Connell's body and Holden's *narrative* had already taken hold of America's fascination with native ink and the experience of living among the cannibals that it represented. Melville established himself in literature as the "man who lived among the cannibals" with *Typee* in 1846, five years after tales of native culture, and the tattoos that authorized them, had taken hold of the American imagination. O'Connell even capitalized on its popularity by having his face tattooed in faux native designs after his arrival in the U.S.[68]

The primitive artifact becomes certifiable through tattooing in *Moby-Dick*. Although Ishmael's pitched, religious ecstasy clearly wears off after "A Bower in the Arsacides," the interplay with the mystical still has a presence. The skeleton, as Ishmael's initial response shows, is much more than a cold scientific artifact, and thus it anticipates Queequeg's copying of his own tattoos into his coffin later in the novel. Both characters carry tattoos on their bodies replete with divine power of cosmic universal significance, and both copy them, Ishmael in his narrative and Queequeg in his coffin, so that the inscriptions might outlive their own lives and be preserved beyond the finite writing tablets of their own skin. Both engage in a gesture that honors those markings as sacred hieroglyphs which they refuse to allow to die with them. Authorship and immortality are very much bound up in these images, reflecting Melville's own enterprise of writing *Moby-Dick*, the transcription of his experience aboard the *Acushnet* tattooed on his soul.

Ishmael's whale-skeleton tattoo takes on greater significance, like *Moby-Dick* itself, given the confluence between science and accurate testimony on the one hand and exaggerated storytelling and religious mysticism on the other. For it is the recording, the precision of the retelling, that provides the very materials upon which the imagination thrives. Ishmael challenges us to test the accuracy of his whale skeleton data by consulting the Leviathanic Museum in Hull, England, along with museums containing whale skeletons in Manchester, New Hampshire, and the sperm whale skeleton privately held in Yorkshire, England, by Sir Clifford Constable. His tone is defensive and legalistic, and thus masks an otherwise direct correlation to the spiritual and religious power of the whale skeleton in the bower in Arsacides, a weaver-god in its plumed temple. That shrine and temple is ostensibly a place of worship, while the museums do not appear that way given Ishmael's shift in tone toward sober argumentation and away from religious ecstasy. Such museums, especially for those at the *Moby-Dick* Marathon reading, are hardly restricted to the function of raw data storage. The giant whale skeletons looming over the reading in the New Bedford Whaling Museum and forming the centerpiece of the sperm whale exhibit for the reading of "Cetology" are religious talismans in their own right, weaver-gods testifying to the creature's transcendent status. Significantly, our only other locale for the reading, the Seamen's Bethel, is evidence of the museum's close link to the divine. The dual function is thus to accurately serve science and history every bit as much as spirituality. Interestingly, no images of the whale are to be found in the whalers' chapel because its rhetorical pitch is toward memorializing human loss, often at the hands of murderous whales themselves. The chapel is thus a shrine to human bravery and heroism (as the ship's bow pulpit and names of drowned whalemen attest) rather than a deification of the whale himself. That function, clearly, is carried out by the museum across the street.

The juxtaposition of the Seamen's Bethel to the New Bedford Whaling Museum is telling not only of Ishmael's play between mysticism and fact but also of our own situation as readers of *Moby-Dick*. Paul Brodtkorb's sense of the novel's tendency to place readers in a bind between precision (which he finds in the formation of allegorical formulas) and formlessness is helpful here: "When the ontological category of nonbeing is evoked by dread in the presence of the numinous, the mind hastens to comfort itself with an allegorical formula that will reduce to static intellectual tractability whatever formlessness it may be facing."[69] Yearning for structure in the face of jarring ambiguity pervades the novel, and particularly the whale himself. The whale is an inspiring god in "A Bower in the Arsacides" and a menacing void in "The Whiteness of the Whale." Left with only perspectives of what the White Whale is to Ishmael, Ahab, and individual readers, "it cannot in itself be named, or structured and explained and categorized," as Brodtkorb observes, since "nothingness floods through the interstices of any conceptual net designed to hold Moby Dick's essence."[70] It is Ahab "who in his drive to *know* cannot bear the pain of eternal ambiguity" and who funnels all ambiguity into "Evil,"[71] and the whale does not contradict him in that characterization.

When not under the influence of Ahab's powerful political sway, Ishmael alternately responds to inscrutability with divergent thought—his tendency is to weave, not funnel—and a loving heart. The gaps in Ishmael's understanding of the whale, like the cultural chasms that separate him from Queequeg, become occasions for wonder that inspire Ishmael's love. The whale escapes his capacity to decipher and thus rationally understand it according to any categorical system of knowledge. For example, Moby Dick has distinctive white coloring, an exception when "blackness is the rule among almost all whales."[72] Sperm whales furthermore are mute and have no face, making them all the more slippery to comprehend. Moby Dick's own isolated characteristics—a crooked jaw, wrinkled brow, harpoons stuck in its sides from failed attacks—can be apprehended in succession, but never all at once in a composite of the complete animal. Ishmael, for example, claims that the "high and mighty god-like dignity inherent in the full front view of the brow is so immensely amplified, that gazing on it, in that full front view, you feel the Deity and the dread powers more forcibly than in beholding any other object in living nature."[73] Since "you see no one point precisely," it appears to have "no nose, eye, ears, or mouth; no face; he has none, proper."[74] Its own range of perception in itself is mystifying, as it can process two images in its head at once, either separately or in a contiguous panorama, because its eyes are on either side of its head. The profound vision it is capable of, combined with its own ungraspability, like the unheard weaver-god silently creating but never answering Ishmael's call to him, gives the whale deific dimensions. Ishmael's challenge to "read it if you can" is nothing less than the challenge of reading our own natural world and, by extension, our place in it.[75]

Far from a blank slate, the whale bears markings, much like the tattoos on Queequeg and Ishmael, which reflect his own connection to the sacred. The whale is "obliquely crossed and re-crossed with numberless straight marks in thick array, something like those in the finest Italian line engravings," appearing as though "they were engraved upon the body itself" beneath its fifteenth-inch-thick transparent protective coating of an "isinglass substance."[76] Ishmael concludes that "the mystic-marked whale remains indecipherable," owing to "the rare virtue of a strong individual vitality, and the rare virtue of thick walls."[77] Such virtues describe and dignify Queequeg as well.

The whalebone temple, the markings of the whale, and Queequeg's identity have thus shown that fact and mysticism collide regularly in *Moby-Dick*. In early November 1851, shortly after Melville had published the novel, Evert Duyckinck, Melville's publisher, sent him a newspaper clipping indicating, "We have just received the following thrilling account of the destruction of the whale ship Ann Alexander, Capt. John S. Deblois, of New Bedford, by a large sperm whale . . . a similar circumstance has never been known to occur but once in the whole history of whale-fishing, and that was the destruction of the ship Essex."[78] Reports emerged falsely assuming that *Moby-Dick* was based entirely on that incident, which of course it was not. Melville's own enthusiasm for the report was sparked by the coincidence of the disaster with the publication of his novel. The report made him feel validated, especially in the wake of a critical reception that had the opposite effect. His wild tale was now rooted in the hard facts of not one, but now two instances of whalers being sunk by their enraged prey, lending his novel, or so he hoped, the dignity of credible testimony that Ishmael yearns for in *Moby-Dick* itself. The two discourses of exaggerated adventure and witnessed event coalesce in his response to Duyckinck. "I make no doubt it *is* Moby Dick himself, for there is no account of his capture after the sad fate of the Pequod about fourteen years ago.—Ye Gods!" Melville exclaimed, putting *Ann Alexander's* destroyer himself on the witness stand, smiling assuredly at the beast's testimony. "What a Commentator is this Ann Alexander whale. What he has to say is short & pithy & very much to the point. I wonder if my evil art has raised this monster."[79]

Although only in jest, Melville's respect for the *Ann Alexander* whale shines through, for he grants him the distance and space to speak for the truth of *Moby-Dick* in his own terse way. In some ways, Melville seems to be telling his culture that whales can and do fight back, that captains go berserk, that terror exists in the world, and that these are the risks inherent in global trade. What we learned from 9/11 was that the United States, due to its dominance in global trade, is not limited to its national borders, but rather is entangled with foreign nations through its spheres of influence. As now, two things were ostensibly visible on the streets of New Bedford in 1841: wealth and racial hybridization. Global economics has now become the predominant medium through which races relate to one another. The *Ann Alexander* whale speaks to the unforeseen perils of global business as much as Ishmael's shock at the folkways and appearance of his roommate are reflections of current views of the Muslim religion and terrorism.

Melville posits a possible solution to entanglements with foreign cultures as well as to the confrontation with the alien world of the sea. The solution comes through Ishmael's refusal to colonize, or even domesticate, the ethnic other. Similarly, he respects nature's power to be potentially deadly and crushingly blank yet capable of revealing the presence of the weaver-god. He offers the distance and space necessary for profitable and mutually beneficial race relations to occur. For in *Moby-Dick*, the dynamics of race relations are not just labor-focused as with blacks in the South, or land-focused as with Native Americans in the West. Instead, race relations in the novel are trade-focused between whites and people like Queequeg of the "global south" both abroad and at home, as Sanborn phrases it.[80]

Cultural and economic isolationism is not the solution to the dilemma of deciphering the inscrutable according to the logic of *Moby-Dick*. In the 1840s, the racial and cultural hybridization of global trade had whites increasingly finding themselves amid diverse ethnicities, working alongside and sharing intimate domestic space with them, as Ishmael does, from the streets of New Bedford, to the bed in the Spouter Inn, to the bunk, deck, and chase boats of the *Pequod*. Transforming ethnic others from distanced aliens into coworkers and potential lovers, Melville's respect for, rather than imperial domination of, remote cultures shines through. As "The Ramadan" illustrates, Melville avoids the trap of excessive idealization of foreign cultures into which so many antebellum fiction writers fell. The fantasy of an equal friendship between Queequeg and Ishmael that might serve to erase any liability to white oppression is a cliché of interracial buddy narratives to which Melville never succumbs. In the same sense, we never witness in Melville such a grotesque domestication and sentimentalization as Harriet Beecher Stowe did to the protagonist of *Uncle Tom's Cabin*, effectively transforming a grown black man into a perpetual angelic child.

Global trade brings inclusive nonidealized racial politics in *Moby-Dick*, framing the complex challenge of reading ethnic identity in relation to dominant culture. So where does that leave the whale? The creature is more deeply understood, given the exploration of global trade, but does that make him a god or a natural resource? Today, the concern for how to interpret our natural environment is critical, as our understandings of it determine the policies we carry out. The trouble, as *Moby-Dick* so effectively dramatizes, is that natural environment, like other ethnic cultures, is profoundly ambiguous. One needs to look from California's to Japan's current orientation toward whales for a sense of how radically diverse the views of this majestic creature are. He has been raised to a godlike status in New Bedford mainly because of his connection to the past, whereas at San Diego's Scripps Institute for Oceanography, he resides very much in the present and future of scientific research, but virtually lacking any sense of his storied past, and as such he becomes a mere clinical subject. The contradictions emerge in light of New Bedford's valorization of whale hunting, which plundered and all but extinguished from existence the largest mammal on earth, not to mention depleted our first nonrenewable oil resource. Today's Japanese whale hunters are considered villains by most nations; ironically, they also look to history to dignify their current whaling, but the gesture is totally anachronistic. Japan had the richest seas and left them untouched for the longest, ironically enough, given their cultural and economic isolationist government. (John Manjiro was the first to leave Japan, interestingly, and returned to play a vital role in opening up the nation's isolationist policies. He ventured into the wider world aboard an American whaler that rescued him from a shipwreck in 1841, the same year Melville shipped out with the *Acushnet*.) Now Japan is savagely hunting whales with the equivalent of aircraft carriers as brave, if not reckless, environmental activists on tiny pontoon boats throw themselves in front of attacked whales like so many secret service agents shielding dignitaries from danger.[81] Melville himself foretold this future in the chapter "Does the Whale's Magnitude Diminish? Will He Perish?" where he considers seriously the threat of extinction.

The Dilemma of Reading an Inscrutable World

THE INTERPRETIVE challenges raised by *Moby-Dick* point to the distinctly contemporary issues of the natural environment and foreign, especially Islamic, cultures. The novel, as I have shown, is concerned with the ambiguity of foreign cultures and the natural world and with the dilemma of forming meaning and thus policy toward them. Has the novel shaped their attitudes toward the environment, global trade, and foreign policy? How do readers resolve the tension at the heart of the ambiguities of cultural hybridization between xenophobic fear and loathing versus love and appreciation? How does *Moby-Dick* inform the reader's understanding of the whale's current destruction by Japanese and Norwegian whaling fleets and of his status as IMAX movie star, as pet food on the one hand and exalted celebrity on the other? Does the novel help resolve such a paradox?

At Wyn Kelley's lecture for the 2009 reading, Peter Gansevoort Whittemore, bearing Melville's strong brow and cheekbones, and penetrating, deep-set eyes—a look so Melvillian that he provided the model for the Melville bust prominently displayed in the lobby of the museum—addressed, in a way only the author's great-great-grandson could, the sickness at heart in a culture clinging to binaries and habitually drawing the line in condescending judgment of the world. "Don't judge, just behold," he said, describing Ishmael's method of dealing with the unreadable or the nonsensical. "Stop drawing the line," Whittemore said, "or we'll be enveloped in the chaos." His pattern is embodied by Ahab in *Moby-Dick*, whose yes/no, right/wrong categories do not measure up to the infinite inscrutability of the universe, but relentlessly are bent on destroying their nuances.

That very sense of tolerance of ambiguity was corroborated by Melville Society members Mary K. Bercaw Edwards, author of *Old Cannibal Me: Spoken Sources in Melville's Early Works* (2009), and Chris Sten, who astutely characterized the frame of mind necessary for approaching this reading ritual. Obsessed as Melville readers at the marathon ostensibly are, tracking and comprehending every word of the novel for the full twenty-five hours, they allowed, was virtually impossible, and further, beside the point of the gathering itself. They openly admitted that one "can only read portions of the novel," and that "nobody reads the whole thing" during the *Moby-Dick* Marathon. They both allowed that the quality of the reading performances, furthermore, had been notoriously uneven, and that particularly bad delivery could cloud or obscure the audience's comprehension of a chapter. However, what "counterbalances the bad readings or missed meanings" in their view was "the beauty of the language and the humor that emerges out of the competent readings." Sten and Edwards shared Whittemore's Ishmaelian approach to the inscrutable, taking an open-minded pleasure in what came, regardless of the depth of insight it offered. When asked about the lack of time for reflection on the subtleties of the novel, they said that virtually everyone at this event had read the novel before and presumably were here precisely because they had poured over such nuances under other circumstances. In a late-night chat, Whittemore, the bloodline relative of Melville, opened up about the supple meaning of the novel, remarking about Melville's stunning capacity to dive into the dark. When asked if he had a favorite chapter or passage, he said, "I pick up a new chapter each time as a favorite," true to the pragmatic notion of Ishmael's intellectual questing, which eschews teleological dogmas or preset critical schemas in favor of taking and using what is readily available if useful and worthy.

Just as the tapestry of meaning of *Moby-Dick* certainly poses readers with interpretive challenges, the display content of the New Bedford Whaling Museum also raised some vexing questions. John O'Connor, journalist for the *London Financial Times*, grappled as I did with the various meanings in the museum itself, in particular its lack of space dedicated to conservation, a subject disproportionately underrepresented compared to that of the history of whale hunting, from the materials used to the products made from the precious whale oil. The issue of conservation was sorely lacking in 2009, since Museum President James Russell had declared this year that the institution was "going green," a fact ironically announced on paper and ink bulletins, which were green, encouraging paperless communication. However awkward the transition, the triumphalism of the whaling history displays (one refers to whalers as "heroes")—offset as they are by newly acquired mother and baby right whale bones, as well as a display referencing outlaw whaling by Japan and Norway—will be remedied by Madeline Shaw's reworking of the sperm whale exhibit under the heading "Pursuit to Preservation." Shaw's plan in some ways represents New England catching up to the vanguard of contemporary cetology stationed on the west coast. Further, the New Bedford Whaling Museum deserves credit for its extensive partnerships and programs in environmental and cultural awareness and education; they are ardently at work in making their display cases reflect such progressive strides.

Those New England and California perspectives form a bicoastal paradoxical view of the whale, at once lamented on the west coast for its destruction to near extinction in the scientific and biological context of San Diego's Scripps Institute of Oceanography, a place where whalers are uniformly vilified, to this east coast glorification of the whaling past which is only beginning to acknowledge conservation issues. Steeped in environmental activism as the west coast is, it is relatively insensitive to the profound richness and artistry of the whaling past. (One will never find a scrimshaw exhibit at Scripps, for example.) Likewise, New Bedford will greatly benefit from the infusion of progressive California environmental politics into an institution so rooted in antiquity. Once Shaw's plan is implemented, New Bedford promises to have the more balanced view of the situation, incorporating more of its missing element of conservation than Scripps will ever achieve in the way of honoring the noble past of American whaling. Though whales were hunted nearly to extinction as a result of the antebellum market revolution during a key surge in the development of industrial capitalism, we should remember that they were never hunted for sport or entertainment in the way the buffalo were, thanks to American killers like Buffalo Bill, who garnered his fame, in large part, from picking off the peaceful beasts from train cars to wow travelers with his stunning marksmanship. ("How do you like your blueeyed boy / Mister Death," e. e. cummings asks in the poem "Buffalo Bill's."[82]) Conversely,

Ahab's is a blood feud, a grudge match that grew from a commercial whaling injury, and thus he should never be confused with a sport fisherman.

The conservation themes that were present in 2009 at the New Bedford Whaling Museum were brought to my attention by professor, author, and Melville Society member Tim Marr, who insightfully linked the mother and baby right whale bones to "The Grand Armada" in *Moby-Dick*, which tenderly portrays such maternal serenity. The skeletons hang from the ceiling, the baby's bones positioned where they were when the pregnant mother was found beached after colliding with a boat. It is poignant and profound in an expression worthy of Melville himself, that this baby in the womb so emphatically signaling life should be in reality a harbinger of death, a sign of its imminent extinction as only 350 of the creatures are left. Part of Melville's appeal in *Moby-Dick* is his capacity to unfold all the dimensions of death. They issue from Ahab's role as the quintessential American killer, to the mass destruction of whales, and ultimately to the demise of mankind through such monomaniacal pursuits that lead to the depletion of natural resources. A major multimillion-dollar lawsuit has been filed against the ship captains who crashed their oil tanker into the Bay Bridge on a foggy November morning in 2007, spilling thousands of gallons of oil into the San Francisco Bay, bringing an end to the Bay Area's pride of protecting what had been among America's cleanest bodies of water next to such a sprawling megalopolis of 13 million people. The spill polluted over 200 miles of shore and killed thousands of birds and sea creatures, but would pale in comparison to the horrific BP oil leak that sent over 50 million gallons into the Gulf of Mexico in 2010. These catastrophes, along with global warming and the 2008 economic collapse, were caused in part by an overdependence on oil consumption.

Early January 2009 was a time abuzz with the threat of global economic collapse in the wake of terrorism and exploitative transnational exchange. Peter Whittemore was candid about seeing the current economic crisis in transnational terms, noting that the U.S.'s failed diplomacy throughout the Bush administration prompted China to make a symbolic show of strength at the 2008 Olympics they hosted in Bejing as a prelude to their economic domination of the U.S. In a late-night conversation, Whittemore and I agreed that where Melville supported global trade's transcultural, mutually beneficial exchanges embodied by Ishmael and Queequeg's relationship, he bitterly denounced the narrow pursuit of capital, figured in the U.S.'s Ahab-like pursuit of oil profits that, in part, led to the Iraq war. Whittemore astutely noted that Melville's leanings were revolutionary (though I said he tended to hedge his bets on the plebs as the source of meaningful political change), citing the interesting historical fact that Melville's father-in-law, Judge Lemuel Shaw, legalized worker strikes in shoe factories during the antebellum era at a time when Orestes Brownson was remembered as virtually the sole figure on the avant garde, if not the lunatic fringe, of positive change on behalf of the economically downtrodden. Melville, we agreed, was more interested in exposing imperialism and the use of colonial force, both foreign and domestic, than he traditionally is given credit for. His attack on missionaries, we concurred, was particularly subversive, despite the disastrous commercial consequences it wrought for his career. Reading Melville's politics, indeed, can prove as difficult as reading Queequeg's ink. But with a like-minded Melvillian, clarity can be attained, not as restful consolation, but as an uncomfortable, or as Al Gore would have it, *inconvenient*, truth. "My friends tell me to lighten up," Whittemore quipped, using a phrase that has appeared on the bumpers and T-shirts of today's countercultural warriors, "but I tell them, if you're not upset, you're not paying attention."

Melvillians love to dive. As such, they are unafraid of confronting the inscrutable and pondering their own unknowing. The hidebound bipartisan political climate has factionalized the populace, driving people away from conceptual challenges into the rhetoric of their own already established beliefs. The spirit of Ishmael moves in precisely the opposite direction as he reverts our narrow-minded view of the world to the open-minded quest for it; he is willing to flounder, grapple, stumble, and even make a fool of himself. For even the noblest efforts of finding meaning, as in Queequeg's transcription of his tattoos, is but a copy of a copy, and who among us can claim any higher authority than a Sub-Sub-Librarian? How, if at all, could a live, continuous reading support a text which demands quiet reflection—"you cannot run and read it"[83] superficially, Melville said—and rereading of the broader questions of our contemporary world? The challenge is there: "read it if you can," Ishmael says of the whale's brow.[84] At this pace, how does one decipher the inscrutable, if at all? The forward progress continues heedless of unresolved questions, much in the way Ishmael's narrative does, with subsequent chapters modifying or enlarging upon problems raised in prior ones. Is the process of reading *Moby-Dick* like Ishmael's fruitless desire to conceive of the whale as a composite image? As such, does the marathon reading format (at least temporarily) remedy that problem through the speed with which we glimpse its successive parts leaving us with a larger impression, a gestalt, than if we were to slowly peruse it over weeks? Mayor Scott Lang thought so, pointing out how one of the privileges of staying for the full twenty-five hours is the unique insight it offers into the full narrative sweep of the novel's build-up to the chase, and a "better sense of the splash" at the end.

As Part 1 has shown, the anticipation of departure, its idealistic visions and "everlasting itch for things remote" meet with bizarre, unforeseen circumstances and seemingly alien individuals and creatures. This pattern is part of the epic journey we see in Homer's Odysseus, who ventures forth to encounter a dizzying array of witches, sea creatures, and gods, all of whom test his mettle and wit. Ishmael's journey is no different. The first individual he must come to grips with is Queequeg, and the main inhabitant of the sea he must understand is the whale himself. As the novel progresses along with his journey, the sea creatures and characters he encounters proliferate, as he ponders porpoises, sharks, and squid (a creature so astonishing to Ishmael that he regales it with the noteworthy superlative of "the most wondrous phenomenon which the secret seas have hitherto revealed to mankind"[85]) as well as Tashtego, Fedallah, and Pip. Among Ishmael's shipmates, ironically none is more outlandish than the American Ahab himself, a domestic rather than a foreign product. He and his mates Starbuck, Flask, and Stubb, form the top brass of the *Pequod*, a kind of group identity with which Ishmael not only must come to terms, but actively joins himself. The body of readers at the marathon event also constitutes a group identity representing nothing less than the lifeblood of *Moby-Dick* and Melville's memory. It is toward a consideration of those subdivisions of whalers and readers, and to their social matrix, that we now turn.

PART II

Readers and Crew

Illustration of Captain Ahab on the quarterdeck, by Rockwell Kent. Copyright © 1930 by R. R. Donnelley and Sons, Inc., and the Plattsburgh College Foundation, Inc.

·3·

Captain and Mates

Honored Readers

*I*N 2009, SCOTT LANG, Mayor of New Bedford, was among the featured readers at the *Moby-Dick* Marathon reading. As the ambassador of this historical whaling city, Lang enjoyed a privileged position among the readers that day. If there were ever a "captain" of the marathon reading, the mayor would appear best suited for that role. The event, however, reaches well beyond the civic significance of New Bedford's whaling past, as Melville's colossal reputation has brought the reading into the national spotlight. As such, several federal elected officials have made a point of participating in the marathon reading. Congressional Representative Barney Frank served as a featured reader in 2009, continuing a tradition of participation by such distinguished Capitol Hill figures as Senator Edward Kennedy, who appeared in 1998. The Massachusetts state House of Representatives even expressed its deepest dedication to Melville's great novel in October 2008 in a way only state legislators can: they passed a law. Further cementing the state's association with its whaling heritage and Melville's literary prestige, the bill was approved to make *Moby-Dick* the official novel of the state of Massachusetts.[1] Are these government officials the real captains of the reading? Or do those honoring Melville's past deserve the distinction, such as the author's own great-great-grandson, Peter Whittemore, whose authentic Melvillian lineage makes superfluous, and even ridiculous, any thought of including an author impersonator at the event? Or does the event showcase the artistry of the novel by spotlighting readers like Richard Ellis, author of *Monsters of the Deep*, whose whale art is prominently displayed at the event? Or should it be today's mariners, such a schooner captain Amanda Madeira, the only 2008 reader to actually bear the occupational title of captain? Or are the real honored guests Captain Madeira's theoretical counterparts who ply their trades in universities rather than at sea? As such, are distinguished scholars Carolyn

Karcher, John Bryant, and Wyn Kelley, who have lectured before the reading, the real stars of the event? Then we also have Ishmael himself, as played by Raymond Veary, a former assistant district attorney, who is annually honored with intoning the very first words of the novel. Is he our captain?

The dizzying range of figures here points to the destabilization of authority dramatized in the very pages of *Moby-Dick* itself, which forms the subject of part II of this book. Melville was always interested in the social matrix of status, of "how human beings organize themselves into ranks, and at how those doing the organizing always reserve a place for themselves at the top," as Delbanco observes.[2] To be sure, the new president of the New Bedford Whaling Museum, James Russell, did not pass up his right to read the most coveted passage of the 2009 event, assigning himself the "Epilogue," to be read from the platform above the crowd on the stairway shaped like a ship's bow. (In his defense, who among this conglomeration of zealous Melvillians would have squandered such a privilege?) Such contested meaning—is Melville the bastion of sea captains or scholars?—also speaks to the unstable enterprise of literary history and biography itself.

Indeed, the figures named above aptly represent the many hats worn by Melville himself, from seafarer to metaphysician to national representative. He is an inspirational patriotic leader and even a legal advocate of American literature in "Hawthorne and His Mosses," a review praising his Pittsfield neighbor's collection of short stories. Functioning as U.S. representatives of sorts, authors like Melville have long been considered the cultural and intellectual faces of the nation, especially in the nineteenth century, and were often appointed to ambassadorships at foreign consulates and embassies. Melville's own legalistic posturings in his writing along with his familiarity with the machinations of the law (his own brother and sometime literary agent, Allan Melville, was an attorney) suggest his strong tie to the legal profession. Authors have also been confused with their fictional counterparts, as they pour so much of their own identities into characters they often regard as "the me that is not me." Melville has been alternately called Ishmael and Ahab; he is truly both and neither, but certainly not one or the other. The question of which is the real Melville is much like the problem of identifying the real "captain" of the *Moby-Dick* Marathon reading. Both bear on the highly contested and unstable nature of authority, which the novel specifically interrogates and deconstructs. This chapter explores Melville's dismantling of authority and seemingly stable, codified law in *Moby-Dick* as a window into the politics of a mass reading like the *Moby-Dick* Marathon. The ritualized leadership of the egalitarian, noncoercive marathon reading sharply contrasts with the arbitrary and self-justifying nature of power in *Moby-Dick*, especially in Ahab's manipulation of the crew through black magic in "The Quarter-Deck" and of economic principle in "Surmises."

Obsession Confession

ORDER AND control through hierarchy is reflected in the reading order and in the authority of the author himself, whose influence over the event is evidenced by the positioning of Melville's own great-great-grandson at the beginning and very end of the novel. Figures of civic and political authority read, as do senators, representatives, and mayors; the legal community also gives its blessing to the event, as the former assistant district attorney dons the persona of Ishmael himself. (Thomas Pynchon was right when he demonstrated through his famous postmodern novel, *The Crying of Lot 49* [1966], that all lawyers are essentially amateur actors of one variety or another. Legislators and clergy, it would appear, are no different.) It is our obsession with laws, their development, and their slippery quality that gives rise to so many of Ishmael's best ruminations. He frequently speaks in the voice of a lawyer, advocating "The Honor and Glory of Whaling" and even the reputation of Moby Dick himself. It is Ahab's confession of his monomaniacal quest that casts doubt upon, and throws into question, all those supposedly stable laws: His obsession for the whale problematizes civilization's obsession with the politics of developing and upholding laws, whether judicial, aesthetic, or theistic. Indeed, the reading creates an oracular theatre for the law, a stage set for the theatrics and ethics of jurisprudence and the posturings of legislation from the ship's deck to national governments.

In "The Quarter-Deck," Ahab confesses to his fully personal stake in the capture of Moby Dick. Captaincy, at this point, is no longer defined by the prevailing codes and conventions of antebellum whalers, since he turns his obsession into its primary function. Instead of hunting all whales to enrich themselves and the industry while also illuminating the parlors of America with the creatures' clean-burning oil, Ahab proposes to hunt but one, whom the harpooners readily identify from past confrontations. His persuasive oration is prefaced by the invocation of the capitalistic muse through a gold coin replete with exotic iconography: "Look ye! D'ye see this Spanish ounce of gold? . . . whosoever of ye raises me that same white whale, he shall have this gold ounce, my boys!"[3] The doubloon's significance fades in the scene as Ahab's charismatic harangue against the White Whale takes over, deftly transposing his own obsession into the hearts of his men. (Later, in "Surmises" and "The Doubloon," he will exploit the profit motive to maintain morale by pretending to hunt all whales rather than just one.) Using the quarterdeck as the stage for his theatrical display of power, Ahab mystically unites the crew through his black magic and heretical fanaticism, binding them to his murderous vengeance.

Ahab effectively blends his exuberant, outlandish audacity—"I'd strike the sun if it insulted me"[4]—with conventional leadership techniques common among sea captains at the time designed to stir the crew into a frenzy. A favorite dictum among captains of American whalers was "this side of land [toward home] I have my owners and God Almighty. On the other side of land, I am God Almighty."[5] Like a general inspiring his troops for battle, Ahab "stood for an instant searchingly eyeing every man of his crew."[6] But his purpose is solipsistic, and his compassion for the lives of his men is wholly lacking, as his designs exploit their very mortality: "But those wild eyes met his, as the bloodshot eyes of the prairie wolves meet the eye of their leader, ere he rushes on at their head in the trail of the bison; but, alas! Only to fall into the hidden snare of the Indian."[7] On antebellum whalers, motivational techniques and even conniving tricks, designed to wed the crew to the voyage's prime objective, were only limited by the captain's imagination. If captains were unable to hold sway over their crews by winning the men's respect through their bearing and rank, they would resort to other "tools to maintain order," as Dolin reports, "from a tongue lashing to extra duties to, in the extreme, being shackled, strung up by one's thumbs, or flogged," the latter practice proving so brutal that it became illegal in 1850 according to federal law.[8] Melville's fascination with leadership tactics extends to his fictional portrait of the British Navy's Captain Vere in "Billy Budd," who is concerned about the threat of mutiny and thus recruits Billy, the reputed "fighting peace-keeper," aboard his vessel.[9] When Billy is accused of killing a superior officer, Vere vacillates, but eventually opts to execute the youth to dampen any glowing embers of mutiny that the perception of weakness in the ship's authority might fan to life. Ahab also shapes his crew to his will, but unlike the above examples, he never directly harms them, but rather more subtly, and thus powerfully, tricks them into imperiling their own lives with far more deadly consequences. He is fully aware that he must have his men's complicity if he is to complete his plan to destroy Moby-Dick. Thus his confession of his obsession becomes a manipulative tool to acquire the entire ship's faith, and indeed its zeal, in carrying out his mission. Even Ishmael confesses his "shouts had gone up with the rest; my oath had been welded with theirs; and stronger I shouted, and more did I hammer and clinch my oath, because of the dread in my soul." With the exception of Starbuck, Ishmael speaks for the crew when he says, "a wild sympathetic feeling was in me; Ahab's quenchless feud seemed mine."[10]

Melville is calling into question the ethos of charismatic authoritarian leadership here as much as he is bringing to the fore the arbitrary and self-serving process by which power is constructed. Indeed, Ahab completes his carefully choreographed Faustian pact by imposing his own obsession upon the crew and sealing it with a ritual quaff from the sockets of the three harpoons. This scene darkens the entire novel by dramatizing the destruction of the sacred brotherhood of mankind, which Melville believed was the best chance at survival in a dangerous world made so by an uncaring God and ruthless laissez-faire capitalism. Any potential for transnational, multiethnic democracy nascent in the crew is usurped by Ahab's singular obsession. In a letter to Hawthorne, Melville himself called for a "ruthless democracy on all sides," reflecting his bitterness toward class pretension and arrogance, which he believed the voice of the people could subvert.[11] What plagues the brotherhood of the crew is the misanthropic undercurrent with which Ahab forges his black art, willingly sacrificing their lives for his own vengeance on Moby-Dick. Melville sensed that even the most radical democratic spirit with the best intentions was not immune to such misanthropy, commenting in the same letter to Hawthorne that "It seems an inconsistency to assert unconditional democracy in all things, and yet confess a dislike to all mankind—in the mass. But not so."[12] Melville also knew that the worst autocratic intentions often masqueraded as empowering populism. Ahab's most trenchant skill, for example, is the appropriation of populist rhetoric to underwrite his monomaniacal quest.

Melville's concern for democracy's abuses by authoritarian charismatic leadership stems from the events surrounding him during his composition of *Moby-Dick*. The North was backing down to Southern demands at the time, as evidenced by the Compromise of 1850. Melville also had the odd predicament of watching his father-in-law, Judge Lemuel Shaw, send runaway slave

Thomas Sims back into slavery in a highly publicized case that upheld the unconstitutional Fugitive Slave Law that progressive Northerners vehemently opposed. As Hershel Parker explains, Melville "was a man with obligations as a . . . son-in-law," yet was "not blind to the great national sin of slavery."[13] In *Moby-Dick*, Melville appears callous to the abolitionist cause when Ishmael asks, "Who ain't a slave?"[14] But the question comes in the context of rumination on the necessity of labor and on the psychologically recuperative power of hard work, especially for Ishmael's dampened and near-suicidal soul. He happily submits himself to the "universal thump" of labor under a managed system of capitalist enterprise in which all are "in one way or other served in much the same way," and for whatever pains suffered in the process, "all hands should rub each other's shoulders and be content."[15] Further, Ishmael is careful to distinguish his work at sea from slavery, for the very next paragraph is devoted to how much more pleasure he takes in "*being paid*" rather than in shipping out as a paying passenger. He emphasizes that his employers "make a point of paying me for my trouble," thereby distancing his labor as a common sailor from that of unpaid Southern black slaves.[16]

Melville's deep sympathy for the oppressed reflects an idealism that should not be overshadowed by his skepticism toward tyrannical, self-serving power. Idealism and skepticism are complexly braided throughout *Moby-Dick* according to Robert Milder's formulation of Melville "as a skeptical idealist: an idealist in his hopes for humanity and his outrage at the abuses of human rights and dignity; a skeptic in his estimate of actual human motives and behavior and in his distrust both of entrenched power and of violent attempts to dislodge it."[17] His heart is with the crew at the beginning of the novel, and their subjection to Ahab's tyranny is a post-Napoleonic picture of power prophetic of the rise of Nazism in 1930s Germany. Melville condoned rebellion in such situations in which individuals had been unjustly stripped of their natural rights. Melville's belief in such human rights emanated from his "growing social and cultural awareness," according to one reader, especially from the early novels to *Moby-Dick*, which reflected his understanding "of the fundamental sameness of all human kind."[18]

Melville's affinity for multiperspectivism as concept and favorite literary technique prevents him from a flat, uniform advocacy of the crew throughout *Moby-Dick*. Ahab's vulnerability comes to the fore later in the novel, for example, as Ishmael describes the captain's loss of his sexual function upon the accidental piercing of his groin by his prosthetic leg. We see Ahab cry, as

Ishmael tenderly waxes poetic about his humanities, particularly in his sentimental portrait of the captain's yearning for his wife and child ashore who await his return. Ahab even becomes a kind of surrogate mother to young Pip. Yet Melville allows Ahab's politics to resurface in subtleties leading up to the final clash with Moby Dick, especially in the black castaway's parting words: "O master, my master, come back!"[19] The diction in his plea subtly mocks proslavery propaganda perpetrated at the time by such Southern pundits as George Fitzhugh. Indeed, Pip's very attachment to Ahab has been conditioned forcibly by the crazed captain through the guise of benevolent paternalism. Ahab, for example, exploits Pip's madness as a source of self-justification, admitting how "I do suck most wondrous philosophies from thee."[20] Those dark philosophies which he has pulled out of Pip have all but overwhelmed Ahab, "so far gone am I in the dark side of earth, that its other side, the theoretic bright one, seems but uncertain twilight to me."[21] When Pip does not embrace Ahab's obsession for Moby Dick, he threatens to murder him, as the boy might weaken his vengeful purpose. Pip's resistance to Ahab's mission elicits a death threat that echoes the same method used by Southern slaveholders to assert their authority over recalcitrant or rebellious slaves. Frederick Douglass's slave narrative testifies[22] that such threats commonly eventuated in murders of African Americans.

A distinct compassionate egalitarian sentiment can be found in Melville's exposure of Ahab's self-indulgent exploitation of Pip. But Melville's skepticism prevents a decisive solution to the dilemma, rendering the more mature outlook of *Moby-Dick* darker than that of *Redburn* or *White Jacket*. Too pragmatic to yield to easy answers, Melville's sympathy for the politically oppressed never had the militant inflection of Walt Whitman, for example. The poet's democratic embrace of a runaway slave in *Leaves of Grass* is reinforced by his willingness to kill for him, as figured in the "firelock [that] leaned in the corner" of the room in which the narrator harbors the fugitive.[23] Killing was never so unproblematic for Melville, as he typically was more cautious than quick to espouse a military solution. For as much as he was critical of tyrannical force, he was no advocate of bloody revolution either. But caution itself is no solution either; it can cost more lives in some cases than decisive action. This moral dilemma is best showcased in the chapter "The Musket," which depicts Starbuck's Hamlet-like paralysis when faced with the opportunity to decisively kill his nemesis and achieve universal political and moral justice aboard the *Pequod*.

Melville's own skepticism frequently undercuts his "ruthless democracy"[24] in the novel. Ishmael's fair-minded, even-handed approach, for example, continually and openly undermines its own authority, often to a fault. He is thus vulnerable to tyranny. "For the most part," as Dolin reports in his recent history of whaling, "captains were reasonably benevolent despots, treating their men firmly, but fairly, but there were also more than a few who were foul-mouthed, spiteful brutes who relied on intimidation rather than leadership to run their ships."[25] Ishmael naïvely speculates that since all captains knock about their sailors, calling them aft and aloft, so "what of it, if some old hunk of a sea-captain orders me to get a broom and sweep down the decks?"[26] By dismissing the brusque, demanding demeanor of sea captains as universal and thus inconsequential, Ishmael unwittingly lowers his guard to the powers of persuasion Ahab unfurls upon making his dramatic entrance on the quarterdeck. The flourish of dark, theatrical charisma would mesmerize Ishmael, moving him to confess his complicity with Ahab's will. Ishmael's confession that "Ahab's quenchless feud seemed mine" is a far cry from his flip dismissal of any concern for authoritarian captains.[27] Ishmael would be lucky to be faced with a relatively harmless taskmaster and scold who orders him about, but instead he finds his soul possessed by Ahab's vengeful purpose. Ishmael's indictment of Moby Dick has him playing lawyer to Ahab's will, as he launches into a character assault on the beast in the chapter "Moby Dick," unleashing his considerable intellect on behalf of his captain.

Mystical Persuasion and Rational Consent

THE IMAGE of the crew consenting to Ahab's will presents us with "a despotism over the spirit that relies on the consent of the very men whose lives, liberty and pursuit of happiness will be sacrificed to the will of the leader," as one reader has aptly phrased it.[28] What draws them in is precisely the illusion of democracy, indeed, a ruthless one, with revolutionary energies and implications. When the men all confirm sightings or conflicts with Moby-Dick and attest to the beast's tyranny over the seas, Ahab calls for the men to stage a bloody revolution to end his rule. The crew's sense of empowerment is thus political, a calling forth of all men to reclaim the seas not just for Ahab, as he would have them believe, but in some ways for themselves, for the people, and for democracy. The trouble here, and the source of the dramatic tension of the novel, is that the people, as figured in the crew, are hoodwinked into what appears to them a justifiable contract. In this way, Melville ingeniously casts doubt on the seeming security of John Locke's theory of social contract as articulated through Jefferson's principle that legitimate government rests upon the rational consent of the governed. The will of the majority to hunt Moby Dick indeed prevails, but what's missing is precisely the component left out of the national democratic credo of how to wed democratic means to moral ends that respect the rights of man. Locke's view that organized society offers an advantageous situation for individuals who would otherwise suffer comes into question in *Moby-Dick*, raising the issue of how the absence of moral restraint derails democratic ideals.

That lack of moral restraint so appalling in the Faustian deal struck on the quarterdeck is made possible not only through Ahab's sham democracy but also through his powerful pagan mysticism. A persistent tension runs through *Moby-Dick* between the capitalist impulse to run the ship like a floating oil factory and Ahab's desire to transform it into an instrument of vengeance. The latter is shot through with mysticism, while the former, from mat making to deck scrubbing, reflects the sober and sedate routines that became common in the business world of the 1850s. The capitalist enterprise of hunting all whales rather than one, indeed, promises to save the lives of the crew from Ahab. "How many barrels will thy vengeance yield thee?" Starbuck asks Ahab,[29] in a curious twist in which capitalism becomes a moral rather than a corrupting agent. In this sense, the pursuit of money can save him from his insane obsession with the White Whale. Ahab's anticapitalist response, interestingly, invokes the romantic distrust of the profit motive so pervasively embedded in the culture at the time, from slave narratives, to transcendentalist writing, to sentimental novels, and even the fiction of Nathaniel Hawthorne, Melville's closest friend during the composition of *Moby-Dick*. But in this case, the antimarket sentiment comes from the villain. "If money's to be the measurer," Ahab barks at the quavering Quaker Starbuck, "man, and the accountants have computed their great counting-house the globe, by girdling it with guineas, one to every three parts of an inch; then, let me tell thee, that my vengeance will fetch me a premium *here!*"[30] Ahab exults, pounding his chest in a way far more passionate and spiritually vigorous than Starbuck, the most pious man aboard the *Pequod*. The deliciousness of the irony here is that given the saliency of the antimaterialist argument at the time—which still holds sway over the denouements of innumerable Disney movies in which characters invariably choose love over money (if only the binary were ever that simple)—Ahab trumps Starbuck with his reply. Star-buck retorts by calling "vengeance on a dumb brute"[31] blasphemous, imply-ing that his Quakerism is superior to Ahab's pagan mysticism as a religious moral standard. But Ahab refutes the claim of idolatry, instead urging that Moby Dick's very materiality (and his attendant "inscrutable malice sinewing in it"[32]) is the thing he wishes to obliterate. The pasteboard-masks speech thus resoundingly asserts his hatred of "all visible objects," the fraud of ma-teriality, and the prison it has placed him in, as the whale himself is a "wall, shoved near to me."[33] Escaping the material prison to a spiritual world even he himself is uncertain of, for "sometimes I think there's naught beyond," becomes paramount for Ahab, as he asks rhetorically, "How can the prisoner reach outside except by thrusting through the wall?"[34]

Adam Smith, who theorized that markets and the profit motive provide incentive for civility and moral constraint, never looked so small as when the bloodless, cowardly voice of Starbuck reminds Ahab about the *Pequod*'s re-sponsibility to the Nantucket market. The force and inertia of Ahab's speech buries Starbuck's cries to stop this fatal quest first for money's sake and then for God's sake. Like Jocasta begging King Oedipus not to inquire further into the identity of Laius's murderer, who of course is Oedipus himself, Starbuck's pleas are in vain. As King of Thebes, Oedipus wields considerable power and authority over his people, much in the way Ahab entrances his crew with his charismatic swagger and sheer force of will. Ahab dominates the scene, emerging as more spiritually potent and wildly at odds with the dull drudg-ery of getting and spending, a life tethered to the accountant's ledger that Starbuck pathetically invokes. In an undertaking inspiring for its willingness to confront death, Ahab eschews the socially prescribed pursuit of gainful employment in the free market, of stocking barrels and dutifully returning them to shore for profit. His inspirational rebellion here is reminiscent of John Milton's Satan of *Paradise Lost*, who famously, if inadvertently, steals the show of the biblical epic poem with his dynamism and transgressive flair. In terms of what he does to desecrate Smith, Locke, and Jefferson—not to men-tion Starbuck and his tepid Quakerism—Ahab could not be more satanic. He gleans his appeal to both the crew and readers from his commitment to a spiritual challenge that rejects materialistic motives every bit as much as Ishmael's romantic renunciation of the civilized hypocrisies and bland deceits he associates with conventional life on shore. Two escapes thus emerge in the first third of the novel: first Ishmael's from shore, and then Ahab's from the prison of the whale. Both energies strike out and away not only from shore but also from institutions, conventions, and accepted occupational value sets. Ishmael's sleeping with a cannibal, taking a pagan for a friend, and recanting his spirituality is but a mild and humorous preface to the bravado of the gale force entrance of Ahab, who "says NO! in thunder," a phrase Melville once used to describe Hawthorne.[35]

Ishmael gives his consent to Ahab's mission, but Melville is careful to portray it as being unnaturally coerced out of him through a kind of witchery or sorcery, like Brabantio's accusations regarding Othello's wooing of Desdemona in Shakespeare's *Othello*. Just as Ishmael's soul is possessed by Ahab's mysticism on the quarterdeck, Melville's skepticism of the entrenched power of *Pequod* owners Peleg and Bildad, the captain's captains, hinges specifically on their use of religion to justify their brutal business ethics that lead to their economic dominance. They pay virtually nothing to Ishmael and Queequeg to ship aboard the *Pequod*, and initially shun the pagan for religious reasons. Ishmael's claim that his partner is a member of the First Congregational Church is refuted by Peleg, who says, Queequeg "hasn't been baptized right either, or it would have washed some of that devil's blue off his face."[36] The Quaker gentlemen quickly drop their religious concern when Queequeg demonstrates his harpoon-throwing skill that sends them scrambling for the ship's papers, promising to "give ye the ninetieth lay, and that's more than ever was given a harpooner yet out of Nantucket."[37] The Quakers' hypocrisy is almost too easily exposed, as religious principle is quickly scrapped when money is to be made. These pacifists drool over Queequeg's killing potential, which flies in the face of their belief in the inner light of the living and that to kill is essentially to kill God. Bildad and Peleg do not hunt on Sunday, but if a whale comes in their proximity, they will not turn it down, for they see it as the Lord's bounty. Melville humorously highlights what they really worship.

In this and other scenes sending up the folly of humanity's pursuit of profit in *Moby-Dick*, Melville seems to protest "that commercial avidity has supplanted once-paramount religious concerns."[38] However, conventional, organized religion is hardly what Melville calls for in the novel. If anything, he privileges a pantheistic spiritualism like that which Ishmael achieves at the bower in Arsacides as he worships the whale-skeleton shrine. Scenes abound in *Moby-Dick* in which economic activity provides the occasion for religious reverie. Such scenes are not presented in a way that idolizes or fetishizes the financial return of the work, but rather in a way that finds the kinetic, physical process of the tasks themselves, in almost Thoreauvean ways, to be pregnant with meaning. The capacity to engage in an economic activity within an industrial context and transform it into a spiritually enriching experience, complete with sonorous, cadenced meditative incantation is typified by the mat-making scene.

The chapter title of "The Mat-Maker" immediately calls attention to the process of weaving and the dominant imagery of lines, yarn, and tapestry as a metaphor for Ishmael's own narrative process. Like "Loomings," "The Mat-Maker" self-reflexively points to Ishmael's process of creating art by weaving concrete experience with abstract thought, a task on the assembly line of production on this floating whale factory yielding a product, like the narrative itself, that is an image of multiplicity in unity. Production, in this case, provides a liberating outlet from the tyranny of Ahab's quest. In it, Queequeg and Ishmael produce a sword-mat without falling into the solipsistic reveries liable to the watchman aloft in the masthead, where narcissistic escapist dreams threaten a violent and watery death of intellectual self-consumption. The "dreaminess" of the scene tempts Ishmael to gravitate into a solitude in which "each silent sailor seemed resolved into his own invisible self." But the "intermittent dull sound of the sword" keeps him alert to the task at hand, his interdependence on Queequeg with whom he weaves, and the force of chance his sword represents.[39] As a kind of editor-publisher to Ishmael's weaving author, Queequeg guides Ishmael's shuttle rhythmically and in tandem, so "the interblending of threads with Queequeg's own" give shape to experience as a storyteller might. We discover along with Ishmael the spiritual in the material "mess and chaos of life," as John Bryant writes on the chapter "Stowing Down and Clearing Up," an "extraction of ideality out of materiality," a realization of sudden convergences and coherencies.[40]

While Ishmael discovers intellectual and spiritual outlets in the tasks driven by whaling's commercial necessities, Ahab is acutely aware of the power of the culture of capitalism, and thus manipulates it to subdue his crew from potential mutiny during the long, uneventful interstices during the hunt for the White Whale. During a time in American history that prompted Henry David Thoreau to question in *Walden* (1846) why we work the way we do and the Frenchman Alexis de Tocqueville to sketch poignantly in *Democracy in America* (1835) the anxiety and desperation etched into the faces of Americans as he toured the country, money menaced Melville as well. Frustrated at his attempts to win the financial rewards of his first novel, *Typee*, by the time he wrote *Moby-Dick*, he was unnerved by the pressure to succeed in the literary marketplace. "Dollars damn me," he wrote, "the calm, the coolness, the silent grass-growing mood in which a man *ought* always to compose—that, I fear, can seldom be mine."[41] That calm, however, can breed rebellion among a crew on an audacious mission to avenge their captain's feud with a frustratingly evasive, seldom-present creature. The force of the quarterdeck theatrics can only carry so much momentum, as Ahab turns to the business of whaling and the routine of its attendant tasks to quell any rising spirit of rebellion among the crew. "Temporary interests and employments should intervene and hold them healthily suspended for the final dash," Ahab concludes.[42] Indeed, the dark underside of the lyrical and magical mat-making scene is not its productivity or tie to the business of whaling. Rather, that euphoric moment is only possible precisely because Ahab underwrites it as one such "temporary interest" to thwart rebellion caused by "protracted meditation unrelieved by action," a task to give them "some nearer things to think of than Moby Dick."[43]

But far from simply keeping the crew's idle hands busy, Melville knows that those busy hands pay homage with their busy-ness to the profit motive through activities and routines that function as "food for their more common daily appetites."[44] Ishmael even confirms that "man is a money-making animal" in the context of Stubb admonishing Pip to stay in the boat, for he should not expect to be rescued since "a whale would sell for thirty times what you would, Pip, in Alabama."[45] Fraternal benevolence ceases in the face of the profit motive, just as the piety of Bildad and Peleg vanishes at the sight of Queequeg's prowess as a producer. Ahab knows what a motivator money is, and that his anticapitalistic quest for Moby-Dick can hold sway for only so long before the crew erupts. "They may scorn cash now," he reasons, "but let some months go by, and no prospective promise of it to them, and then this same quiescent cash all at once mutinying in them, this same cash would soon cashier Ahab."[46] Such considerations come in light of Ahab's awareness that they can "with perfect impunity, both moral and legal . . . refuse all further obedience to him, and even violently wrest from him the command."[47] Ahab thus pours his personal grudge against the White Whale into the commercial "customary usages" of the *Pequod*. He feigns interest in "the general pursuit of his profession" to harness the power of the ship's "natural" commercial purpose as well as his crew's nature as money-making animals.[48]

Melville offers a clear acknowledgment in "Surmises" of the civilizing, if often bedeviling (especially for authors), power of capitalism and its socially mollifying commercial culture. Indeed, common economic interest not only bonds sailor to sailor—cutting, mincing, rowing, weaving, swabbing—but it tacitly conjoins them to their captain. Indeed, money is one of the biggest enemies to Ahab, more so than morality or religious principle especially as it rests in the hands of Starbuck as he considers killing Ahab in the chapter "The Musket." In sharp contrast to Ahab, Peleg and Bildad are not so much ship captains but captains of industry. Ahab's spirituality, concussive and embroiled as it may be, is better wedded to his pursuit of the whale. In this regard, his heart is pure—purely black, to be sure—in his total lack of capitalist self-interest as evidenced not only in "Surmises" but also in "The Doubloon," where he only exploits the marriage between mysticism and money, piety and profit motive, to make the crew conform to his monomaniacal and murderous design. Money in the novel is thus like the mysterious iconography on the Spanish coin itself: Its value is inert, even neutral, until imposed upon by an individual's will. Interestingly, the men only remain subject to Ahab's tyranny so long as they are blind to how they have been cheated of their right to capital through the systematic deprivation of genuine commercial and professional purpose. As such, the genuine free market (as opposed to Ahab's sham of capitalist pursuit) functions as a curative cleansing agent.[49] To be well employed—not coerced, harried, or hoodwinked—is indeed one of the most peaceful states of mind alluded to in the novel. It is fleeting, however, and as maddeningly elusive as the whale himself. Ishmael, for example, looks up to the grand mansions of New Bedford's whaling elite but is careful to note that such riches were dredged from the abject depths of the sea. The undercurrent of irony, nonetheless, does not dissipate his applause for the achievement of such prosperity and security.

Next in Command: The Mates

WITH THE failure of his appeal to Ahab to back down from his frantic chase after the White Whale and Ahab's own appropriation of economic tasks for his mission's masquerade as furthering the financial function of the *Pequod*, Starbuck reaches for another weapon—a musket. It also proves ineffective in his hands. What confounds Starbuck is an epistemological crisis: in order to execute the captain and thus create a revolution, he must undergo an internal revolution, which he lacks the nerve to do. "I stand alone here upon an open sea, with two oceans and a whole continent between me and law," he muses, feeling totally isolated from any set of guiding principles developed by mortals on land. Thus he turns to heavenly guidance but only confronts ambiguity when he asks, "Is heaven a murderer when its lightning strikes a would-be murderer in his bed?... And would I be a murderer then, if...?"[50]

Ahab is sure he has no legal recourse for his actions in "Surmises" and openly worries that the crew will discover his tyranny and retaliate. "Having impulsively, it is probable, and perhaps somewhat prematurely revealed the prime but private purpose of the *Pequod*'s voyage, Ahab was now *entirely conscious* that, in doing so, he had laid himself open to the unanswerable charge of usurpation; and... refuse all further obedience to him" and even physically retaliate with the full backing of the law.[51] "Usurpation," in this sense, means the unlawful appropriation of or illegal use of property violating proper and intended use, especially as agreed upon in a contracted position defined in papers he signed with Captain Peleg and Bildad. In this case, of course, it is the ship and crew that Ahab has illegally seized for his "private purpose," flouting its use as a tool of trade in the public free market.

According to antebellum maritime law governing the conduct of ship captains, however, Ahab had less to worry about than he supposed. Since he never put the sailors directly into harm's way until the final confrontation with Moby Dick—and even then, the battle could have been excused as part of the business of whale hunting, representing to an outsider nothing out of the ordinary—he was operating within the letter, if not the spirit, of the law. The law stipulated that "an abused sailor had virtually no redress against a tyrannical captain, other than the promise of retrospective succor in the admiralty courts on land."[52] According to *A Treatise of the Law Relative to Merchant Ships and Seamen* from 1810, and the 1844 lawsuit, *U.S. v. Givings*, a captain like Ahab would have been permitted to use even unreasonable punishment on his crew, as long as it did not accelerate into "cruelty and oppression."[53] Only in the limited instance in which the sailor's "life or limbs" were under direct threat could he defend himself from the captain physically.[54] Indeed, "any action of the captain threatening less than imminent death," which of course would only apply in the last three chapters of the novel, "or permanent bodily injury must be submitted to" until the case could be heard by a home tribunal.[55] Starbuck has no recourse in positive, or written, law; his only hope is for divine inspiration from natural or higher law's idealized code of conduct.

Starbuck's tragic inaction and fatal paralysis in "The Musket" is not portrayed as a moral man straitjacketed by positive law. Instead he appears to be a pious man failing to boldly break that law in service of the higher law to which he is so devoted. It is not the strength of positive law as a constraint on his potential retaliation but his "wrestling with an angel" that stymies him. The force of Ahab's conviction to his mission that has him calling out in his sleep humanizes the captain and thus weakens Starbuck's resolve, much in the way Claudius's peaceful slumber breaks Hamlet's will to murder him. He lowers his musket precisely when Ahab cries, "Stern all! Oh Moby Dick, I clutch thy heart at last."[56] The gesture culminates Starbuck's deference and capitulation that began when he first averted his eyes and cast his visage downward the moment the crew made Ahab's vengeance their own on the quarterdeck.

Not just Starbuck but the other mates, Flask and Stubb, represent varying degrees of opposition to Ahab's authority. All are acutely aware of Ahab's tyranny, as "by all their minutest gestures and expressions, they plainly showed the uneasy, if not painful, consciousness of being under a troubled mastereye."[57] The mates all show the stress of their situation in different ways. Flask's diminutive and shallow pugilism is the least threatening to Ahab. Starbuck's Christianity and musket have the best revolutionary potential but die the hardest and require Ahab's most complex soul-wrenching utterances to dispatch. By contrast, Ahab easily banishes Stubb to his quarters for asking him to stop pacing because his whalebone leg has kept him awake. "Down, dog, and kennel!" he shouts in tones brutally degrading to his officer.[58] Stubb's retort, "I will not tamely be called a dog, sir," elicits Ahab's venom: "Then be called ten times a donkey, and a mule, and an ass, and be gone, or I'll clear the world of thee!"[59]

The pragmatism of Stubb's perfectly reasonable solution to buffer the prosthetic tip to dampen its knocking into the deck is an irritation to Ahab, because it assumes he should conceal and compromise his tormented condition for the good of the crew. Indeed, the request insults the grandeur of his inner turmoil, his somnambulant wakeful dreaming, with its quotidian fastidiousness. Stubb only speaks up against the captain when his blissful domestic space below deck, marked by untroubled and utterly peaceful sleep, is disturbed by Ahab's pacing. If the otherwise wholly noncombative Stubb is to defend anything, it is his insulated lair, since "he was as particular about the comfortable arrangement of his part of the boat, as an old stage-driver is about the snugness of his box." This is in keeping with his domestic regard of whaling as "but a dinner, and all his crew invited guests."[60] Ahab throws his pipe angrily overboard in an aborted attempt at achieving domestic peace and leisure; Stubb never was seen without his pipe and would put it into his mouth before "putting his legs into his trowsers."[61] Stubb's love of leisure and slumber, his carefree attitude also represent an affront to Ahab, who suffers his anguish with every bit of the pugilistic resolve of third mate, Flask, but with the soul ache of Starbuck.

Together, the mates represent the warring perspectives that color Ahab's inner crisis. Melville was fascinated with the dynamics of leadership and the lengths to which captains go to mold attitudes and behaviors. The bearing of a ship captain was all-important to the way the crew, and more important, his mates, received him. Starbuck, Stubb, and Flask cannot bear to look him in the face, quailing "before his strong, sustained, and mystic aspect. Stubb and Flask looked sideways from him; the honest eye of Starbuck," the only of them to openly protest, "fell downright."[62] Ahab's nightmare is too difficult to behold let alone destroy. It is "a vulture that feeds upon his heart forever"[63] and leaves him sleeping "with clenched hands; and wake with his own bloody nails in his palms."[64] It is the voice of this living nightmare of "the trances and torments" of one "consumed with one unachieved revengeful desire" that drives asunder Starbuck's revolutionary plans, a voice made more powerful as it emanates from the unmediated palpitating soul, a voice independent of his rational mind that triangulates the calculus of the chase in the charts.[65]

Deference to the sheer strength of Ahab's monomaniacal vision is dramatized in the chapter "The Cabin-Table." Hierarchy is fully reinforced, ritual is obeyed, and a crushing silence quells any potential rebellion from rising in the throats of the three mates who dine with Ahab. The men sit around Ahab, who "presided like a mute, maned sea lion on the white coral beach, surrounded by his war-like but still deferential cubs."[66] Ahab's own silence expresses his power to silence his mates and his will to make them abide by his will. Ishmael's description then shifts its comparative imagery from the animal kingdom to German royalty, as he likens the scene to the "Coronation banquet at Frankfort, where the German Emperor profoundly dines with the Seven Imperial Electors, so these cabin meals were somehow solemn meals, eaten in awful silence."[67] One *Moby-Dick* reader observed that "Speech is gagged and no threat of revolution can arise, for Ahab presides over his table as portentously as a king or slaveholder."[68] The silence of the mates is their tacit, yet forced, endorsement of his command, as they "participate in his hierarchy" and as "each accepts his rank without protest, consuming his portion of the spoils, however small it might be."[69] In the ensuing chapter, hierarchy is turned upside down in the "frantic democracy of these inferior fellows the harpooneers."[70]

Noncoercive Knowledge and Democracy

DEMANDING THE opposite of deference, *Moby-Dick* invites readers to be coauthors of the text and to inscribe our own meanings and experiences upon it. Peter Whittemore, the only one at the live reading among us with Melville's blood coursing through his veins, said it best when he noted that each time he encounters *Moby-Dick* he discovers not only new threads of thought but a new novel. We live with it, and it grows with us. This divergent, radical plurality of meanings that we all actively and freely access, and indeed, which draw us to the reading, runs precisely counter to the stanching, silenced predicament of the three mates under Ahab. Our silence as we listen then should be read as an ecstatic one, fully open to our liberal and conservative, progressive and decadent, civilized and wild selves. "I have even participated in the marathon readings of *Moby-Dick*," John Bryant confesses, "along with other bleary-eyed companions, up all night reading their assigned chapters out loud, hopped up on Melville's jazz."[71] If this is a jazz club, it is an epistemological one, equal parts steady intellect and runaway passion. For what stuns us and what excites us are those moments of coherence in the novel itself, a vast, tangled, unfinished mess of a novel in many respects, a "draught of a draught," a mishmash of sources jumbled into beautiful chaotic coherence.[72] But if the novel does not mind its manners, if indeed it does not silently sit in deference while Ahab finishes his meal, if its ungodly and unearthly linguistic riffs, like improvisational jazz (played well) begin to cohere over the twenty-five-hour period, patterns emerge, and visions can be attained. Only with the liberty of our own individual reading backgrounds, our own senses of the history of whaling, our own store of knowledge of Melville's life, our own assemblage of life experience and applications we have all made and continue to make through this great novel, can those visions be attained.

Ahab's will to coerce his reading of the whale onto the crew emerges into a crisis of meaning reflecting the ship's political tensions. Thus the biggest political threat to him lies in Starbuck's interpretation of his wounding as arbitrary and random, and not deeply significant. Peretz has gone so far as to claim that "what the whale means is unknown, the event of its encounter is a surprising event where knowledge collapses, but it is almost certain to Ahab, and only to him (and he is therefore the only witness to this near-certainty) that it means something different than what it signifies to everyone else."[73] The cosmic significance and psychological urgency Ahab attaches to his wounding is totally at odds with Starbuck's understanding of it as a whale-hunting accident, unfortunate yet hardly writ with such profound significance. This perspective presents a threat to Ahab's political power and is the main source of tension between captain and mate.

Destabilized authority onboard the *Pequod* points toward destabilized laws, creating a tangle of interpretation that boils down to the notion of rights and ownership, the subject of the chapter "Fast-Fish and Loose-Fish." That chapter is Ishmael's wonderful exposition of the folly and conundrum of property rights regarding the rights to whales that are being actively pursued, versus those that are anyone's fair game, or "loose-fish." The business of forming coherent arguments in such a murky miasma emerges as a rhetorical burlesque at best, which Ishmael jokingly performs himself in "The Honor and Glory of Whaling" in the hyperbolic, exaggerated tones of a rookie lawyer stridently overstating his argument. Yet Melville being Melville, the darker and more subtle joke in Ishmael's advocacy of whaling as the stuff of high art and nobility is that many of his points are ironically plausible. Here and elsewhere in the novel, Melville exposes the absurdity of argumentation, despite its apparent persuasive powers as coercive knowledge. Melville instead advocates a noncoercive form of knowledge marked by its openness, as in Whitman's pastoral poetry. "The Pacific" and "The Prairie" chapters particularly allow for pluralized rather than narrow legalistic argumentation. Noncoercive knowledge is embraced through Ishmael's expansive lyrical language rather than a narrowing delimitation of it. Space is essential to this noncoercive paradigm, as Melville himself said "you must have plenty of sea-room to tell the Truth in"[74] and "it is hard to be finite about an infinite subject, [since] all subjects are infinite."[75] Yet this is no invitation for complacency or sloth—we leave that to the likes of Stubb in his fastidiously appointed and highly domesticated bunk area and his ever-present pipe—for Melville loved, as he said of Emerson, "all men who dive," who seek truth at great depths, "for any fish can swim close to the surface, but it takes a great whale to go down stairs five miles or more; & if he don't attain the bottom, why, all the lead in Galena can't fashion the plummet that will."[76]

The ambiguity and plurality built into the multiple perspectives of the whale are precisely what Ahab aims to destroy in a gesture every bit as political as it is epistemological. The "thinking that takes the address of the whale and its implications into account," and its attendant "enigmatic . . . revolutionary disorientation of the senses," as Peretz urges, "always demands the introduction of a certain inevitable vocabulary of power and forces."[77] That which we cannot control brings out the language of power, and Ahab lashes out against the passivity of his body symbolized by his wound. In "The Whiteness of the Whale" a consideration of the whale's multiple meanings raises the issue of power, as the tyranny of monolithic interpretation crumbles under multiple perspectives. Peretz astutely notes of this chapter that "no meaning which an emperor, a judge, or a priest assigned to whiteness can ever stop Ishmael's discourse, which is to say dominate it; these authorities and institutions are all erased and washed away by the huge white wave that carries Ishmael's language," which humbles Ishmael's own attempt at mastery and dominance.[78] The closer we examine reality, the more we engage issues of power, which under scrutiny also deconstruct before our eyes. The great wave of readers—literally millions of them from 1851 until now—represents that vast sea of understanding and knowledge, which overwhelms the narrow iron-rails view of the world in its immense vastness, so that by the end of the novel, "helpless Ahab's head," the center of his monomaniacal thought, "was seen, like a tossed bubble which the least chance shock might burst," a tiny vulnerable speck in a universe of thought whose weight he cannot bear.[79] As Thoreau said, "the universe is wider than our views of it."[80]

In keeping with Melville's own adherence to noncoercive knowledge at the heart of American pragmatism, no such singular reading as Ahab's is coerced on us at the *Moby-Dick* Marathon; this is a celebration of a diversity of readings and even of art works inspired by the novel. What one of us finds arbitrary and random in the novel, another will surely see as deeply significant. Indeed, we tolerate and encourage such diversity of thought, such open-mindedness, as it is consonant with the pantheistic multiperspectivism and omnivorous intellectual hunger of Ishmael that is as starry as Vere and as grounded and earthy as Queequeg. As a collective whole, our perspectives form the constellation of ideas that make up the world—at least the whole of western civilization—reflected in *Moby-Dick*. This characterizes the politics of a mass reading like the 2009 *Moby-Dick* Marathon, and it is toward the details of that event that we now turn.

The Politics of Mass Reading, 2009

THE CAPTAIN(S) and mates of the 2009 reading, those distinguished and celebrated readers of the event, attracted a great deal of attention. How did they envision their leadership roles? Why would a politician be interested in promoting 150-year-old fiction? Is there a nationalistic agenda at the reading to promote American patriotism, especially considering that *Moby-Dick* was recently legislated as the state novel of Massachusetts? Is this event democratic? How does it ritualize its own hierarchical structure? What can an event like this do for our political institutions or civic engagement and citizenship? What is the advantage of reading a book like this as a group rather than alone? Is this a remedy to "bowling alone," the emblem of eroding group engagement in civic and public events, clubs, and activities that Robert D. Putnam has lamented about modern American life?[81] If so, how does this build social capital? The 2009 reading promised to provide some clues to the answers to these questions.

The top brass of the reading were on display in the first hour of the 2009 event, with Mayor Lang and Congressman Frank bearing the honorific titles on the schedule. Veary and Lang opened with sonorous, stirring readings from "Loomings" in the first two slots, delegated to honor the novel's theatricality—with Veary dressed as Ishmael—and its local civic ties represented by the mayor. The room was abuzz in anticipation of Frank, representing the novel's statewide and even national significance. He was to read next, but to the disappointment of all but the veterans, one of whom later assured me that he was "notoriously late" in past years, he did not show up for his passage. Those in charge of managing the reading order, the "watch officers," a cadre of museum friends and volunteers, most of them elderly, did not miss a beat, deftly substituting Whittemore for the absent Frank.

Of all the top brass in the room, Frank clearly possessed the most star power, coming fresh from spending significant time on the national stage as a key player in the federal economic stimulus package designed to assuage the 2008 financial crisis. A bona fide celebrity, Frank is the only member of the House whose remarks have been collected in a book, irresistibly entitled *Barney Frank: The Story of America's Only Left-Handed, Gay, Jewish Congressman* (2006), and was voted the "brainiest, funniest, and most eloquent congressman" by Capitol Hill staff in a poll published by *Washingtonian* in 2006. More recently he was the subject of a *New Yorker* feature-length article in January

2009. Thus, with his status rising to such heights so recently, his fashionably late arrival turned heads, as a hush swept over the excited crowd. The Massachusetts representative to Congress approached the podium and in his characteristic gravelly voice, with a soft "r" worthy of Nathan Lane's best Disney voices, lit up the room with his rendition of Ishmael's fearful first encounter with harpooner, cannibal, and Spouter Inn roommate, Queequeg. The humor of the passage, centered as it is around Ishmael's fear of Queequeg's primitive sexual power, made visible in his phallic harpoon, was well matched to Frank's own bawdy wit. At a gay rights fund raiser, for example, a speaker onstage said her Texan father thought that L.G.B.T. "sounded like a sandwich," to which Frank shouted from the audience, "Sometimes it is!" bringing down the house in gales of laughter.[82] Melville's humor emerged brilliantly at the live reading, thanks to Frank's impeccable, yet human delivery. Midway through the passage, the succeeding reader, Emily Prigot, clad in her paramilitary New Bedford Whaling National Historical Park uniform, approached the podium next to him, waiting her turn. Frank, seeing her out of the corner of his eye, halted and gaped at her, saying, true to his peace-loving democratic politics, "The uniform makes me nervous," to the audience's delight. Prigot smiled and swung into her passage when Frank finished, representing the reading's second tie to the federal government, this time via the National Park Service. She too benefitted from a fresh and full crowd, which responded with raucous glee to the line, "better sleep with a sober cannibal than a drunken Christian," a line made all the more savory, read as it was on the heels of the first openly gay congressman's reading of a passage lampooning Ishmael's homophobia. Prigot's own military bearing and uniform were undercut by her affable female voice and unrestrained joy in Melville's attack on conventional religion. Melville would have adored the tableau cast by these two readers and its attendant iconography, as the federal government itself openly joined in his merciless satire of heterosexual normativity and conventional mainstream Christian dogma. If only the entire federal government, and not just these two of its representatives, had such sympathies, perhaps the nation might be better off.

The lineup of readers from Prigot to "The Sermon" at the Seamen's Bethel represented the second tier, a kind of corps of officers, beneath the stars of Barney Frank's caliber. Not quite dignitaries, each reader in this set represented a significant faction of the Melville faithful. One would expect higher education to be represented in this group through a president of a local college or university. But aside from Professor Wyn Kelley, representing professional

Melville scholars in her prefatory lecture, the first reader listed in affiliation with higher education, interestingly, was neither university faculty nor administrator, but a student, Xaele Perez, who was an undergraduate at the nearby University of Massachusetts at Dartmouth. In this high-profile spot, she fittingly represented the ample portion of the 1,300 visitors and 168 readers in their early twenties. A graying Ray Veary responded to the high numbers of undergraduate-aged spectators and readers with unhesitating support: "That's a good thing," he affirmed, glad in knowing that the novel's memory promises to live on through this ritual reading. After Perez came Cile Hicks, a trustee to the museum, representing the multitude of donors providing the vital economic base that underwrote the entire event from its origins thirteen years prior. Indeed, donations such as hers supported the salary of key museum staffers like the late Irwin Marks, the man who originally brought the reading to New Bedford. Such donations, of course, continue to keep the museum afloat. It is notable that, of these first two tiers of readers, Kelley was the sole professor, yet she chose to list her affiliation as a representative of the Melville Society rather than with her home academic institution. In conversation, and on the ledger, few presented themselves as "Melville experts," as they had just one week prior at the Modern Language Association's Melville panels in San Francisco, where Kelley presented a paper. (I was fortunate to have attended that event.) Status, in other words, was not conferred through academic credentials at the reading, but indeed through a reader's love—inflected through the voices of political representatives, a park ranger, a student, a relative, and a generous donor to the museum. Despite the quality and quantity of scholarship by Melville Society loyalists, Sten, Bercaw Edwards, Kelley, and Tim Marr, which easily might have entitled them to dominate the event, they graciously chose to blend in to the egalitarian community in which one group did not angle for the spotlight more than another.

Bercaw Edwards put it incisively: "This is a cross section of people, most of whom bring their own copy of the novel to the event," she said, noting that here, as at the Mystic Seaport marathon reading of *Moby-Dick*, we find an eclectic mix of twelve-year-olds, punkers, and auto mechanics, all of whom "found the novel in different ways, and were there because they were excited to see others like themselves." She affirmed that "everyone who has been touched by the novel is here." That sense of community and democracy through the common, unsung readers and the obsessed amateurs, thus forms the subject of the next chapter.

Life in the Forecastle. Courtesy MIT Museum.

·4·

Harpooners and Sailors
The Unsung Readers

*T*HE HIERARCHY OF THE *Acushnet*, the vessel with which Melville shipped in 1841, like most antebellum whalers, was built directly into its architecture. The highest ranks enjoyed the luxury of occupying sleeping quarters positioned farthest toward the rear, or aft, of the ship. Unlike in an airplane, the aft of a whaling vessel was far preferable to its bow, because of its nearness to the ship's fulcrum as it rocked against incoming waves. The most tumultuous position aboard a ship at sea is to the fore, and thus the roughest ride in a gale below deck on a whaler was in the forecastle, the cabin housing the lowest ranking crew, including harpooners and common sailors. Most of those common sailors, representing the four corners of the globe, would sleep cap-a-pie, heads forward to avoid the nauseating nocturnal cadences affected by the ship lifting the feet rather than the head, a predicament that works against the natural flows of blood circulation and digestion. For eighteen months, Herman Melville slept cap-a-pie in these quarters, measuring fifteen by fifteen, with twenty other whalemen. Captain Valentine Pease and his mates slept at the opposite end of the craft in the least rocky and most roomy compartments, while the skilled men—boatsteerers, carpenter, cook, and cooper—were also to the rear of the ship, but forward of the top brass.[1]

The common sailors of the forecastle made up the bone and muscle of the whaling industry much in the way common readers, and there are many, constitute the grass roots of the *Moby-Dick* Marathon. They are the critical mass of the masses, the energy and synergy of the crowd, wedged in little niches under the stairs with pillows and comforters, some awake and engaged at 3 AM and others sound asleep and audibly snoring like their counterparts 150 years prior in their forecastle bunks. The school teachers, singers, sculptors, and scientists now become obsessed amateurs of all stripes, many of them first-timers who board this lexical and semantic ship at the New Bedford

Whaling Museum with sleeping gear, creating makeshift bunks in odd corners and splaying themselves across benches. Who are they? How do they
"do" the *Moby-Dick* Marathon? What rituals do they cling to, and what does
it say about the print culture of Melvillians? Certainly, the men aboard the
Pequod have their own culture, as did the real men of the *Acushnet*—and it is
just as much generated by language as that of the audience at the reading.
Print culture—especially its cross-pollination with song, visual art, and oral
storytelling—spawned *Moby-Dick*, and print culture keeps it alive with readings like this.

Whereas the prior chapter examined the nature of authority in the novel
and the reading, this chapter focuses on the culture of the common sailor and
reader. I investigate the folkways and lore of the common sailor—the climate
conditioning life astern in the world of the forecastle—to reveal how language
is at the core of their culture, from songs to sexuality, from gams to alcohol. I
specifically look at "Midnight Forecastle" and "The Cabin-Table" to discern
the mentality of the masses who populate the contiguous social worlds in
and around *Moby-Dick*, from the *Acushnet* to the *Pequod* to the New Bedford
Whaling Museum. What is the nature of the "frantic democracy" that initially
unleashed and continues to sustain the life of a novel whose radical voice so
brazenly defies the "tolerable constraint" and "invisible domineerings" that
color Ahab's dining quarters?[2]

Frantic Democracy

WHEREAS THE dinner setting of Ahab and the three mates described at the
beginning of "The Cabin-Table" is marked by constrained silence, submerged
discord, and repressed resentment, the dining atmosphere of the harpooners
is unvarnished, transparent, and spontaneous, a truly unrestrained and noisy
affair. Power is evenly dispersed among Tashtego, Dagoo, and Queequeg,[3] as
the three harpooners tyrannize and bedevil their white server, Dough Boy,
the son of a "bankrupt banker and a hospital nurse," darting forks at him
like harpoons, ordering him about, and upbraiding him for failing to deliver
the food quickly enough.[4] Their rough play with the steward pantomimes
their people's past violent triumphs over whites, from capture to scalping to
cooking, "snatching him up bodily, and thrusting his head into a great empty
wooden trencher, while Tashtego, knife in hand, began laying out the circle
preliminary to scalping him."[5] The "tumultuous visitations of these three

savages" made Dough Boy's "whole life . . . one continual lip quiver," as "hard fares the white waiter who waits upon cannibals."[6]

The scene's comic appeal masks Melville's deeper concern for the contrasting faces of democracy, which sets Ahab's despotic and orderly table against the harpooner's unrestrained and frantic feast. As liberal and tolerant as the harpooners' cabin table appears, it is nonetheless a mockery of a civilized dinner. The scene's chaotic cacophony combines the harpooners' shouts at Dough Boy with the very act of consumption itself, a "barbaric smack of the lip in eating—an ugly sound enough," as they "chewed their food with such relish that there was a report to it."[7] They intentionally chomp with audible relish to elicit Dough Boy's xenophobia. Right on cue, he "looked to see whether any marks of teeth lurked in his own lean arms."[8] Intermittent crescendos of clashing pots and pans erupt, which "all but shattered the crockery," when Tashtego sings out for the waiter to produce himself. Though democratic, this is a mob, and a boisterous, infantile, unruly one at that. Like a bunch of wild adolescents, the sea dogs know very little indoor civility because they are out in the open air except for sleeping and eating in the cabin. Their democratic energy knows no real power, as it is so disorganized. The mates know no power, for they quail in Ahab's autocratic presence.

Melville always found something adolescent and even boyish about most whalemen; the seasoned sophistication of Ahab, dark and tortured as it may be, is not to be mistaken with the blunt naïve world of the common sailor. For all his abstract reveries and wise considerations of social and whaling conventions the world round, Ishmael, a rookie whaler, demonstrates his share of galling shortsightedness and naïve optimism. Elsewhere in Melville's writings, "undergraduate" striplings like the title characters of *Pierre*, *Redburn*, and *Billy Budd*, are prone to abysmal blunders that are at once laughable and profoundly regrettable collisions of innocence with a fallen and treacherous world. In *Moby-Dick*, Queequeg is like an overgrown adolescent, "just enough civilized to show off his outlandishness in the strangest possible manner. His education was not yet completed. He was an undergraduate."[9] None of these characters have the potential to organize or spearhead any sort of effective or lasting revolution, however apparently subversive (even inadvertently so, especially in the case of Billy Budd) their actions appear. "Yes, as a class," the narrator of *Billy Budd* confirms, "sailors are in character a juvenile race. Even their deviations are marked by juvenility,"[10] as portrayed by the raucous harpooners' dinner scene in *Moby-Dick*.

The rambunctious whale equivalent to this adolescent energy is the forty-barrel bulls, whom Melville characterizes as a bunch of undergraduate rowdies in the chapter "Schools and Schoolmasters." These whales are bent on their own nautical version of the campus mayhem that was making headlines during the antebellum era, which frequently turned grim as riots broke out leading to at least one professor's murder. "Full of fight, fun and wickedness," the "riotous lad at Yale or Harvard,"[11] like leviathan, indeed "carries a surplus stock of vitality in him."[12] The lad's outbursts are too frequently ill timed or misdirected to become concerted into revolutionary power. The rebellions are sporadic and intense, usually spearheaded with little sense of principle, amounting to directionless surplus vitality randomly expressed as reckless mayhem. So, as Fanning writes of the harpooners' gleeful subjugation of Dough Boy, "hierarchy is in this manner turned upside down, for a white servant now serves dark masters."[13] Yet in Melville no easy political answers emerge, as his satirical pen is aimed as much at the panic-stricken waiter as at the lip-smacking and exuberant, yet politically inconsequential, subversive theatrics of Tashtego, Dagoo, and Queequeg. Cast in a similar humorous light that expresses ambivalence toward unrestrained revolutionary force, the black cook, Fleece, delivers a speech to a group of sharks, which he berates as if they were a white congregation. He exhorts them to "kick up de dammdest row as ever you can; fill your dam bellies 'till dey bust—and den die."[14]

Kings of the inverted world though they may be for the moment, these sea dogs can be seen as venting their frustrations only for the time being, mainly because of their positions at the bottom of the wage-earning hierarchy. Charles Olson asserts that "whaling started, like so many American industries, as a collective, communal affair. . . . But it was already a sweated industry by the time Melville was on hand on a lay (1841–43) . . . THE TRICK—then as now: reduce labor costs lower than the worker's efficiency. . . combine inefficient workers and such costs [as food at fifteen to thirty cents a day per crew member] by maintaining lowest wages and miserable working conditions."[15] Ishmael corroborates this evidence with the observation that "though man loves his fellow, yet man is a money-making animal, which propensity too often interferes with his benevolence."[16]

Despite their shameless exploitation, sailors and harpooners represent the business end of the enterprise of catching whales. They constitute the physical point of contact between man and animal, between *Pequod* and Moby Dick. Without them the precision instrument of the whaling vessel is rendered useless. Factory workers for Nike in Malaysia play a similar industrial role in the transnational corporate world, just as in the world of U.S. education, the overworked and unsung public school teachers bear the brunt of the work of educating the future of America for scant material reward. These are the people who make such industries go; sailors and harpooners were the John Henrys of whaling whose sweat produced the fantastic wealth enjoyed by the New Bedford ship captains and owners. In terms of their relation to building wealth, as Thoreau notes, "It certainly is fair to [credit] that class [i.e., the working class] by whose labor the works which distinguish this generation are accomplished."[17] However essential to producing the distinguishing works of a generation, the working class, like the one Olson identifies in the 1840s whaling crews, "were the bottom dogs of all nations and all races."[18] The *Pequod*'s crew reflects the brutality of the work and its overwhelmingly youthful ranks. Melville referred to the thirty-eight-year-old William Maiden as the *Acushnet*'s "old cook."[19] Surrounded by whalemen whose ages ranged from eighteen to twenty-four, with the majority of them in their early twenties, Maiden appeared "old" to the twenty-one-year-old Melville. This is not surprising given that child laborers of developing countries toil today in various factories and that the average age of U.S. soldiers in Viet Nam was nineteen. The pattern has persisted, as the exploitation of youth labor has not escaped the attention of lyricists from eighteenth-century poet William Blake ("The Chimney Sweeper") to contemporary musician Paul Hardcastle ("Nineteen").

Among the mass of youth that comprised the first revolving-door industrial wage laborers, "Of the 18,000 men [who sailed aboard whalers annually], *one-half* ranked as green hands and more than *two-thirds* deserted every voyage."[20] What accounted for such high rates of desertion was more than the youthful wayward global hitchhiker spirit discussed in part 1, "Shipping Out." Driving the incentive to leave was the work itself. When it was not an exciting and transcendent adventure, the work of whaling was notoriously thankless, dangerous, and mind-numbingly monotonous. The low wage and lack of power in the ship's management relative to the captain and mates stripped common sailors of any economic or political incentives to stick with their voyage. With little in these ways to keep them on board, the prospect of women, terra firma, a warm bed, and a decent meal after months at sea magnetically compelled the seaman ashore.

Roll Call

THE FATE of the crew of Melville's *Acushnet* speaks to this pattern of transience. Similarly, waves of comings and goings are also built into the culture of the *Moby-Dick* Marathon reading, as there too might be a situation that grows tiresome if the novelty of its adventure were to wear off. In yet another category of desertion, many on the roster never ship out. Certainly, like any athletic marathon, there are those entries listed after the race as DNS, or "did not start." The *Acushnet* was no exception, as two common sailors deserted before the ship even departed from Fairhaven. As with the *Acushnet*, the captain abides by his ship (and goes down with it if he must), and the top brass will almost invariably return to the home port in fulfillment of their professional obligation and, perhaps most important, the opportunity to cash in on the voyage's profits. At the marathon reading, the extremely high profile attendees, such as members of Congress, of course do not stay for the duration of the full twenty-five-hour reading, but instead make an appearance, read their passage, spread good cheer, and make haste back to the beltway.

Likewise, the officers and captain of the *Acushnet* returned home, with few exceptions. The forty-three-year-old Captain Valentine Pease would bring back with him the second mate, John Hall, who at 5'11" was considered very tall, as most men aboard the ship stood no taller than 5'8", with Melville being considered among the tallest, at 5'9½." The English-born Hall would venture out to California during the gold rush while Captain Pease enjoyed a quiet retirement at Martha's Vineyard, where he lived in 1853. Boatsteerer William "Barney" Barnard also returned as did the "old cook" William Maiden. Joseph Warren, the twenty-five-year-old cooper also returned and settled in his native Boston. Of the green hand common sailors, only two returned. They were eighteen-year-old Bostonian Joseph "Little Jack" (or "Jack Nastyface") Broadnick, and the twenty-year-old Henry F. Hubbard from New Hampshire. Among the experienced crew to return were a twenty-four-year-old mulatto from Ohio with "wolly hair," according to Melville's description, and another ethnic American born in New York named Carlos "Bill" Green, who was nineteen. Foreigners returning with the *Acushnet* included John Adams, twenty-one and born in Cape de Verde Islands, and Joseph "Jo Portuguese" Luis, the twenty-year-old Fayal-born Portugal resident. Parker calls these seamen more "stable and reliable members of the crew, or the less adventurous," as they docked in Fairfield to complete the *Acushnet*'s voyage in May

1845, unlike Melville, who deserted in Nukuheva in the Marquesas Islands with Richard Tobias "Toby" Greene in July 1842.[21] The eleven returners of the *Acushnet*'s original twenty-five shared experience and rank, as all but two who came home were either officers or experienced whalemen.

Those who deserted, like Melville, tell a different story, or rather, a variety of stories. Boatsteerer David Smith deserted in Peru in June 1841 and wound up committing suicide in Mobile, Alabama. Others fled in San Francisco, Rio de Janeiro, Lahaina, Roa-pua, and Oahu. Two went out in search of medical aid, likely to no avail. Seventeen-year-old Henry Grant of Portland, Maine, crawled ashore at Oahu "half dead, spitting blood," and John Wright, an eighteen-year-old from Vermont also likely suffering from tuberculosis, known then as consumption, "went ashore half dead at the Marquesas," according to Melville's log.[22] Steward Henry Harmer, perhaps Melville's model for Dough Boy, fled at Lahaina in May 1843 and was seen by Toby Greene managing a hotel in New Orleans thirteen years later. Apparently for Harmer, stewardship to a bunch of brawling whalemen inspired him to a healthy ascent in the hospitality industry.

The list of names and their fates was important to Melville; *Moby-Dick* in some ways is his love letter to these men with whom he "spent more hours . . . than anyone except the closest members of his family; these were men who knew him better, in some ways, than anyone outside his family ever knew him," Parker astutely observes.[23] Indeed, Melville in some ways knew that the crew was replacing his own family members. He sensed this in a letter reassuring them that he "was not dissatisfied with his lot" of men he was thrown in with, "the fact of his being one of a crew so much superior in morals and early advantages to the ordinary run of whaling crews affords him constant gratification."[24] There is hardly a simple correlation between "moral superiority" and "early advantages" in *Moby-Dick*, as Ahab's wisdom and education clearly do not constrain him from his moral abominations. In many ways, the *Acushnet*'s crew was precisely representative of the "ordinary run of whaling crews," but Melville sympathized with them and also had his own mother's concern for his safety in mind in the letter. The stark contrast to this portrayal of the *Acushnet*'s crew being so exceptional is his disgust with their unwillingness to unite in a mutinous common front: "unfortunately, with a very few exceptions, our crew was composed of a parcel of dastardly and mean-spirited wretches, divided among themselves, and only united in enduring without resistance the unmitigated tyranny of the captain."[25]

Melville does not deliver an unproblematic celebration of the sea dogs in *Moby-Dick*, as the earlier discussion of their political limitations attests. Instead, he revels in their culture, from its bizarre foibles to its fiery fierceness and solemn dignity. He adroitly plays with the idiosyncrasies and contradictions of that forecastle culture, simultaneously mocking its appalling brutality and reveling in it. To define Melville's attitude toward the common sailor is like defining his attitude toward revolution and captaincy: he was above all compassionate for the humanity that lurked beneath the regrettable predicaments that social and political conventions placed it in. He had compassion for the sea dogs, for indeed he was but one, yet he could not put his faith in them as a revolutionary force. Melville's total honesty in his ambivalent and vacillating feelings for the common seaman emerges in his truthful portrayal of the seedy underside of life at sea and in his respectful dignity toward the spiritual survival woven into the mats, scrimshaws, songs, and stories of forecastle culture.

If Melville was frustrated by the common sailor's inability to organize into a political front, it was only because he saw such tremendous potential through their community and brotherhood. Chapter 40, "Midnight, Forecastle," is one such scene depicting the garish conviviality of the crew's brotherhood. More complex than it looks, this chapter extends well beyond what Olson and others have written off as the "bottom dogs" of a "rough and bastard crew . . . made pretty" in a "balletic chapter."[26] Though he never openly discusses it, Olson's diction of "balletic" and "pretty" to describe an all-male locker room atmosphere of profanity and macho bravado hints at the paradoxical sophistication of the scene, particularly with respect to its gender politics. Melville gleefully skewers rigid gender roles later in the novel in the chapter "Stowing Down and Clearing Up," which depicts the men scrubbing the ship with all the fastidiousness of women preparing for a tea party. It satirically calls into question the rigid segregation of sexes according to types of work, in this case, public production and domestic housekeeping, as the burly whalemen flamboyantly relish the opportunity to straighten and scrub the ship to a suitable shine after a messy kill. Their community in their work—evidenced by their willingness to playfully transgress gender roles— also points to the close bonds of their leisure hours in the forecastle.

Doing the Forecastle Jig

CHAPTER 40, "Midnight, Forecastle," does more than just invert gender roles; it looks deeply into how the sexual frustrations of the womanless crew channel into song, sexual fantasy, racial strife, and work. It opens with a lament of the lost sexual life addressed to the dearly departed women on shore, a kind of dirge bidding "Farewell and adieu to you, ladies of Spain! / Our captain's commanded."[27] The men at this point are united according to the stage direction, *"all singing in chorus,"* and continue in harmony as a Nantucket sailor steps in to change the tone with a merrier tune to counter the dreariness. His cheery song, celebrating the whaling life like a true Nantucketer should, has them dancing hand over hand so "your hearts never fail! / While the bold harpooner is striking the whale."[28] The men now swing into an impromptu cabin dance party, jigging to the beat of Pip's tambourine. The sounds of whaling are directly integrated into the high-spirited scene of song and dance, as the call for the watch becomes a sung voice to the musical accompaniment of ringing bells. Interestingly, some men sleep through the shenanigans, as the Dutch sailor suggests waking them to "Tell 'em to avast dreaming of their lasses. Tell 'em it's the resurrection," a bawdy play on their fantasy-induced erections.[29] Their dreams indicate the unquenchable desire for women will not be erased by this momentary fool's paradise, as one Maltese sailor calls for "Partners! I must have partners!" to which a game Sicilian sailor readily plays along as a girl, "girls and a green!—then I'll hop with ye."[30] A Long-Island sailor realizes the homosexual potential: "Well, well, ye sulkies, there's plenty more of us." He urges the men to make use of each other, to figuratively "Hoe corn when you may, say I" and seize the opportunity before them, so that "All legs go to harvest soon."[31]

The kings of the upside-down world, as Melville would have it, preside over the forecastle with no stuffy constraint, as joy is expressed as openly as anger. Hostility arises when Tashtego, for example, will have none of the merriment, as the tone of the scene shifts toward racial strife. His sullen dismissal, "That's a white man; he calls that fun," elicits the old Manx sailor's fancy that "the whole world's a ball . . . so 'tis right to make one ball-room of it." But the sailor's vision of song and dance as global harmony fades as the wind rises and the sky darkens with the mood. The men's sexual frustrations yet again surface, this time not through song, but through the sweetly tantalizing projections of their imaginations. "Those swift glances of warm, wild bosoms in the dance," they can almost taste with their "lithe swayings—coyings—flutterings! . . . all graze: unceasing touch and go!" A Tahitian sailor laments the fading images of naked dancing girls woven in the wood of his mat, "green the first day I brought ye thence; now worn and wilted quite." It pains him to see them fade, their visual images becoming disembodied, "transplanted to yon sky."[32]

The sea roars against the hull and shakes the men from their fantasies, as they yield to the reality of the ravages of time and the persistent mockery of the sea. The initial fear at the rising storm transforms into anger, which brews from the stark realization of the celibate masturbatory sexuality of the common crew life. Dagoo and a Spanish sailor then square off after an exchange of racial insults, leading to a fight that is only broken up by the mate's call from the quarterdeck to man the sails in the storm. The call to duty pulls them from their symphony of pastimes reflective of their deepest anxieties and unfulfilled desires, and their bitterest racial hatred. The movements of the chapter reflect the culture of the harpooners and sailors, and the endless interlacing of the seaman's culture—his songs, carvings, tale-telling, fantasies, and fisticuffs—with his duty to the ship.

The movement of the chapter evokes the vacillations between harmony and discord among the men in a kind of locker room environment that ranges from pathetic fantasy to ridiculous horseplay to silly dancing to vicious fighting. Never once in the chapter do the men truly converse except to fight; either their voices rise together in chorus as they sing, or they speak almost in soliloquy throughout the chapter. It is the world of work that unites them, and even there, little is spoken aloud, as in "The Mat-Maker" and "The Monkey-Rope." However silent, their bond, trust, and love for one another radiates through their concerted physical actions and their very coordination as a team.[33] Indeed, adversarial language would threaten to dominate the entirety of *Moby-Dick*—from metaphysical squabbles between Ishmael and Queequeg (as in "The Ramadan") to the executive debates between Starbuck and Ahab—were it not for the power of storytelling, especially at gams. Men in this novel, especially the sea dogs, relate not only through their work but also through their stories. Melville's birth as a writer came at precisely one such exchange while occupying the life and culture of a common sailor hearing a fantastic but true tale of the sea.

Gams, Yarns, and Print Culture

AMONG THOSE stories told at gams, social gatherings of ships sharing the same cruising ground, Melville heard for the first time the tale of a white whale sinking the *Essex*. On July 23, 1841, the seeds for *Moby-Dick* were planted in what Dolin calls "the most consequential gam of all time."[34] Tall tales, always the order of the day for gams, were exchanged, yet one particular story struck Melville as stunning for many reasons, not the least of which was that it was entirely true. What set the story apart from the usual yarns told at gams, whaling culture's key unifying ritual, was that it was told by Owen Chase, the teenage son of *Essex* captain William Henry Chase, and was corroborated by his father's book, *Narrative of the Wreck of the Whaleship Essex*.[35] After hearing the verbal rendition, Melville was so enthusiastic that the young Chase promptly pulled the volume from his stowage and presented it to his astonished listener. Indeed, the tale's initial telling of a sperm whale's destruction of the vessel and its men rowing for their lives for three months over thousands of miles, eventually resorting to cannibalism, riveted Melville. Young Chase and Melville, both common sailors at the time, spoke about the incident throughout the night, as their captains chose to extend the gam until daybreak. Thus Melville and Chase were likely in deep conversation about the event, as Melville's voracious appetite for wonder was unleashed on the storyteller. He also had more time than the usual several-hour visit that gams encompassed to absorb the full scope of the tragedy and the dimensions of human interaction, leadership, and enraged sea life it evoked. Indeed, the story of *Moby-Dick*'s origin is the story of a gam, during which a story was exchanged and transformed into the most ambitious novel ever written. *Moby-Dick*'s author was born that day.

It makes sense that *Moby-Dick* would become a novel very much interested in the culture of the common sailor, because its inspiration arose directly out of one of the most embedded and unifying rituals of forecastle culture. Gams, to be sure, should not be underestimated for their social role in the whaleman's life. On one level they were a microcosm of mutually beneficial economic collaboration. They rarely transformed into collusion against other ships but instead provided the opportunities for neighborly aid, sympathy, and external support of colleagues in the same business. For the mates and captains, business was a priority. Information was exchanged between captains regarding weather patterns and sea currents mitigating the location of whales. Captain Ahab's incessant questioning ("Hast ye seen the White Whale?") attests, albeit in an exaggerated way, to the utilitarian function of gams for captains and mates that took precedence over the aesthetics and entertainment of storytelling. Information about the location of whales and past mayhem were conveyed through stories, like that told in the chapter "Leg and Arm." Yet such tales were designed less for entertainment than as a form of executive consultation to help steer the objectives and methods of the voyage at hand. Ahab's inquiry about the White Whale prompts Captain Boomer of the *Samuel Enderby* to regale him with the gripping tale of the loss of his arm, capped by his vow to avoid Moby Dick at all costs, a sentiment diametrically opposed to Ahab's response to his dismemberment by the same creature. Significantly, Ahab does not tell his story to Boomer because his haste spurs him on to continue his search. For the common sailors, stories instead functioned less as moral or executive guidance than they did as fascinating entertainment and fuel for their frequently overactive superstitions, to which many seamen were prone. Common employees are rarely present at business meetings where managers exchange principles, often told in stories, to help guide future executive decisions. But on whalers, a full complement of those employees is present by necessity and thus are free to treat the meeting as an opportunity for entertainment, to hear new sailors tell new stories with fresh voices for a welcome relief from the constant company of their own crew.

Moby-Dick itself is organized by several gams, and its marathon readings can be thought of as a series of gams as well. Melville himself scarfed down, and yet paused to savor every morsel of Chase's *Narrative*, reading the single book that arguably would change his life more dramatically than any other he had ever read. The setting, as is also true of the *Moby-Dick* Marathon, was crucial to Melville's heightened sensitivity to and absorption of the book he began reading as the dawning summer sun warmed the decks of the *Acushnet* on July 24, 1841. Indeed, *Moby-Dick* "happened" on his voyage with the *Acushnet* as reflected in the premier marathon reading's decision to commemorate its January embarking from nearby Fairhaven. Print culture intersected with the common sailor's oral storytelling ritual at this late July gam to inspire the writing of *Moby-Dick*. As Melville's recollection of reading Chase's narrative attests, "This was the first printed account of [the *Essex* disaster] I had ever seen. The reading of this wondrous story upon the landless sea & close to the very latitude of the shipwreck had a surprising effect upon me."[36] And that surprising effect, the magic of that first morning when he read of the *Essex*'s dreadful fate, powered the writing of the novel itself.

Indeed, common sailors keep such stories alive; the fictional Ishmael represents them, starting his narrative as if he were introducing himself at a gam, with all the directness and swagger of a sailor with an amazing tale to tell. "Call me Ishmael," he says, in a moment where whaling culture, its songs, artistic expression, and gams all coalesce to keep the story of the White Whale alive, as he is the sole survivor of the *Pequod*'s crew. Like Billy's memory at the end of *Billy Budd*, the *Pequod*'s story is kept alive through the grassroots culture of the common whalemen. The story of its voyage is ironically best told by Ishmael, a common sailor, just as Billy is best commemorated by the sea dogs' song "Billy in the Darbies," which proves as accurate and movingly sympathetic as the newspaper report of his death is preposterously erroneous and callous.

Certainly, all gams were not created equal, as is true of individual transactions in any economy of exchange. The currency in gams is the tale and the information it conveys; Ahab willingly steps outside of the economy of exchange by ascertaining first all information about the whale he feverishly chases, and then stepping aside, leaving his interlocutors empty-handed. Human sympathy drives the profusion of stories told at sea; they will stagnate and cease if all act as Ahab. But Ahab only tells one tale, the tale of his wounding, and it is for the ears of his crew only; other ships only represent obstacles to him if they cannot directly aid his mission. The *Rachel* is the best example of a gam gone awry, as it leaves the desperate Captain Gardner pathetically begging for help in finding his lost son. Ahab coldly rebukes him and moves on in one of his most galling and profane moments in the novel. Other gams fail as mechanisms for the exchange of information, degenerating into deceitful transactions, such as Stubb's fleecing of the French ship captain of the *Bouton de Rose* in "The *Pequod* Meets the *Rose Bud*." Stubb tricks the French captain into thinking their blasted whale is not only worthless but also diseased, given its foul smell. The opposite is actually true, as the whale's bowel contains the precious ambergris, a substance that, while fetid and rank in the whale, once extracted could be refined into perfume. Ishmael's discourse on such a fair-smelling substance coming from a most foul source, interestingly, was an inside joke Melville shared with Hawthorne (to whom he dedicated *Moby-Dick*). The two often marveled at how such a sweet cherub as Hawthorne's daughter, Rose, born on May 20, 1851, could produce such noxious diapers.[37]

Moby-Dick structures itself around a series of imperfect gams begetting a series of diffuse stories, many without balanced exchange and closure. Old news is often transferred, recycled, and distorted. Some gams, like successful sexual encounters, bloom with passion and exude mutual satisfaction. The very names of the ships evoke a sexualized, narrative vehicle for desire, as the etymology of "gam" also alludes to a cracked tooth, the jaws of the whale, the front of the ship, and a head-to-head meeting. The *Bachelor*, *Delight*, *Jungfrau* (German for virgin), and *Rose Bud* all connote sexual fecundity. Further, symmetry is established as the first three ships the *Pequod* meets mirror the last three in their Nantucket origin so that the beginning of the voyage reflects its end. The notion of desire through a balanced economy of exchange is attached to both the symmetrical pattern of the gams and their sexual connotations. Gams function as a medium for desire and thus the intersection of passions. Given Ahab's entirely self-serving abuse of gams—he takes but does not give—the *Pequod*'s multiple meetings with other ships never live up to Ishmael's ideal of the ritual as a site of mutual exchange. The ship once again proves truly an anomaly at sea, rendering yet another lexicography, along with cetology, a hoax.

For the *Pequod*, gams represent a series of necessary markers of whether the whale is near. The first three render either silence or a negative response, and the last four affirm sightings of Moby Dick, accelerating the narrative and hunt through the end of the novel. It is fitting indeed that a gam would provide the original inspiration for the novel and also be the wind in the sails of the narrative, dictating the course of the plot. Gams change complexion throughout the novel and often counterbalance each other. The silence of the *Albatross*, for example, has its foil in the *Jeroboam*'s tale of the archangel of God shrieking the truth; the devil-may-care *Bachelor*'s crew are ideologically untethered and wayward in sharp contrast to the *Delight*, a ship named for the Calvinist delight of exposing the secret sins, looking under the robes, as it were, of priests and politicians. The *Delight*'s mentality is as ideologically committed to doctrine as the *Bachelor* is free from it. As spiritual and intellectual free agents, the bachelors who use their freedom to dive into the world of knowledge outshine their roguish counterparts in Melville's formulation. "The great men are all bachelors, you know. Their family is the universe," Melville wrote in *Pierre*.[38]

Along with memorable gams like the one Melville enjoyed in July 1841 that brought him the story of the *Essex*, a good many were forgettable affairs, as some sailors testified. One was "getting sick of gamming. It is impossible to get any sleep ... when you have a boats crew gamming in the forecastle." Another, Sylvanus Tallman of the *Canada*, groused on January 11, 1848, about multiple gams with "that Confounded ship again the Lion. I wish to the Lord she was somewhere else. Well, well, we must do the best we can." Yet another complained of how "the time is generally spent by the Capts in spinning the greatest lies about their personal engagements with whales how far they can throw the lance and kill a whale. In the forecastle [common sailors] talk about those of their acquaintances who had been killed or maimed by whales, and the different island ports they had visited, of women and wine [and] whoring & hard drinking."[39] Although such tales provided precisely the kind of entertainment a sea-weary sailor could look forward to, more social contact could have just as easily irritated as inspired the crew.

Scrimshaw, Sex, and the Common Sailor

No ONE likes forced social engagements, and indeed, sailors and harpooners took refuge from the incessant presence of their shipmates through solitary pastimes like reading, writing letters (sent on homeward-bound ships), keeping a log, or crafting their own unique brand of art called scrimshaw. Scrimshaw was the practice of carving and etching images, often of whale chases or sexual acts—no somber still lifes or arcane abstractions for these sea dogs—into whalebone, baleen, and teeth with sharp, pointed implements resembling dental instruments. Their subjects mirrored the yarns exchanged in gams, functioning almost as pictorial representations of those tales of epic battles with whales, exotic ports, and "of women and wine [and] whoring & hard drinking."[40] Scrimshaw functioned as an outlet for creative and artistic expression, and some raised it to an impressive and sophisticated art form, much in the way Melville transformed a tale told at a gam into the colossal novel of the White Whale. In the hands of Nantucket whaleman Frederick Myrick, who produced some of the most impressive works, scrimshaw was much more than garish images of the whaleman's youthful fantasies of sexual and heroic conquests. He created domestic scenes—elaborately detailed etchings of ships, portraits of presidents—and included mottos and phrases in his productions. Myrick became well known for etching over thirty whale teeth during one voyage aboard the *Susan*, from 1826 to 1829. The collection is referred to as "*Susan's Teeth*," notable not only for its quality of artistry but also for the soaring creative ambition a common sailor, not unlike Melville himself, could discover while serving on a whaling expedition.[41]

If scrimshaw and tall tales were the whaleman's folk art, Myrick and Melville proved they were also the stuff of high art. Like Myrick, Melville made art out of the materials of his labor. This process echoes the moving sculpture that fictional factory laborer Hugh Wolfe crafts out of the refuse of iron ore, known as korl, in Rebecca Harding Davis's *Life in the Iron Mills*. His sculpture, the Korl Woman, is remarkable because of its profound rendering of the expression of hunger in her face and extended arms. This is a hunger, as Hugh describes, that is not for food but to fill a spiritual void. Ahab and even the depressed and nearly suicidal Ishmael in the early stages of the novel also express their inner hunger and unquenchable thirst, which interestingly emerges from working conditions that might prevent the realization of such ambition.

Scrimshaw, like the readings and writings of the whalemen, did not generally channel into publicized and celebrated art but instead had a more private psychosexual function. According to Andrew Delbanco, sailors and harpooners were so rife with sexual tension due to their confinement to their all-male condition on the ships that they turned to scrimshaw depicting sexual intercourse as masturbatory aids, using "toothpicks, whistles, and pipe-tampers [that] were carved out of whale teeth in the form of a woman's leg [to] suck or fondle in the absence of the real thing."[42] After all, these were young men in their teens and early twenties whose testosterone levels, and attendant erotic imaginations, were at their lifetime peaks.

Echoing such metonymic sexual longing is Tim O'Brien's fictional Lt. Jimmy Cross, of the Viet Nam novel *The Things They Carried* (1990), who carries a pebble sent by his girlfriend back home, turning it over lovingly with his tongue in an erotic fantasy fueled by the hope that she still loves him. Like Viet Nam soldiers, whalemen also left love interests at home to whom they remained devout, but still more sought out anonymous physical encounters. Captains often brought their own wives along on voyages to join them in their spacious private quarters on the ship. Stops in ports were taken as occasions for common sailors to seek out sex. Houses of ill repute sprouted at whaling ports to capitalize on the demand. In Honolulu, for example, one such brothel was cheekily named Cape Horn. More commonly, men did not have to pay for sex, especially in the Marquesas Islands. The journal of the *Samuel Robertson*, for example, paints a picture of "about 30 or 40 girls all standing on the beach with their white tappa or cloth in their hands or thrown around their necks perfectly naked" beckoning incoming whalers, their crew leaning over the rail, eager, wide-eyed, and erect. This meant "girls 1 to a man for and aft Cabin boy and all included and after a night's debauchery put them on shore and repeat the same night after." But the paradise of willing native women without any of the cultural stigmas or repressive attitudes toward sex of the western Victorian world did not come without a price. Though no money is lost in the transaction, "plenty of young men are ruined by this and catch a disorder [of a sexually transmitted disease] which . . . makes old men of them," an image that frighteningly darkens the attraction of sexuality in port.[43]

During extended cruises away from shore lasting up to several months on well-stocked vessels, men resorted to other forms of release. While homosexual acts were indeed punished on board whalers—captains had no tolerance, especially for forcible, nonconsensual sex[44]—mutual masturbation was not. Melville's metaphorical ode to this practice in *Moby-Dick* is the chapter "A Squeeze of the Hand." The chapter quickly moves from the operations and duty of cutting, hoisting, and bailing necessary to the processing of the whale oil to a decidedly romantic reverie coinciding with the business of squeezing lumps of spermaceti back into fluid. The perfumelike aromas rising in the air transform an otherwise narrowly defined mindless task of repetitive labor into magic—"literally and truly, like the smell of spring violets"—and velvety sensuality: "such a softener! Such a delicious mollifier! After having my hands in it for only a few minutes, my fingers felt like eels."[45] The wet smoothness of tactility provides an escape from the psychological pressures of duty, much in the way Jimmy Cross transposes his desire for Martha into flipping and sliding her smooth pebble (a token of remembrance she had mailed to him) in the moist chasm of his mouth. Whereas Cross's fantasy is solipsistic and thus dangerously detaches him from the troops he is charged with protecting, Ishmael's escape from the search for Moby Dick on behalf of Captain Ahab—"I forgot all about our horrible oath"—draws him nearer to his shipmates,[46] "unwittingly squeezing my co-laborers hands in it" in such a way as to inspire "an abounding, affectionate, friendly, loving feeling," as he caught himself "looking up into their eyes sentimentally."[47]

The moment significantly bridges the chasm of capitalist competition increasingly dividing and alienating male relations. "Melville's own society of the nineteenth century offered no model for adult male relations except those of competition," according to historian Robert K. Martin, "[since] affectionate friendship was permitted between adolescents but had to give way as boys became adults" and professional responsibilities arose, such as Melville dramatizes in *Pierre*.[48] In the following chapter, "The Cassock," in which the mincer goes about his work cloaked in the pelt of the whale's penis, there is no shortage of satire regarding the rigidity of gender codes, specifically the separation of the public male sphere of work from the private female sphere of leisure and thus communal pleasure. Sexuality in Melville, Martin explains, "must be divorced of its links to possession and power, must be decolonized" so that the erotic can be playfully performed rather than depicted at a distance. This crucial element of play, in many ways the key to Melville's signature discursiveness, often constitutes "expressions of sexual exuberance," Martin writes, "that threaten to break out of the boundaries of prose," and indeed reach exalted heights of lyricism.[49] Here and elsewhere in the novel is a "reorganization of erotic activity to a greater range of possibility" so that "transgressive sexuality of any kind"—as in "A Squeeze of the Hand"—"by putting conventional order and authority in question, offers a subversive . . . potential."[50] What is being subverted, above all else, is the notion that work must be drudgery. Opening up the possibility that the rhythms of work can become the rhythms of art, men can touch and be touched by their fellow mates meaningfully during the process. Ishmael's reveries, indeed, are invariably initiated by his engagement in his whaling duties, and as such are associational and not isolationist. Hester Blum perceptively points out that such vision should not be confused with Emerson, for whom "the transparency of the [Transcendental] eye allows it both to see without interference from the corporeal self and to be adapted by others for whom the disembodied eyeball would pose no barrier. The sea eye in maritime narratives," like *Moby-Dick*, "however, provides a model of vision that does not erase the embodied eye." Indeed "the sea eye," especially that of Ishmael's lyrical interludes, "provides a vision that is predicated on the sailor's experience of maritime work."[51] This perspective, Blum convincingly argues, disabuses readers "from taking too romantic a view of maritime life—the kind of idealized view offered by those who viewed the sea as a metaphor, say, rather than a sphere of labor."[52] The hallmarks of domesticity, sympathy, and sentimentality, further, find their way into this public sphere with work that does not make the men callous but rather heightens their sensitivity to each other.

Erotic play fuels Melville's satire of narrowly defined gender codes of

behavior. For example, the industrial, decidedly public-sphere task of liq-
uefying spermaceti in the chain of productivity leads Ishmael to vow eternal allegiance to the domestic sphere—"the wife, the heart, the bed, the
table . . . the fire-side," as a site of "attainable felicity" much more pleasurable
than "anywhere in the intellect or the fancy."[53] Not to stop at the cultural
sacred cow of domesticity, Ishmael, and Melville by extension, marches directly onto religion. Ishmael's hyperbolic cries echo biblical exclamation
and preach the platitudinous piety of peace and love—"Oh! My dear fellow
beings, why should we longer cherish social acerbities, or know the slightest
ill-humor or envy"—reaching an absurd, delirious, downright sacrilegious
pitch when he imagines "long rows of angels in paradise, each with his hands
in a jar of spermaceti."[54]

Such mischievous mayhem only a common sailor could drum up, and Melville loved playing that role. For embedded in his burlesque of gender codes
is a distinct anxiety over his own craft of authorship failing to provide him
with the pleasures so palpably present in the domestic sphere or out in the
country. Of course, Melville shut both bucolic and female domestic worlds
out of his daily life as much as he could during the composition of *Moby-Dick*,
locking himself in his study for ungodly stints of uninterrupted literary labor,
utterly draining the "attainable felicity" from "anywhere in the intellect or
the fancy." The attainable felicities of domestic and country pleasures of his
farmhouse and the rural setting of his Arrowhead estate, ironically enough,
were ever present outside his writing chamber and more than accessible.
Drawn to his novel with drive and obsession, he eschewed these pleasures,
but clearly wrote his longing for them into its very pages.

While composing *Moby-Dick* at the age of thirty-one, Melville yearned
for the simple days of the gams he enjoyed as a twenty-one-year-old green
hand tar when the powers of his mind did not torment him with aesthetic
complexity and existential anxiety, days composed of outdoor physical work
during which he looked forward to a spritely yarn, supper, and a fair measure
of potables. Peace of the most wholesome physical and spiritual sort Melville
understood as the condition of doing "the hardest possible day's work, and
then com[ing] to sit down in a corner and eat my supper comfortably," as he
wrote in a letter to his best friend in November 1851, "my peace and my supper are my reward, my dear Hawthorne."[55] A simple economy of exchange
in which he expects nothing more than peace and supper for his hard work
makes "appreciative praise" a "bonus over and above what was stipulated for,"

he reasons, "for not one man in five cycles, who is wise, will expect appreciative recognition from his fellows."[56] Authorial anxiety over the prospect of fame and notoriety, which Hawthorne's *The Scarlet Letter* had won in 1850, were clearly plaguing Melville, whose commercial and critical success had been steadily declining since *Typee* (1846). Looking for nothing more than the soul satisfaction of supper honestly earned in many ways is Melville yearning for such simple needs and attainable satisfactions. As a mature and far more sophisticated professional author, his needs grew and became exceedingly complex. Lost in that complexity was the simple pleasures of forecastle life, not the least of which was the ale and grog consumed therein, as he sorely missed the conviviality of sharing in the inebriated camaraderie of his mates. As such, he sought out collegial quaffing with a fellow laborer, only a literary one, in the figure of Nathaniel Hawthorne. Melville's January 1851 invitation to host Hawthorne for an evening at his home specifically links spirits and storytelling—two inseparable and essential elements to any good gam—as the evening's main attraction. "Hark—There is some excellent Montado Sherry awaiting you & some most potent Port. We will have mulled wine with wisdom, & buttered toast with storytelling & crack jokes & bottles from morning till night," Melville promised, with the playful threat to "come . . . if you don't—I will send Constables after you."[57] He once told his friend to "have ready a bottle of brandy, because I always feel like drinking that heroic drink when we talk ontological heroics together."[58] Melville savored the pleasures of drinking with Hawthorne at these new landlocked gams.

In the life of the common whaleman, alcohol also functioned as social glue and lubricant for storytelling. And, as it had in Melville's life, it also killed the pain as a form of escape. Like "A Squeeze of the Hand," "The Decanter" is an ode to forecastle culture, this time to its ritual quaffing, again as practiced not by mates and captains but by their lower ranked counterparts, the sailors and harpooners. "The Decanter" serves up some of Melville's finest admiration for the simple pleasures of imbibing spirits, to which he sings praises in *Billy Budd*, as well as the "Paradise of Bachelors and the Tartarus of Maids." Stuffy as those bachelors may be, or as buttoned up as British Navy Lt. Radcliffe is about impressing Billy onto his ship, none suffer from excessive aridity. The happy-go-lucky London crew of the *Samuel Enderby* in *Moby-Dick* adopts their captain's demeanor in the wake of a tangle with the White Whale that cost him an arm. Unlike Ahab, it taught him to studiously avoid the beast at all costs. "He's best let alone," Captain Boomer concludes. In keeping with the ship's London hospitality and careful evasion of precisely those strident animosities of life—"social acerbities . . . ill-humor or envy"—Ishmael also gleefully escapes while ruminating on the job of squeezing spermaceti into liquid.

With Ahab's monomaniacal mentality emphatically put aside by the *Samuel Enderby*'s alternative lifestyle and attendant perception of Moby Dick, the party is set to begin. And begin it does, as Ishmael reports that during the gam they "drank good flip down in the forecastle . . . Yes, and we flipped it at a rate of ten gallons the hour," a pace that would command the respect of most college fraternities. Called above to reef the topsails as a squall rolls in, the "drunken tars . . . ignorantly furled the skirts of our jackets into the sails, so that we hung there, reefed fast in the howling gale" sobered by the chilling wind so "that we had to pass the flip again" and warm the embers once below deck. The mixture of duty and drunkenness (and feasting, for these roast beef Brits offered a fine spread of meats and "indestructible dumplings" that rolled about like billiard balls in one's stomach and "if you stooped too far forward, you risked their pitching out of you like billiard balls") inspires Ishmael to research alcohol on ancient whalers. His findings report some 10,800 barrels of beer shipped in Dutch whalers centuries prior, which amounted to "two barrels of beer per man, for a twelve weeks' allowance, exclusive of his fair portion of 550 ankers of gin." These men apparently drank more barrels of beer than they secured in whale oil. Such numbers raise the question of professional competence, as does the episode of the drunken sailors inadvertently allowing the wind to tether them to the sails by their coattails in the squall. But Ishmael urges that the brisk northern climate kept the men alert, and the harpoon accuracy stayed true, as he speculates that equatorial climates would have left them "sleepy at the masthead and boozy in his boat." Dismissing the question of compromised skills and increased dangers, Ishmael concludes that "if you can get nothing better out of the world, get a good dinner out of it at least."[59] Ishmael being Ishmael, he is not content to rest complacently on such a numb perspective on life. He thus immediately moves to higher sources of sustenance, shifting away from forecastle culture into anthropological science and ultimately to ecclesiastical zeal in the very next chapter, "A Bower in the Arsacides." The unexamined life is worth visiting, according to the narrative progression here, but not worth leading indefinitely.

Ishmael tries all things, and as such reflects the diversity of thought and modes of living proliferating in the mid-nineteenth century. Indeed, the sexual and drunken lifestyles of sailors and harpooners were by no means the only mode of living at sea at the time. From the eighteenth to the early nineteenth century, most whalers carried a huge complement of liquor, but by the 1830s, many boats reflected the temperance reform movement afoot at the time and carried no alcohol. These "temperance ships," as they were called, apparently were such only at sea, as when the men went ashore, as Reverend Daniel Wheeler observed of the Tahitian port in 1835, they drank lustily. Such behavior should not overshadow, however, the presence of "clean-living and God-fearing" men at sea, whom Melville no doubt encountered, and modeled Starbuck after.[60]

The common whaleman's culture, like that of young men and women in military combat today and during O'Brien's Viet Nam era, bears signs of rec-reation as a struggle to find vitality amid the stress of random calls to action in highly dangerous conditions, attempts at killing the pain of geographical and cultural dislocation, alienation, and isolation. The common sailor of the antebellum era found relief—sexual, artistic, narrative, and alcoholic—anywhere he could. There have certainly been other tales of such culture, from Anthony Swofford's *Jarhead*, which renders a nonfictional inside look at the grunt's life during the 1991 Gulf War, to the films *The Dirty Dozen*,[61] *North Dallas Forty*, and *Bull Durham*. Booze, bawdy talk, brawling, racism, and sexism run through the barracks and locker rooms of these narratives. Melville may romanticize some of that culture, but his satirical bent and visceral reminders of the exigencies of the work of whaling undercut any rosy ideals. For all its exalted transcendence, "A Squeeze of the Hand" ends with the sober reminder that "the spademan's feet are shoeless" as he works and thus "toes are scarce among veteran blubber-room men."[62]

Moby-Dick marathoners are a well-behaved crowd; this is not Sturgis or even an NFL game. But the diversity in its ranks—nonetheless essentially united through the romantic choice of attending this event in the first place—echoes the diversity of the common sailors themselves, who resemble not a little the roster of a minor-league baseball team: many are young, tattooed, transnational, in their late teens and early twenties, physically tough, com-petitive, and ethnically diverse; they earn low wages, share cramped close quarters, and are constantly on the move, traveling from city to city through-out their season, having notorious associations with women and beer, and devoting themselves to a nonlinear romantic, even unreasonable, occupa-tional choice.

While the culture of the dugout of minor-league ballplayers and their real lives bears a striking resemblance to the Jack-Tars of Melville's era, the common literary whalers of the *Moby-Dick* Marathon may be in a league of their own. But they are not without their similarities to these two rough-and-tumble groups. Their culture is no less distinct and idiosyncratic, as I describe in the section that follows on the common reader's experience of the 2009 event. At the 2008 reading, for example, a Unitarian Universalist minister reported:

> At around two in the morning, I was awakened by loud voices outside our apartment building. There are a lot of bars in the neighborhood so we get more than our share of drunks walking by our house. But these voices kept on and on; and besides, it wasn't a Friday or Saturday when we usually get the loud drunks. I went to the front windows and looked out. Three guys stood just under one of the windows, all bundled up against the bitter cold, and one of them appeared to be sipping out of a large can; but they didn't sound drunk, merely high-spirited.
>
> I opened the window a crack. "People trying to sleep up here, guys."
>
> "Oh, sorry, sorry," said the one with the can, and they scampered off towards the Whaling Museum. The only thing I can figure is that they were at the *Moby-Dick* Marathon and decided they needed to take a break outdoors; but it seems odd that they would come across the street and stand under our windows.[63]

Looking for a release from the reading, not unlike the whalers running amok on shore, these marathoners ran out for a dram of grog and unfortunately chose a parson's window by which to imbibe it. They later identified themselves "in nomine diaboli" in this online reply to the minister's blog:

akirk Says:
January 6th, 2008 at 8:14 PM
Hi–
Sorry
That was we. We were in high spirits, worshiping the bard. And there was not a can but a bottle involved, and containing more than beer. The sailors had their share of rum, did they not?

We extolled the bard, reveled, got too loud, left at your request.
We are glad it was another lover of Melville who so laconically sent
us on our way.
Non in nomine patris, sed in nomine diaboli
–The Drunks[64]

The spirit of "The Decanter" lives on, and the *Moby-Dick* Marathon's unsung readers keep it alive. They do so with all the edginess of Melville's own tendency to brush the profane up against the sacred. Indeed, that late-night toast was likely a token of sacred homage, as indicated in the rejoinder, to Melville and the sea dogs who regularly partook of spirits. Blessed are both the awoken minister and the devilish rabble-rousers. Both are Melville's marathoners sharing the voyage true to the author's vision of decidedly different perspectives converging to form an unexpected connection. Their comic encounter resonates with the culture of the sort of common sailor that Melville himself was more than a century and a half ago.

The Common Crew of the 2009 Reading

THE EQUIVALENT of the forecastle during the *Moby-Dick* Marathon, without doubt, was the upper deck overlooking the reading area. For in it were the majority of the twenty-two hearty souls prepared to spend the night with makeshift provisions, making the very best of the meager accommodations. If their idiosyncratic attempts to find comfort did not disclose their full characters, then certainly it revealed a telling glimpse at their dispositions toward the voyage. This was the high holy day for Melvillians, as they engaged in their ritualized set of folkways before my eyes. Almost all could be characterized as obsessed amateurs, the sort that keeps subcultures alive, like that of the common antebellum whalers. The common readers are the essential force driving the event itself. To discover the essence of this forecastle culture, I searched for clues to how the book had touched the average reader's life, and what drove them to share the reading experience with others. How far had they traveled? How long did they stay? Did they come to see any famous readers? How do they regard the event's management? Were they well taken care of? Were they granted their request for a reading spot? Above all, I wanted to know what drove their amateur obsession, and how they perceived their place at the event with respect to the featured "top brass" readers—did they emulate them, or rally around them as surrogates of Melville himself?—to discern their place within the context of the reading's management and structure.

Not one of the all-night readers was a celebrity or honored reader. One can hardly imagine Barney Frank and Scott Lang among these huddled masses. Although in fairness, Lang had said he would consider staying for the duration as a civilian. The high profile reader who came nearest to joining the twenty-five-hour crew was Peter Whittemore. It was close to midnight when I asked if he would spend the night. An obsessed, daring look swept across his face before he caught himself in the romance of the voyage, replying dryly that he had "to hold onto what little sanity was left." When I saw him again at noon the next day as he presented me with the signed graphic pop-up (!) edition of *Moby-Dick*, he fixed me with his eye as if gauging the effect of the twenty-five hours—enlightening or unhinging?—on my soul. He could see that I was, though rumpled and disoriented, no less a survivor, having been through plenty of other protracted experiences of equal parts heaven and hell as a father of three children and veteran of six athletic marathons. The night before, once he stiffened his resolve, Whittemore tossed me a ripe lead as consolation for not sharing the evening with me. "No," Whittemore said as the witching hour approached, "I won't spend the night. The guy you want to talk to though is Mark Wojnar. A true Melville guru—Hershel Parker cites him, and he's truly obsessed with the novel. He's stayed all night in eleven out of thirteen of these marathons." Sensing an intriguing story, I urged Whittemore to unearth more. "He works on and off, sometimes helping a group of disabled people; he's been homeless for some time. He usually has trouble getting a ride to the reading, since he doesn't own a car." The description called to mind the brilliant homeless gnomic protagonist, Romulus Ledbetter, of Charles Dawes Greene's *The Caveman's Valentine*, a seer whose vision is so deep that it derails him and leaves him professionally unhinged. "Much Madness is divinest Sense," as Dickinson wrote;[65] and there was Pip, and there was Elijah in the Caveman's wake, a stream of seers left damaged by the sheer force of their wisdom.

Glad to have a fast fish to pull me through the midnight hour, I decided to make Wojnar my White Whale, secretly holding a vigil for the man, contemplating swinging out into the dark night in my absurd white Pontiac Vibe rental car (the young African-American hipster at the rental lot exit couldn't restrain his mocking glee at my selection of what I realized by the expression on his face was a ride coveted by gum-snapping sixteen-year-old [OMG!] girls) to provide him the transportation he likely needed. Wojnar was reader 77, set to man the podium at 12:40 AM. Parker had consecrated his genius, and the American workforce had marginalized him; the insights he held could be nothing less than miraculous. Perhaps the most uncommon of the common readers, Wojnar ironically did not paralyze me with anticipation, as I somehow turned my attention toward the thriving culture of the group in front of me. Why wait for Godot and become Beckett's Pozzo when Melvillian seers of all sorts abound, "coming in the goddam window," as Holden says in *The Catcher in the Rye*,[66] replete with stories of their own for how they had been touched by what everyone in this building tonight knows to be the greatest story ever told?

Once I was enmeshed in their world, any barrier caused by my role as a detached observer rapidly disintegrated. Many drew me in, wanting to talk more about me than themselves, for I was the true curiosity. Most asked why I had come all the way from Iowa and what sort of book I wanted to write. As I opened up to them, they freely and amiably embraced me, and I discovered a rich, diverse, and vibrant readership, a contemporary print subculture performing its highest sacrament on its holiest day. These were readers transforming classical American literature into lived experience in a way not forced and dutiful, but as frank and human, as nonchalant and even cocky, as Walt Whitman's self-possessed pose on the frontispiece of the 1855 *Leaves of Grass*. In the spirit of Whitman's poet figure and Ishmael, the populace of the *Moby-Dick* Marathon, democratic as ever, was not afraid to voice its opinion and question authority. "I don't like the unpredictability of it; I read chapters 28–32 and was assigned chapter 27!" one reader complained on Saturday evening at 5:10 PM, clearly wanting that preparation time back, neglecting the insight she may have gained from the other five chapters. "We could have just come, seen Barney Frank, and gone home," she said only half-sarcastically, her patience worn thin now almost six hours into the reading. Her friend sympathized, predicting that her assigned range of chapters would also change. This lack of confidence in the marathon's management is more acute among the younger readers, if at all. Most are flexible and, like me, are grateful at the opportunity to read any of the novel at all from the podium in such a grand setting.

By the time this conversation took place, the crowd had thinned out considerably since the opening of the reading. Noon to 2:20 PM, from "Loomings" through "The Sermon," is the prime time of this event; after that, the crowd reduces by half. All masks were off at this point, and people were commenting freely how the chapter "Cetology" was "the only chapter in high school that I skipped"—quite a feat considering how many more chapters teen readers commonly skip. The next breath, "But I've read it now several times," affirmed the reader's current relation to the novel, typical of most of us in attendance at that moment. The tableau of a young female reader genuinely inspired by a chapter like "Cetology" is wondrous in its own right, and even more so given that the museum's president, James Russell, even underestimated our love for that chapter. He admonished us to have patience and wait, beyond the culminating last line of the novel, to hear him deliver a litany of staff acknowledgments. "If you could all sit through 'Cetology,'" he quipped, "then you can stick around a few more minutes." Little did he know that most marathoners present share the sentiments of the aforementioned young woman reader toward "Cetology," which clearly make it a source of inspiration, much less a chore to sit through. Like any intense and dedicated subculture, like distance running or rare-book collecting, there are even those purportedly on the inside not entirely in tune with the ethos and motives of the group's hard-core constituents.

But what appears hard-core, sitting through the anguish and teeth-gnashing tedium of the equivalent of a whaling encyclopedia, is really a love affair marked by its poignancy, softness, and play. For here, in the Sperm Whale Gallery that we occupy for the reading of "Cetology," we are given the pleasure of encountering this chapter in front of a giant sperm whale skeleton that materializes the words we hear. Sitting on the floor next to the enormous skeleton is a four-person family, two teen-aged girls, one with her own edition of *Moby-Dick* and one clutching a gift bag with a stuffed whale peering out of it. They listen in harmony and contentment, their father reclined on the floor, fingers laced behind his head, legs crossed at the ankles, and eyes brilliant, visualizing and animating the mass of bones looming over him. I look over my shoulder and see a balding, middle-aged man with book open, several lines underscored with a circled asterisk and exclamation point inked in the margin, likely marking one of Ishmael's many jocose quips in the chapter. The mark is a sure sign of this reader's active vigorous apprehension of a creature who can range from "gregarious" to savage, sporting a cunningly evil "Mephistophelean grin," hiding an essence that "eludes both hunters and philosophers." Whales are so subtle that they "catch their food with sudden bursts of sound produced and amplified in their heads."[67] All this, yes, even in "Cetology." A sense of wonder vibrates through the room. A woman in a wheelchair to the rear of the whale beckons me. "Get my phone," she says, lifting herself up to reveal her cell on her chair just out of reach, like the whale itself, tantalizingly beyond our ken. I oblige, feeling a peaceful sense of family in this diverse bond of Melville aficionados. The connectedness between word and thing, book and whale, reader and reader is palpably present at this moment. The playfulness of the language, further, has me wanting to jump on the skeleton in the crook between his spine and skull and ride him, like Dr. Strangelove on the bomb, exulting in, of all places, the Sperm Whale Gallery of the New Bedford Whaling Museum surrounded by the blackness of January in southern New England. This, I didn't expect.

However swept up in the moment I became, Richard Tonachel, retired editor at Harvard University Press and veteran reader, assured me that the marathon, despite its growing popularity, "is not cultish." The event's capacity to retain its dignity is attributable, in part, to the character of the ever more youthful spectators and readers packing the house each year. The forecastle culture of the reading as seen through the common reader, indeed, will not likely sink to the level of a Star Trek convention. Attendees do not dress up — those who do are the designated "performers" of the reading, like Raymond Veary (Ishmael), Edward Dufresne (Father Mapple), and Arthur Bennett (Captain Ahab). The common crew of all-nighters, furthermore, is not an exclusive clique or even remotely clubbish; all are welcome to join their ranks. Like marathon runners, this circle universally and instantly grants social acceptance regardless of youth, age, or pedigree. Ivy leaguers and waterfront workers alike openly intermingle in communion, a kind of literary version of a Grateful Dead show without all the petty bartering of homemade (and homegrown) goods. Tonachel's affiliation with elite literary and scholarly culture does not keep him from considering joining the ranks of the forecastle, for example, as he says "I'd like to do the whole thing" and experience the full twenty-five hours with the hard-core set.

That intergenerational diversity is the common thread connecting so many tableaus throughout the reading. Dick Settele, a watch officer managing the pacing and sequencing of the reading, is a grey-haired gentleman clad in a navy sport coat. He scanned the text with a magnifying glass monitoring the reading of a high schooler, grey sweatshirted, voice just changed, yet delivering his chapter with confidence and authority. Steven Noel, Jr., in his early twenties, stocking cap and facial hair on the beard side of a five o'clock shadow, leaned into the mike like a dance club emcee, his voice charismatic, loud and filling the room with kinetic energy. A democratic patchwork shapes the text from "The *Pequod* Meets the *Rose Bud*" to "Ambergris" to Pip's price brutally laid on him by Stubb in "The Castaway." Readings are uneven, but so is Melville's prose, I realize, as he makes up words and delivers some lines so flat that one is tempted to credit him with irony where likely there was only fatigue. Take, for example, "Stubb was the second mate. He was a native of Cape Cod; and hence, according to local usage, was called a Cape-Cod-man."[68] Readers also stumble, and butcher lines, making up words—"levinian" for "Leviathan" and about four other variations by one elderly woman had the entire second row barely repressing their laughter at the Monty-Python–esque absurdity of it all. But Melville himself was notorious for inventing words, "oblivionated" and "predestinated" being among his favorites.

At 2 AM, I return to my seat among the spectators, wisps of what looks like twine lie on the floor, the scraps of a cadre of organic hemp weavers seated in front of me. One sports a hemp-hewn hat, as these natural bohemians one associates with whole food grocery stores weave to the sound of Melville's weavings, a narrative yarn in which lines and tapestries, loomings, warp and woof are so central. The hempen products swell beneath their rhythmic hands, their loomings contiguous with Ishmael's. I return to the upper level, our "forecastle," to discover a couple in their early twenties on a date, snuggling at the rail overlooking the podium, reminiscent of Leo DeCaprio, arm swung around his lover at the bow of the *Titanic*. The man's hand is under the hem of her shirt, caressing her bare skin rhythmically to the cadence of Melville's prose, rising dangerously high. They wander away from the rail to look at a few exhibits and eventually leave. Another couple, also early twenties, lay on their backs, bedrolls propping their heads, side by side, knees up, shoulders and thighs touching, arms crossed, quietly chatting and giggling as if at a slumber party. Our forecastle culture, subdued and absorbing this stream of prose poetry, consists of single middle-aged men and women and young couples, many cross-legged on the carpet, nested by blankets. A father and son, both in jeans and running shoes, stand on the balcony at the top of the stairs, each with his own edition, son in a purple T-shirt with the words "Moby-Dick" emblazoned on the back in gothic style. They read along to the sound of a young woman's voice, almost comically adolescent. Her "Have you seen the whale?" sounds as if Ahab were asking, "Do you have any gum?"

Hers is not the only performative slip, as Ahab's cries on "The Quarter-Deck" earlier in the evening were delivered matter of factly and with a sense of quiet poise utterly foreign to the tone of the lines. But the mismatch somehow works; I am reminded of Jesse Jackson, earnest race advocate and founder of the Rainbow Coalition, reading with his trademark seriousness *Green Eggs and Ham* by Dr. Seuss on *Saturday Night Live*, rendering a priceless kind of poetic absurdity, the sacred meeting the profane, a burlesque of tomfoolery like the common crew's forecastle antics.

This is what our great American novel looks like from the vantage point of the forecastle deck, replacing scrimshaw for hemp weaving, where Melville's colossal work resonates in the voices and hearts of the people. As Keith Hilles-Pilant commented, the all-nighters "do not stay for the stunt of it, but for the love of the novel." This love is the glue that truly bonds such a diverse crew together, bridging generations, transforming a 160-year-old novel into a source of passion for readers like the woman in her early twenties who sits near me with a nose ring and high top Chuck Taylors shaded with yellow magic marker and letters spelling "Grace" in gothic black calligraphy on the sides. She is a fan, yet unmistakably sophisticated, a new generation of *Moby-Dick* reader that promises to take the massive accomplishments of Hershel Parker's generation into exciting uncharted waters for the twenty-first century. This is the source of energy that not only makes Melville live but also promises to keep him alive and well, however changed, for the coming generations.

PART III

Twenty-Five Tumultuous Hours

The Spectre Whalemen, showing sea wreckage and storm images. Courtesy MIT Museum.

·5·

Survival

Enduring the Sledge-Hammering Seas of the Soul

*T*HE POLITICAL CULTURE IN THE grand theatre of both *Moby-Dick* and the marathon reading, from the covered seats to the groundlings, from executive power brokers to the unsung grassroots populace, formed the subject of part II. We now consider the mood of the reading and its readers, tracing in this chapter the turbulent and transcendent moments of the novel and in the final chapter the turbulent and transcendent moments of the 2009 marathon reading. This chapter concerns itself with the anguish inherent in the disaster that Ishmael witnesses, as well as those disasters and rough seas of readers' lives that attract them to Melville's novel for its power to cleanse and cure.

For many, the marathon reading of *Moby-Dick* has a particularly cathartic function. The novel probes the depths of global trauma and catastrophe as figured in the wreckage of the *Pequod*, a disaster that captures the impending doom of our news headlines that loom over our lives daily. The week of September 15, 2008, some three and a half months prior to the 2009 marathon reading, marked one of the most significant economic crises on Wall Street in a century. Some of the oldest corporations vanished, while others were rescued in the eleventh hour by the deus ex machina of the U.S. federal government. Our worries over the Iraq war and military missions to Afghanistan also do not abate, as those conflicts painfully persist in a protracted series of battles older than *Moby-Dick* itself.

Melville published *Moby-Dick* in the decade before the Civil War, as political controversies and anxieties ran high over the Mexican-American War and the revolutions sweeping Europe in 1848. Nothing less than the very fabric of American life was called into question by myriad social reformers, many of whom, such as Orestes Brownson and proslavery pundits of the South like George Fitzhugh, openly questioned the limitations of individualism in the free market economy. Melville himself questioned the aims and directions of American democracy. He was demoralized by the spectacle of violent labor riots in the streets of New York City involving the bloodying of broods of newly arrived Irish immigrants. Bearing witness to the brutality of the Astor Place Riots led Melville to conclude that Protestant theologian John Calvin was right in his conviction that humans were depraved since the fall of man in the Garden of Eden. The controversy over hard currency and the widespread corruption involving the proliferation of loans, promissory notes, and paper money eroded confidence in banks, leading to the mass run on financial institutions known as the Panic of 1837. Pantheism and paganism were openly discussed as alternatives to Christianity, as comparative religious views emerged in light of communal living experiments such as Brook Farm, famously fictionalized in Hawthorne's scorching 1852 satire, *The Blithedale Romance*, the year following the publication of *Moby-Dick*.

In light of this social, political, and economic sea change of the antebellum era, Melville's willingness to face directly his own mortality and the limitations of the democratic life bear the mark of his honesty in negotiating such tenuous anxiety-ridden times. Today, the United States is facing profound change, as a new president takes control of the White House within months of the writing of this chapter. Melville himself juxtaposed global military conflicts and pivotal presidential elections with the smallness of Ishmael's tale, at once mocking the insignificance of his own efforts and aggrandizing them with cosmological significance beyond the scope of newspaper journalism. Ishmael makes the former gesture by showing how puny he looks upon insertion into such headlines—in a stunning replication of our current ones—that he imagines as the "grand programme of Providence that was drawn up a long time ago":

> *Grand Contested Election for the Presidency of the United States.*
> WHALING VOYAGE BY ONE ISHMAEL.
> **BLOODY BATTLE IN AFFGHANISTAN.**[1]

In a line of almost surreal prophetic power, Melville seems to have written that very "programme of Providence" himself. Although Ishmael's voyage looks absurdly diminutive here, several paragraphs later it becomes clear that the best lens through which to view bloody battles in foreign lands and grand contested presidential elections is Ishmael's multiperspective, politically engaged, psychologically fearless narrative. His narrative can and will cast such events on the even larger canvas of "the overwhelming idea of the great whale himself."[2]

The novel can lend clarity not only to outer worries but also to inner ones. Readers have often turned to *Moby-Dick* in their darkest hours to reclaim a sense of direction in a life of loose fish, to fix ourselves with Ishmael's irreverent and outrageous humor, and finally to share in the bizarre predicament of coping with our material circumstances. To assuage the powerless feeling of being on a ship out of our control, we get closer to death through the aesthetic power of literature to better feel the life in us. We take refuge in our books: "I've been to every single book I know / To soothe the thoughts that plague me so,"[3] as poet and accidental rock star Gordon Sumner admits; one renowned academic has confessed that Whitman's *Leaves of Grass* served as his courage teacher in his darkest hours, commenting that reading is "the most healing of pleasures" because "Imaginative literature is otherness, and as such alleviates loneliness."[4] The wind on the frosty deck of the *Pequod* links us to the brutal gales that buffet our lives in a way that can and does provide a corrective emotional response. And that we read it together, listen to it live in each other's physical presence, brings forth a solidarity of endurance not unlike those of pace groups in athletic marathons, magical coteries designed to wring out our collective doubts in a miracle of belief. This chapter traces those life buoys of survival against perilous waters in *Moby-Dick* and in the lives of the marathon readers, for whom the book enacts the process of wounding and recovery at the very core of its narrative.

"The Horrors of the Half Known Life"

CHIEF AMONG the things *Moby-Dick* saves us from is the mind-numbing effect of the landlocked life and its sedate, highly regulated routines that shut us off from our deepest selves and indeed encourage a kind of superficial unexamined life. Our current age of abundance begets a mastery of our environment, from its freeways to its shopping malls, that insulates us from what Ishmael calls, in the chapter "Brit," the untamed chaos of "the masterless ocean that overruns the globe." The ocean he imagines is a natural force opposite that of the controlled and "superficial western" world Columbus discovered.[5] Ishmael's argument is that the sea, unlike land, is unknown and thus contains unspeakable invisible horrors. The sea can swallow up ships and crews in a "universal cannibalism" in which all "creatures prey upon each other, carrying on eternal war since the world began,"[6] not unlike those in the Afghanistan of his headline. He turns the extended metaphor, in a gesture akin to those of John Donne and the metaphysical poets, to "a strange analogy in yourself," "as this appalling ocean surrounds this verdant land, so in the soul of man lies an insular Tahiti, full of peace and joy, but encompassed by all the horrors of the half known life."[7] Ishmael warns the reader to stay put on that island, for "thou canst never return" once those horrible depths are probed.[8]

Ishmael's admonition is a narrative ploy to keep us reading, to do precisely the opposite of what he has advised, in a sort of gothic tease to the reader. Do not continue with this dark tale, he advises, for the consequences, the psychological horror and shock are entirely too much to handle. Remain in the sunlit domestic sphere, the superficial and controlled terra firma, he says, and at all costs avoid the horrors of that half known life. Of course, Ishmael himself continues to dive deeply into them throughout the narrative, and Melville by extension corroborated the impulse in his assertion that "I love all men who *dive*."[9] Our best example of the disingenuousness of the statement comes from Melville's frequently misunderstood facetious tease to his Pittsfield neighbor Sara Morewood to stay away from his excessively male book. (As demonstrated in his gender play throughout the novel, however, the book is anything but.) Melville employs the same rhetorical strategy as Ishmael to seduce Sara into reading the novel by arguing that it would be a rough and scary transgression from her safe domestic world, so forbidden that it becomes precisely the kind of escape a nice New England lass would relish. Indeed, we must at all costs dive into the wreckage and witness the horrors if only to quench our morbid curiosities, which Poe particularly enjoyed stimulating. Ishmael lures us into venturing away from that "insular Tahiti" to learn about our darker self, the one Hawthorne knew existed in even the most seemingly pious public figures, and that Thoreau discovered in the meanness of life he drove into a corner at Walden Pond.

That adventurous and risky outer world is precisely what draws Ishmael to sea in the first place and is what prompted Melville to revisit his own voyage aboard the *Acushnet* in the space of fiction. The novel sets that world up as forbidden territory—"quick to perceive a horror," Ishmael says, "I love to sail forbidden seas, and land on barbarous coasts"[10]—that is nonetheless irresistible. It is not a guilty pleasure of indulgence in voyeurism, but a hard and edgy glimpse into one's world and one's self. In that world and self is the human capacity for evil, especially its closeness to, and participation in, the pervasive reach of death. Those unknown depths can also lead to a blank void of "a colorless all-color of atheism from which we all shrink," as Ishmael notes in "The Whiteness of the Whale."[11] This blankness reverses Emerson's genial spiritual world: "though in many of its aspects the visible world seems formed in love, the invisible spheres were formed in fright."[12] In such invisible spheres lies perhaps the most frightening truth to apprehend, for such colorlessness implies the loss of a spiritual center and being caught untethered and rudderless in an inconsequential abyss.

The call to confront our darkest selves is an invitation, as in "Brit" and Melville's letter to Mrs. Morewood, to read *Moby-Dick* in the deepest manner possible. The unexamined life, according to this logic, is not worth living. The "horrors of the half known life" thus come to represent, ironically, not so much that cruel and surrounding sea that remains unknown in contrast to domesticated terra firma; instead those horrors are the unwillingness to explore it. Ishmael, like Melville, provides great motivation not to hide and speculate about such horrors but to seek them out. Like Thoreau, he wants to "get the whole and genuine meanness out of it and publish its meanness to the world."[13] Like Virgil in Dante's *Inferno*, Ishmael is our tour guide to that "half known life" and the abominations of the deep sea that tend to shed more light on human behavior than on natural history.

The key to surviving those "sledge-hammering seas"[14] of the soul is a willingness to face our own mortality, to confront it directly and unflinchingly in such a way that not only demystifies it but also wrestles and even plays with it. Fear, in the right measure, is of course advocated in the novel as the healthy alternative to Ahab's reckless example. But excessive fear, as discussed in chapter 3, is paralyzing, especially in the case of Starbuck. To remain safely ensconced in an insular Tahiti leaves us blind to the world and to ourselves. In *Moby-Dick*, the greatest sin is to be afraid of exploration, both outer and inner. The warning then that Ishmael gives, and that Melville expresses to Mrs. Morewood, can be seen as nothing less than an invitation to dive, to risk, through the presentation of a liability waiver not unlike those that skydivers and marathon runners must sign before their events. Reading this book, like engaging in those sports, is compelling precisely *because of* the volatile cocktail of fear and desire reflected in their warnings and waivers. It promises to bring us in the presence of our own mortality in an opportunity, as Stephen King has said of the function of horror fiction and roller coasters, to rehearse our own deaths. To fear this is nothing less than to fear ourselves. In John Guare's contemporary play, *Six Degrees of Separation* (1990), confidence man Paul Poitier explains the importance of courage as an act of the imagination. Like Ishmael, Paul solicits the confidence of his audience, only not in a faux warning of the dangers that lie ahead. Paul's objective nonetheless pivots on the same fulcrum as Ishmael's. It is the imagination, the very lynchpin of our existence, which provides us with the lens through which we might be able to tolerate a close, hard look at ourselves. Paul uses Holden's belief in *The Catcher in the Rye* that "it's the worst kind of yellowness to be so scared of yourself you put blindfolds on rather than deal with yourself" to illustrate his thesis: "To face ourselves. That's the hard thing. The imagination. That's God's gift to make the act of self-examination bearable."[15]

The imagination is both what makes the tragic vision of *Moby-Dick* palatable and an effective tool for examining our own lives. Melville never lets us take any of Ishmael's narrative too seriously. For example, the most monstrous of problems—death, the Whale, captivity to tyranny—can be outwitted, deflated, and defanged with a deft turn of perspective, a subtle shift in sensibility. For as shrouded in terror and the stuff of psychological and mythical tragedy as the final three chases of the White Whale are, they also amount to a giant three-round wrestling match with death, a tall tale of a dare, and a challenge to kill death itself. Melville's tone here echoes the confrontational and brazen voice of John Donne's speaker of "Death Be Not Proud." Death, of course, cannot be "beaten" per se, but it certainly can be met eye to eye, if only in a heartbreaking image of clinging to life.

Ishmael renders exactly such an image after the sinking of the *Pequod* itself. The harrowing scene pays homage to the duped, exploited, and slaughtered Native Americans at the hands of imperialistic tyranny figured in Ahab's treacherous mission. The image, a vignette really, is among the most moving of any in *Moby-Dick*. It calls to mind our own metaphorical ships—the group affiliations of nation, profession, ethnicity, gender, and region that keep our identities afloat—we might be sinking with, the masts we might cling to dutifully holding up the appearance of order amid the chaos of a rapidly forming swirling vortex. Whereas the image itself is one of profound human powerlessness in the face of inescapable oblivion, it is also an image of strength. Tashtego has a tenacious grip on physical survival, figured in his clinging to the mast and in his equally fierce refusal to yield to meaninglessness as he hammers Ahab's flag onto that mast: "for that one beholding instant,

Tashtego's mast-head hammer remained suspended in his hand; and the red flag, half-wrapping him as with a plaid, then streamed itself straight out from him, as his own forward-flowing heart."[16] In a "forward-flowing" gesture of dignity dedicated to the continuation of life in the face of death, "in the act of nailing the flag faster and yet faster to the subsiding spar," Tashtego freezes when a sky-hawk intervenes to snatch that flag symbolizing the ship's significance. Tashtego wrestles with the bird for the flag and thus the ship's meaning, pinning the hawk's wing beneath his hammer as his "whole captive form folded in the flag of Ahab," marking the final action as the *Pequod* sinks to the fowl's deathly shriek.[17]

Tashtego attempts to nail the *Pequod*'s flag onto the mast in vain, as waters inundate the decks below him, precipitously climbing the very mast to which he clings. In a heartbreaking tableau of the human pursuit of meaning in a chaotic world, the flag signifies the purpose of life aboard the *Pequod* in the face of imminent death. I see in this a quintessential Melvillian perspective of passionate questing agnosis, reflected in Hawthorne's sense of him as one who "can neither believe, nor be comfortable in his unbelief; for he is too honest and courageous not to try to do one or the other."[18] The flag, now reduced to a meaningless rag given Ahab's death moments earlier, nonetheless holds the Indian captive to Ahab's profane quest. With undying loyalty, Tashtego honestly, courageously, doggedly nails away despite his descent into the dark oblivion below. The gesture anticipates twentieth-century images of the *Titanic*'s band playing on while it sank and Jacqueline Kennedy inexplicably reaching for her husband's brain tissue on the trunk of their parade vehicle, trying beyond reason to contain the chaos that had just broken out before her.

Bundled into Eternity

THE POWER of *Moby-Dick*'s tragic vision has been linked by Charles Olson to *King Lear* and *Macbeth*. But more than this, I am drawn to the way in which it helps us organize our feelings toward death. The unstoppable and inevitable movement of nature echoes Alice's posies that grow on the roof of her cursed and desperate home, the symbol of her blackened lineage in Hawthorne's 1851 novel, *The House of the Seven Gables*, published the same year as *Moby-Dick* and composed on the other side of Pittsfield from Melville's Arrowhead homestead. Alice, the sacrificial lamb to the corruption and real estate monomania of the Pyncheon legacy, is rumored to have tossed the seeds out her window, the wind scattering them over the roof as they took root and miraculously bloomed above the chaos and madness of the house. Nature subsumes, takes over, swallows, inundates, and eventually heals. The *Pequod*, like the house of the seven gables, is the artificial construct, the site for malignant ideas executed at the expense of humanity, which cannot withstand the forces of time and nature. "Then all collapsed, and the great shroud of the sea rolled on as it rolled five thousand years ago," as all but Ishmael are buried in this watery grave.[19] The image exudes a stillness, a held breath, a momentous realization, not unlike the death meditation of Zen Buddhism or the child's prayer before sleep: "if I should die, before I wake . . ."—solemn, yet with a stunning clarity of vision.

Such moments provide ample evidence to refute Lawrence Buell's claim that "no community of devotees has ever received [*Moby-Dick*] as a spiritual authority, nor was that Melville's intent, though he did think of his vocation as truth telling rather than tale telling."[20] The community of devotees of the *Moby-Dick* Marathon reading may view the novel as a spiritual authority, but not in a doctrinaire, rigid way. The novel instead offers a noncoercive tapestry of experience through which readers might reassess their own spirituality, revisit and question any dogmas tyrannizing their guiding set of principles. But more than being a series of knotty ethical dilemmas, *Moby-Dick*'s magic specifically brings us in touch with space, grandeur, and our sense of significance despite our smallness in the broader scheme of things.

The terror inherent in the realization of the enormity of space, as figured in the image of Ishmael floating adrift on Queequeg's coffin, is a staple of the sublime. These forces dominate the Hudson River School's grand sweeping landscapes fraught with cataclysmic cosmic clashes between menacing clouds and bright sun, between craggy outcroppings and soft, green verdure, with tiny specklike figures dotting the terrain, dwarfed by the sheer immensity of space. "Melville felt the pressure of landscape art in his own writing," as Bryan Wolf notes.[21] Inherent in that pressure is the location of the self in the vast expanse, a spatial trope for the soul's relation to eternity and the divine—referred to as "the weaver-god" in "A Bower in the Arsacides"[22]— rather than a formalized sectarian God. "Ishmael's notion of pantheism," Wolf continues, "is a peculiarly romantic one: It emphasizes the *individual*'s oneness with nature while playing down *God*."[23] Such oneness with nature, significantly, bears the threat of total annihilation to which the day-dreaming sailor aloft in the masthead is liable, as no benevolent omnipotent deity will save him. The romantic adventurer, figured in the briefly mentioned Bulkington, regards that open ocean as a better place for his death than the domestic cocoon, since "it is better to perish in that howling infinite, than be ingloriously dashed upon the lees, even if that were safety!"[24] The "deep, earnest thinking" demanded in reading this novel, Ishmael emphasizes, is "but the intrepid effort of the soul to keep the open independence of her sea." Such thinking resists "the wildest winds of heaven" blowing toward shore. Dutiful obedience to the strictures and safeties of shore life, replete with its "civilized hypocrisies and bland deceits," yields a "worm-like" insular death, "craven claw to land!"[25] Ralph Waldo Emerson intoned precisely this note in his address to the Harvard Divinity School graduating class of 1838, whom he castigated for meek derivative habits of mind lacking in such adventurous spirit and thus giving way to a corpse-cold Unitarianism. The opposite emboldened enterprising spirit appears in Bulkington, as "the land seemed to scorch [the] feet" of the demigod restless whaler, who strings voyage upon voyage, ceaselessly seeking out the highest truth, though terrifyingly "shoreless," blank and "indefinite as God."[26]

Most readers take this as inspiration rather than justification of Manifest Destiny, which was embedded in the culture at the time. Ceaseless striving in the face of sublime terror and danger, however, still rings true as a model worth emulating despite what has become something of a critical obsession, as represented by Jenny Franchot's remark that "Ishmael's vocal space mimes cultural invasion, creating a motion of ceaseless imperial summoning and negation that creates in turn an immense, yet abstract, materiality of language."[27] But the drive is not so much nationalistic—Melville himself worried that unrestrained democratic leadership might lead to authoritarianism—as it is spiritual. Shoving off land forces one to engage the rudder, to hoist the sail and navigate; movement does this, hence the heroism of Bulkington. To seek out the weaver-god at work, to witness him at close range and internalize the power of that cosmological creation with an equally forceful cosmological knowledge and vision is profound, if not overwhelming. The point is not to confirm the presence of a benevolent God in such questing, but to ascertain the nature of existence in all its cruel beauty and "joyous, heartless, ever-juvenile eternities." God may turn out to be as indifferent to our value as Stubb is to Pip's when he warns him not to jump out of the boat because "a whale would sell for thirty times what you would, Pip, in Alabama."[28] Such a

God is a fake, "while the true God, called the Stranger or Alien God, is exiled somewhere in the outer regions of the cosmos," according to one reader.[29] Bulkington seeks him, and Pip inadvertently finds him.

Such profound vision is precisely what Pip unintentionally acquires, ironically enough, out of an act of cowardice. Pip finds the weaver-god not only indefinite but also unsympathetic to his plight and vulnerability. Pip's madness, his "weal or woe" reaches an uncompromised expression "indifferent as his God."[30] Among his shipmates, with the significant exception of Ahab, Pip's near-death experience and subsequent madness does not turn him into a seer with special insight into the nature of existence because he cannot express it adequately to attain their comprehension. Pip's gibberish to the sailors is poetry to the *Pequod*'s captain. Only Ahab is attuned to the attitude of total abandonment and willful paternalistic negligence Pip ascertains as the true nature of God. Pip's revelation of God's indifference corroborates Ahab's sense of the whale as a blank wall pushed close. This is Melville's expression of "the ancient Gnostic heresy in which the creator God of this world is a bungler or imposter."[31] Pip's discovery of a cold, indifferent God also reflects the federal government's callous attitude toward slavery in 1851, as witnessed by the Fugitive Slave Law and the Compromise of 1850, both concessions to the South.

Pip's madness appears "divinest sense," as Dickinson would have it, most emphatically in his soliloquy upon the crew's midnight antics, which Olson connects to "the sharp bitter wisdom of the Elizabethan fool" in Shakespeare's *King Lear*.[32] Indeed, his madness is his wisdom, as he has the last word of the pivotal chapter "The Forge." In that chapter, Ahab baptizes his harpooners' lances "in nomine diaboli" (in the name of the devil) thus sealing his fate and ritualizing his damnation.[33] Melville ends the chapter with sound, first of the "ivory leg," then of the "hickory pole, both hollowly ringing along every plank." Finally a "light, unnatural, half-bantering, yet most piteous sound" of Pip's "wretched laugh," like the smiles of Hooper, Wakefield, and Coverdale in Hawthorne's fiction, comprehends the full, horrible weight of "the black tragedy of the melancholy ship, and mocked it!"[34] This laughter is not connected to any coherent language or speech; Pip's knowledge, like that of the Hawthorne characters, is entirely nonverbal and rests in his soul. His Gothic cackle, that of a crazy man, ends the exceedingly dark scene, which functions as the concluding ritual counterpart to the opening oath upon the quarterdeck.

Pip and Bulkington are odd bedfellows, yet they distinctly coalesce through their encounters with the divine more than any other characters in the novel. Charles Olson observed that both were "inactive to the plot" of the novel, forming a dynamic by which "Ahab has to dominate over a world where the humanities may also flower and man (the crew) by Pip's or Bulkington's way reach God."[35] Strikingly, both are wrecked in reaching God. Pip's eyes and reason are burned out as in Emily Dickinson's poem, "Tell All Truth, But Tell It Slant," while Bulkington dies in the abyss of the sea. Pip's cowardly action of jumping overboard to avoid confrontation with the whale leads him to God; Bulkington's brave action of embarking on serial voyages in an unwearied, bold, and energetic pursuit of landlessness brings him to God. Pip's incoherence also counters Bulkington's "deep, earnest thinking" that "is the way of man's sanity, the pure forging of his intelligence in the smithy of life," as Olson poetically expresses it.[36] Significantly, both characters provide "a struggle and a catharsis which he intended, to feel 'spotless as the lamb,'" Olson writes.[37]

Bulkington appropriately remains a "sleeping partner" to the action of the novel. Abiding by and watching over the narrative in silence, he sharply contrasts with the crazy, cackling gibberish of Pip. Bulkington's disembodied presence carries the quiet solemnity of the deaths of the common whalemen Ishmael regards in "The Chapel." "The Lee Shore" is Ishmael's epitaph to Bulkington, a pitched prose-poetry elegiac version of other such remembrances of disappeared sailors that line the walls of New Bedford's Whaleman's Chapel. Indeed, the "bitter blanks in those black-bordered marbles which cover no ashes" and "the deadly voids and unbidden infidelities in the lines that seem to gnaw upon all Faith," horrify Ishmael. It is the notion of death at sea, of lost "beings who have placelessly perished without a grave," its rudderless void, and its terrifying expanse that haunt him so. Like Bulkington, those men "tell no tales, though containing more secrets than the Goodwin Sands." The silence is rooted in the very fact that "there is death in this business of whaling—a *speechlessly* quick chaotic bundling of a man into Eternity."[38] Speed, chaos, and silence produce a shivering cocktail of spiritual destiny here. Death appears in studied contrast to innumerable slow angelic expirations common to Victorian sentimental novels, most conspicuously, little Eva's protracted death in Harriet Beecher Stowe's *Uncle Tom's Cabin* or any Dickens novel.

Ishmael's tale gives voice to the whalemen's otherwise deathly silent experience so eloquently and forcefully that *Moby-Dick* has become a staple for all histories of American whaling. Melville's greatest novel nonetheless refuses to provide any pat answers. It assures, through its multiple perspectives, that the "universe is wider than our views of it," as Thoreau said.[39] The humbling realization that our inner dramas, and even the outer trauma of the political world, are all smaller than nature, however, does not necessarily demand passive surrender. Instead, it offers a fresh and proper perspective on our brief stint within the colossal sweep of time that William Cullen Bryant poetically envisioned at the age of sixteen in "Thanatopsis." Like figures in a Cole painting, individual lives in Melville's fiction appear dwarfed by the expansive grandeur of nature's compass. Yet with a stroke of luck, our experience, our wisdom, and our insight might reach the wider world, with demand meeting supply in a perfect marriage, as the image of the *Rachel*'s rescue of Ishmael so powerfully demonstrates. Indeed, the grieving Captain Gardner saves Ishmael and thus his tale, turning his miniscule and meaningless existence into the stuff of grand tales, mammoth cosmological narratives of immense space. It is not that Captain Gardner gets all the credit for the tale, but he is instrumental as the midwife of its birth and facilitator of its realization into art, not unlike a fortuitous business partnership, such as those joint-stock companies Ishmael fancies as animating the crew while they work.

Gardner's lost son is now found in the surrogate Ishmael, as the epilogue of *Moby-Dick* completes a broken and incomplete family figured in the devious cruising *Rachel*. As such, the domestic world appears as always already inhabiting the public world of the whaling industry. Only its intimacy, as evoked in *Kindred Spirits*, Asher B. Durand's timeless landscape of two figures discoursing on an outcropping in the woods, is often suppressed or submerged beneath the iron-rails mentality of Ahab's business, a metonym for the narrow, dehumanizing pursuit of capital. Melville dismantles the dominant culture's insistence that the two must remain separate. He repeatedly shows ties of kinship and filial love between the sailors. A palpable desire for domestic peace, if not the achievement of it, drives Ahab's attempt at smoking a leisurely pipe and his tearful revelation of his humanity in "The Symphony." What is striking about the concluding scene of Ishmael's rescue is how it foregrounds sympathy, according to Lori Merish's explanation of antebellum novels in general, as "the spontaneous emotional faculty that allows the flourishing of both . . . market society and the 'companionate family' [of] market capitalism and middle-class personal life, as mutually determining spheres, each dependent on the other."[40] Melville's radical re-vision of "middle-class personal life" (re)constructs a patchwork family out of the chaos of the sunken *Pequod* upon the decks of the *Rachel*, deviating from the ostensible objective of her commercial voyage in the public sphere of industry. Of all places, family—the type that saves with its love—comes to the rescue amid a floating industrial wasteland.

Surviving Trials

SYMPATHY AND the ever-whimsical finger of fate appear not only in the form of the devious cruising *Rachel*. They also fuse the forces of life and death in Queequeg's coffin-sea chest that Ishmael uses as a life buoy. Summoning the strength to survive and raise life out of death is as important as the force of sympathy here, as embodied by Gardner's failed pleas for help. The plaques commemorating the dead in the Whaleman's Chapel earlier in the novel make Ishmael sensitive to precisely such a paradox, as he remarks that "Faith, like a jackal, feeds among the tombs, and even from these dead doubts she gathers her most vital hope."[41] During the composition of *Moby-Dick*, Melville himself was pushed to the brink of his psychological strength, and he too found a life buoy in the materials of death that plagued his life.

On June 29, 1851, he wrote Hawthorne, describing his melancholia in an extended metaphor for his endless literary labor on *Moby-Dick* of building some "shanties of chapters and essays" in a "trackless" outpost in the woods fraught with dangerous Indians and "insignificant but still stinging mosquitoes."[42] His self-diagnosis links him to other thought-divers like Hawthorne, "men like you and me and some others forming a chain of God's posts round the world," casting their tough toil as some sort of band of literary missionaries prone to "certain crotchety and doleful chimeras." He resolves to be "content to encounter them now and then" and "to fight them the best way we can," finding refuge in a wilderness of thought, however "boundless [and] trackless," one that is "still glorious."[43]

The rather light-hearted tone of his letter to Hawthorne masks the depth of Melville's struggle at a moment midway through the writing of what would become the most ambitious novel ever penned by an American. During that time when "The 'Whale' is only half-way through for press," Sophia Hawthorne recognized in Melville an agitated state in which he was stimulated by present thoughts of the work in progress and his relationship with Hawthorne, as much as he was haunted by memories of his past.[44] Elizabeth Hardwick, in an impressionistic biographical riff worthy of D. H. Lawrence, recently described Melville at this time as one "who has about him, even in settled married life, much of the renegade, the scars of knowing, choosing, the bleak underside of life."[45] The poet Cornelius Mathews, Melville's contemporary, dubbed him "Mr. Noble Melancholy."[46] The Berkshires were fertile ground for writing, yet fraught with memory traps leaving Melville in what he described as "a very susceptible and peradventure febrile temperament."[47] These were "reminders," as Parker syntactically captures their dizzying associational significance, "of how his life had changed, and changed again—through death (his father's, his uncle's, various cousins', his brother's), impoverishment, bodily changes, seasonal changes, his own travels, his literary achievements, his marriage."[48] The Berkshires conjured memories of his visits to his uncle's farm as a twelve-year-old youth having recently endured his father's too-early death, and later as an eighteen-year-old schoolteacher.

There is ample evidence in Melville's writings pointing to the profound and lasting impact of his father's death. The protagonist of *Pierre*, for example, intersects with his father's checkered past, particularly as embodied by Isabella, the illegitimate offspring of an overseas tryst. Melville wrestled with his father's demons, to be sure, during the composition of *Moby-Dick* as well. He was in many ways the author's fallen hero, a man he aggrandized beyond his real station as a failed clerk and merchant, a man crushed by debt, both financial and emotional. Melville cast him instead as a sophisticated and worldly gentleman whose aristocratic shine reflected his royal ties to the Earl of Melvill House, to the queen of Hungary, and kings of Norway. His death, which Melville witnessed at the age of twelve, was anything but dignified, however.

The nature of Allan Melvill's (as the surname was originally spelled) passing was turbulent and tortured. The well-spoken gentleman in January of 1832 was "*very* sick" according to his brother, Thomas, Jr., who reported the illness was "induced by a variety of causes." None of those causes, however, would ever emerge through any clear medical explanation. Instead, the history of his passing consists of symptoms, not the least of which was a "great mental excitement—at times fierce, even *maniacal*." The physicians agreed that were he to survive the illness, as Thomas painfully lamented, "he would live, *a Maniac!*"[49] A precocious and emotionally sensitive twelve-year-old, Herman Melville likely bore witness to "the melancholy spectacle of a deranged man" in his final death throes.[50] Fueled in part by such crippling memories, Melville poured himself into *Moby-Dick*, exposing what David Leverenz depicts as "the chaos of narcissistic needs and fears in the American middle-class marketplace—the same marketplace that drove his patrician father to bankruptcy, insanity, and perhaps unconscious suicide." In this sense, the novel can be read as Melville's obsession with "avenging his shattered manhood."[51] Leverenz is overzealous and reductive in his attempt to make the novel essentially about manhood, but his point that the novel contends with great pain, especially Melville's own personal pain, is well taken, and indeed corroborated by Peter Whittemore. At the 2009 reading, Melville's great-great-grandson incisively pinned Melville's sense of terror in the color white to the fact that "on the day his [Melville's] father screamed himself to death, there was a massive snowstorm. He forever associated that blank whiteness with the most horrific memory of his childhood" and indeed etched it into his characterizations of the whale at his most menacing, the blank wall shoved near, a psychic abyss signaling a spiritually rudderless state, untethered to all meaning whatsoever. "The White Whale," continued Whittemore, "is violent like that snowstorm was to Melville as a boy." The trauma indeed would find its way onto the pages of *Moby-Dick*.

The suggestion that Melville's father committed a kind of unconscious suicide is compelling in light of his father's financial disasters and subsequent guilt over squandering his wife's fortune. Melville's father indeed had given up, as his decline proceeded directly from economic failure to psychotic derangement, physical debilitation, and eventual death. The incident may have provided the stimulus, whether conscious or otherwise, for Melville's fictionalization of the mortal power of individual will. Precisely the reverse progression of Allan Melvill's decline can be seen in Queequeg's willful return to health in *Moby-Dick*. After suffering from what appears to be a fatal disease, Queequeg rapidly recovers from the protracted illness. Victorian authors were fascinated with how people died and attached profound significance, especially as an indicator of the soul's destiny, to the attitude and manner of the dying figure. Ishmael's description of Queequeg's apparently imminent death reflects this preoccupation, and even obsession, embedded in antebellum culture: "And the drawing near of Death, which alike levels all, alike impresses all with a last revelation, which only an author from the dead could adequately tell."[52]

Melville's father's raving lunacy that defined his passing sharply contrasts with the quirky dignity and noble courage of Queequeg's self-willed resurrection. The scene appears to intone Melville's own refiguration of his father's death in an effort to correct it in the imaginative space of fiction. Melville indeed finds life in death in the very withering of Queequeg's frame, in the paradox of his emaciated figure that "wasted and wasted away in those long-lingering days, till there seemed but little left of him but his frame and tattooing."[53] Even the cannibal himself sees the end nearing, as he requests burial at sea in a canoe rather than the perfunctory hammock in which the bodies of most sailors were bundled and tossed overboard like so much vile shark food. The vitality emerges as his body wanes, preparing for his last sea voyage in a coffin-canoe to the afterlife: "But all else in him thinned, and his cheekbones grew sharper, his eyes, nevertheless, seemed growing fuller and fuller; they became a strange softness of luster; and mildly but deeply looked out at you there from the sickness, a wondrous testimony to the immortal health in him which could not die, or be weakened." Ishmael likens his ever-expanding, "rounding" eyes to "the rings of Eternity," in a beautiful and lyrical natural figure of broadening circles on the water.[54] His soul seems to open and reach out in direct proportion to the withdrawal and shrinking of his own flesh. The sense, at this early stage in the chapter, is that Queequeg's soul is ready for release from his body, preparing to depart on its journey into eternity.

Ishmael's language, in describing Queequeg's eyes as "the immortal health in him which could not die," is a conventional trope common to antebellum fictional death scenes in which the departing spirit outshines the withering body in a show of final exuberance. Under Melville's command, the trope instead functions as a perfect red herring; the immortal in Queequeg is not a paradoxical figure for the flight of the spirit but is refreshingly literalized in the rejuvenation of Queequeg's flesh and blood. As the carpenter goes about measuring Queequeg's dimensions to make his coffin-canoe, Melville puns on the reversal of reader expectations, setting up the comic situation of preparing for a death that does not occur: "No sooner was the carpenter apprised of the order, than taking his rule ... regularly chalking Queequeg's person as he shifted the rule," or his measuring stick. Indeed, the order or rule is that deathbeds are made for those about to die; the carpenter does not want his labor wasted, and proclaims, "Ah! Poor fellow! He'll have to die now."[55] The rule will be shifted in this case to accommodate a mind-to-body connection totally unanticipated by most antebellum readers wedded to a mind/body binary, one so deeply embedded in the culture that it would positively scandalize Whitman's insistence in *Leaves of Grass* of the body's status as animated soul, capable of organic regeneration. Queequeg's vital soul is not reaching out for eternity so much as it is reaching into his physical form and seizing hold with a strength superior to that of the sickness that seems to have overwhelmed him.

All involved are sure Queequeg's death is imminent, which heightens the comic impact of the realization that not only will he survive, but he will leap back into the fray with almost miraculous alacrity. The speed of his recovery mocks the protracted efforts, indeed labors (particularly on the part of the carpenter), to prepare for his passing. Water, biscuits, a pillow, his little god Yojo, and even his harpoon are meticulously arranged about the new coffin, and Queequeg himself lies within, trying it on for size, to confirm its fit. The Egyptian overtones are emphasized here, as all the items signify the "necessities" of the afterlife. But these necessities will transform from symbols into items of practical value in the physical world, the most important of which is the coffin itself. Once he has rallied after the prophetic cry from Pip that "Queequeg dies game! . . . but base little Pip, he died a coward,"[56] the coffin-canoe is remodeled into a sea chest to accommodate his new plans to live. Elevating the coffin out of the realm of such drollery, Melville places profound significance upon that coffin-sea chest in the final scene, as it transforms yet again into a life buoy for Ishmael. That final transformation reverts the useless, heavily symbolic coffin with all its claptrap of Queequeg's favorite things for the afterlife into an object of life-giving, and thus miraculous, significance, animated at once with mystical power and pragmatic purpose. Queequeg's will to survive his sickness eventually saves Ishmael's own life, since it initiates a chain of events figured in the multiple lives and functions of the canoe-coffin-chest-buoy in a wedding of free will and fate of the very sort Ishmael glimpses while mat-making with the cannibal.

Indeed, that act of free will that seemed to kill Melville's own father, now for Queequeg is the stuff of life, a conscious decision, and "a matter of the sovereign will and pleasure." If a man "made up his mind to live," Queequeg explains, "mere sickness could not kill him: nothing but a whale, or a gale, or some violent, ungovernable, unintelligent destroyer of that sort." But the pragmatic (and no less comically so) punch is that Queequeg had realized he had unfinished business ashore, "which he was leaving undone; and therefore had changed his mind about dying." Rising, he shakes, stretches his limbs and "poising a harpoon, declared himself fit for a fight."[57] Queequeg met the match of his unfinished business, whereas Allan Melvill perceived that he was no match for the business that beckoned him from the grave. This angle of perception, with its pragmatic center and comic edges, is precisely the source of survival in *Moby-Dick*. But it is not without the willful suspension of disbelief, for fate, or chance, must come into play and keep the coffin-sea chest from being sucked into the swirling vortex of the *Pequod*'s wreckage. An impulse to survive, like Queequeg's own practically grounded revival, along with fortuitous circumstance, like the buoy remaining intact and accessible to save the drowning Ishmael, can intersect to save all our lives.

Even the best intended philosophies cannot substitute for a well-placed life buoy, the source of a man's will to live and tend to worldly matters. The pragmatic reach of Melville's thinking is visible in a letter to Hawthorne in which he commented on the relative impotence of a maxim like Goethe's *"Live in the all"* when directed at "a fellow with a raging toothache. 'My dear boy,' Goethe says to him, 'you are sorely afflicted with that tooth; but you must *live in the all*, and then you will be happy.'"[58] Such advice fails to address the deeper cosmic pain that feels more like a toothache of the soul than some minor malaise. Emily Dickinson's poem 501, "This World Is Not Conclusion," resonates with the same sentiment that "Narcotics cannot still the Tooth / That nibbles at the soul."[59] This is a psychic and cosmic malady immune to even the most notable of Goethe's maxims.

Moby-Dick certainly offers no coherent formula for recovery, and indeed actively shrinks from unproblematic panaceas to Ahab's existential ache. No easy cure exists for the "damp, drizzly November in my soul" the despondent Ishmael complains of in his landlocked slump on the first page of the narrative.[60] Yet Melville does symbolically arrange his characters, particularly the first mates and Queequeg, around a schema that addresses potential escape from the dark prison of depression. It is no secret that Melville himself was manic-depressive; not only does his fiction bear it out, but also a preponderance of his relatives, the most notable of which being his father, strongly suggest its hereditary origins.[61] The disorder's darkest moments are captured throughout the novel. Through his troubled sleep—he awakens from a night terror in one scene with fists clenched so furiously that his nails dig into his bloody palms—and his incapacity to enjoy a moment's peace, Ahab is tyrannized by his own intolerance of ambiguity, which he projects onto the whale. As Wendy Stallard Flory writes, "No romance writer has dramatized the experience of manic-depressive mood swings more comprehensively than Melville in *Moby-Dick*," particularly in his capacity to capture Ahab's "irresistible coercive power, black moods, metaphysical agonizing, paranoia, rage, obsession with revenge, grandiosity of self-concept, and headlong rush to self-destruction."[62]

Rather than simply presenting a series of symptoms to diagnose the diseased state of Melville's mind, *Moby-Dick* instead invites us to see what channels for recovery exist for the liabilities of leading the examined life, for exploring well beyond the insular Tahiti and into the depths of the soul. Readers of this sort, who tend to be thought-divers of various stripes, are well represented at the marathon reading. The novel poses as one of its key concerns the tolerance of ambiguity as essential for a healthy relation to the universe. In a way that illuminates the function of *Moby-Dick* as the reader's life buoy—a kind of inscrutable, shape-shifting, multipurpose lifesaving device that we cling to like Ishmael holding fast to Queequeg's coffin in the open seas—Flory usefully demonstrates how characters symbolically represent different attempts to escape Ahab's moods. The captain's moods, significantly, are characterized by his desire to kill all ambiguity as embodied in the whale.

Flory's thesis—that Starbuck, Stubb, and Flask represent failed attempts to survive rough inner seas, while Queequeg symbolizes healing and rescue— is especially relevant to the twenty-five-hour *Moby-Dick* Marathon reading as a curative and cleansing experience. That span of time offers plenty of sea room to absorb the perils of ineffective coping strategies and to see the light of psychic survival as figured in Queequeg's actions and Ishmael's open-mindedness. Ishmael, in this sense, provides a model of intellectual exploration, and indeed, of reading, that is capable of overcoming petty prejudices and accepting Queequeg, who turns out to be a lifesaving force for him. As lifesaving forces with textual significance, Queequeg is to Ishmael as *Moby-Dick* is to the marathon reader. The hieroglyphics carved from Queequeg's tattoos, "a wondrous work in one volume," into the coffin lid of what becomes Ishmael's life buoy contain "a complete theory of the heavens and the earth, and a mystical treatise on the art of attaining the truth" and come to stand for *Moby-Dick* the novel, to which we also cling for all its cosmological power.[63]

If Queequeg represents rescue and calm, then Starbuck represents aborted attempts at countering inner darkness through the sheer force of will that might destroy it once and for all. The chapter "The Musket," though primarily an exploration in political philosophy, also bears the psychological resonance of a man coming to grips with his dangerously bipolar self. Flory indicates that Starbuck is "the contribution of the reasoning, conscious mind to with-standing the depressive mood," a "conscious resolve to avert these moods," and a noble respectable impulse at that, one not wholly cowardly or weak.[64] Working from the premise that Starbuck represents the will, albeit failed, to withstand or avert depressive moods is particularly compelling in light of the lengths to which he will go to eradicate those moods altogether in "The Musket." Starbuck's corrective will is no match for Ahab's moods; he cannot talk him out of his mission to kill the whale and so considers killing him as a blunt, desperate attempt at final liberation from the disease of Ahab's quest. Starbuck's will, at this late stage in the novel, is weary and brutalized to the point of reckless drunkenness, as his gun "shook like a drunkard's arm against the panel," in a scene that echoes the serious consideration of suicide.[65] His gun trembling, Starbuck knows his action will cause profound consequences and shifts in the power dynamic of the *Pequod*. So too did Melville know that taking his own life would turn the power structure of his family upside down. On September 10, 1867, some seventeen years after the composition of "The Musket," Melville's own son would complete what Starbuck could only con-sider and pull the trigger to escape his youthful demons forever.

Ishmael himself, in his morose wanderings on land before embarking with the *Pequod*, is less serious to the point of self-mockery when he says he goes to sea as a "substitute for pistol and ball. With a philosophical flourish Cato throws himself upon his sword; I quietly take to the ship."[66] His dark humor notwithstanding, the line still betokens survival and echoes the very act of reading an epic novel of such vast spiritual and philosophical depth. Reading this novel is a form of going to sea, a gesture of self-sustenance that shares Ishmael's motives. It is not the escapist "self-medication" of the sort Stubb and Flask embody with their respective smoking and drinking. Rather it is the process of facing the darkest traumas of Ahab so that we might better be able to face our own with the open-mindedness of Ishmael and bear them with the soothing calm of Queequeg that finally has the desired healing, restorative effect. Queequeg not only provides the life buoy for Ishmael and thus the narrative's survival, but he also saves a bumpkin from drowning and rescues, with his fine "obstetrics," Tashtego from the whale's head after he had fallen in while extracting oil. Queequeg affects Ishmael, who proclaims, "No more my splintered heart and maddened hand were turned against the wolfish world. This soothing savage had redeemed it,"[67] the same way he affects the reader. It is fitting that the narrative have a balm like Queequeg to counterbalance the corrosive, self-destructive bent of Ahab, whose narrow reading of the whale is met with the native's poised embrace of his own death (and revelation that he was in command of his mortality all along). Crucially, the native's faith, however blind to the meaning of his tattoos it may be, drives him to trust in their significance, moving him to copy them onto the lid of his coffin-canoe, at once exerting control over his own death by figuratively writing his own epitaph, and also accepting the unknown. However illegible to him, he copies his tattoos onto his coffin lid because he knows, trusts, believes they contain cosmological meaning linked to his soul's destiny. In this sense, Queequeg displays more than just a tolerance of ambiguity, but an act of faith that embraces it.[68]

Blankness and silence do not confront Queequeg as a challenge to his manhood, as they do Ahab, forming a close confining wall that menaces and mocks him. Instead, quiet and blankness signify peace and tranquility at the Spouter Inn, as Queequeg "seemed entirely at his ease; preserving the utmost serenity" in the face of the utter alienation and panic-inducing chaos of being "some twenty thousand miles from home . . . as though he were in the planet Jupiter."[69] In a place of such busy trafficking, a kind of grand central station for whalers, with a dizzying variety of cultures, ethnicities, and personalities sweeping through Peter Coffin's establishment in a wild rush, Queequeg is the still eye of the storm. As such, he finds peace in the untamable flow of humanity in all its diversity and even perversity. Melville wrote the novel to survive, yet paradoxically it nearly killed him and certainly decimated his career. Reading it is a way into the consciousness and mental health of Queequeg, who embodies an open-minded acceptance also seen in Ishmael. Melville avoids the noble savage stereotype of the ethnic other by making Queequeg flawed, even comically so, especially in the scene when he outfits himself for death and abruptly, almost absurdly, decides it is not time to die, as his body blithely follows the order and snaps back with astonishing speed. The source of Melville's survival is Ishmael and Queequeg; our survival as readers occurs through the brave exploration of our own capacity for madness, the dark underside of our souls far removed from the insular Tahitis in which we live. We acknowledge that darkness through Ahab, who has such a firm grip on the narrative. But his necessary counterpart and balm are in the epistemological and psychological examples of Ishmael and Queequeg. Together they are comic and lighthearted, brave questing souls, pantheistic and culturally diverse in their enriched and global outlooks. At bottom both are made sound by their very relation to the ambiguities of the world, which do not imprison them but set them free.

The quest for survival is inherent in the act of reading *Moby-Dick*; in completing the novel—most attendees of the marathon reading have previously done so in one form or another—readers enjoy a sense of completion that evades the crew of the *Pequod* in its calamitous conclusion. But images of survival and regeneration still flourish throughout the course of the novel, including Pip's near-death experience and subsequent madness, and Queequeg's miraculous willful recovery from an apparently fatal illness. These images speak to how we survive, how we carry our wounds with us, adjusting and adapting to them, or vowing vengeance for the suffering they inflicted. The White Whale himself bears the marks of his experience, a hearty and rugged survivor himself, whose tangles with whalers have made him notorious the world around.

Nothing about the investigation of such facts is perfunctory in *Moby-Dick*; it is instead the epitome of natural science aestheticized into exalted inspiration. For whatever "numerous rude scratches" and "violent scrapings" Ishmael locates on the White Whale, he is not only defining the characteristics of a remarkable animal, but he also is elevating his subject to a venerable and exalted individual.[70] In this way, the whale becomes a figure whose endurance gives pause, for each scratch and scrape, each rusted harpoon hanging from his flanks represents trauma, like that of Melville's own father's raving death, like his own bouts with the diabolical brute of manic depression (which Jimi Hendrix, an artistic genius who also wrestled with colossal demons, dubbed a "frustrating mess"), and like the innumerable, unsung trials we as readers have survived. Pain is behind those marks, but they are badges of honor, for they did not spell the end for the creature.

To revere the whale's capacity for survival, then, as Elizabeth Bishop does in her stunning poem inspired by *Moby-Dick*, is not a "quasi-theological" gesture that mystifies the animal. Quite the opposite, it provides a nearness to the detail of the marks of that creature's experience as a kind of hyperreality, a level of scrutiny so exacting as to cast his resumé of near catastrophe into hyperbolic relief not artificially exaggerated but pragmatically, ecologically true.

> that from his lower lip
> —if you could call it a lip—
> grim, wet, and weaponlike,

hung five old pieces of fish-line,
or four and a wire leader
with the swivel still attached,
with all their five big hooks
grown firmly in his mouth.
A green line, frayed at the end
where he broke it, two heavier lines,
and a fine black thread
still crimped from the strain and snap
when it broke and he got away.[71]

The state of each line that dangles from his mouth, "frayed," "crimped," "swivel still attached," signifies a strength of force that gives the speaker pause, that brings her to a profound moment of reverence, from an initial sense of guilt, eventuating in ecstasy in the creature's will to survive, as reflected in the brilliant rainbow of the fish's triumph. The very materials of its death have now become the tokens of the fish's survival, as lyrical as it is fierce, as primitive and brutal as it is ethereal and transcendent, bringing a profound sense of awe and glory. Like Ishmael, the narrator "stared and stared," until struck by the way "victory filled up / the little rented boat," now colossal, magnificent, rendering the waste of "the pool of bilge" and "the oil" and the "rusted engine" and the "bailer" in the luminous transcendence of the fish's will to survive, bursting through the "sun-cracked thwarts" and finally filling the blasted, beaten equipment of that fish's destruction into pure bliss until "everything was rainbow, rainbow, rainbow!" The anticlimactic last line pulling us back into the reality of the fishing narrator, "And I let the fish go,"[72] is exactly what Ahab does not do, and Moby-Dick makes him pay.

Survivors in 2009

IT IS TELLING that print culture today has become so intensely real in the lives of its participants that there is now a *Harry Potter* help line, a toll-free number desperate readers can call when they need help recovering from the emotional trauma of the deaths of their beloved characters in the seventh installment of J. K. Rowling's astonishingly popular fantasy series.[73] Perhaps there should also be a help line for obsessed Melvillians, for the descent into his darkness is a far graver proposition than a tour of even the darkest recesses of Hogwarts. ("For epistemological crises regarding the visible absence of all color as described in the chapter, 'The Whiteness of the Whale,' press one," a recorded female voice would inform us on the automated system.) Those who stay the full twenty-five hours, in all seriousness, do face inevitable rough patches, for who among us will not admit to feeling weary beyond comprehension, to succumbing to the waves of words hour after hour that just don't stop, like the accumulation of thousands of footfalls in an athletic marathon, a ceaseless cadence, a pounding that becomes undifferentiated and works its way into the soul? But in some ways, *Moby-Dick* is itself a sort of help line, offering to cleanse and cure, as much as it dangerously draws us into its swirling vortex of sublime terror. Embedded in it are the keys to surviving the *Pequod*'s voyage, a predicament aptly described a century earlier in Dr. Samuel Johnson's quip that a sailor is but "a man in jail with a chance of being drown."[74] Melville emerged from writing the novel feeling "spotless as the lamb" though he had just written a "wicked book, broiled in hell-fire." Does that vindication of soul and that cathartic purity transfer itself to the reader? If we are up to the challenge of endurance that the novel poses, especially as it is read in a marathon format, great rewards not only of survival but also of exultation are in order, as the next chapter on breaches discusses.

The *Moby-Dick* Marathon and Ammon Shea's *Reading the OED: One Man, One Year, 21,730 Pages* (2008) perform feats of reading endurance analogous to what Jack Kerouac and the Beats had done in their endless writing stints. Both significantly link the body to print culture for the insights and vision that accrue from the extension of mind and body to ungodly limits. The *Moby-Dick* Marathon reading, like Shea's reading of the entire *Oxford English Dictionary* in one year, is a physically taxing feat of endurance. Something this long inevitably involves the body. Shea reported neck pain, headaches, nausea, and failing eyesight. It hurts to consume books in ways they were not intended; a dictionary was never supposed to be read cover to cover, of course, but used intermittently as a reference tool, one word at a time. Novels are universally divided into chapters or sections breaking down the units of consumption, offering interstices in the narrative for pauses of usually a day or longer. Absorbed beyond reason, many of us have read entire novels in one sitting, but those works tend to be shorter and more manageable than *Moby-Dick*. The marathon reading for those who stay the full twenty-five hours speaks more to human potential in general and to our collective strength than to the accomplishment of the personal challenge to "stay in the building," the requirement to be recognized at the end of the event as a "finisher." Ed Camara rightly pointed out shortly after the opening of the 2009 reading that going the full twenty-five hours can be construed as a mere dare. "I am not an early morning person," he said, distancing himself from the endurance dimension of the reading. "I question their prudence in [seeking] a personal challenge to see if they last that long," he added. "There are people who do it merely as a challenge," his tone now acerbically sarcastic, "there are also people who eat fried cockroaches." The image calls to mind old 1950s footage of college stunts aimed at breaking world records for the number of people to fit inside a Volkswagon Beetle or a phone booth, undergraduates cramming in from all angles in what appears mere fanaticism and goofy lunacy. Little did they know that their mindless fun was exposing, if not pointedly protesting against, the increasing compartmentalization of human beings by the mid-twentieth century into privatized spaces for transportation and communication, both formerly intimate pastimes — the omnibus and the train; the front porch and the agora — in which people physically occupied the same space. Such stunts exposed a cultural anxiety about the loss of intimacy with the rise of the machine age.

Similarly, the all-night feature of the *Moby-Dick* Marathon reading functions not as an eccentric solipsistic dare so much as a way to collectively expose the cultural anxiety about the death of literature, the death of reading great works unabridged, sans Cliff's Notes, summaries, digital or online shortcuts of any sort. In this light, the New Bedford reading functions almost like a sit-in protest against the technological threat posed to the love of long, difficult literature and the patience, endurance, and long attention span it demands. The reading defies such trends lampooned in Howard Moss's poem, "Shall I Compare Thee to a Summer's Day," written through the voice of our abridged contemporary culture to demonstrate the flattening, dulling, blunting, and colloquilizing of Shakespeare's lovely original sonnet into something like a dry charcoal briquet, all chemicals and dust, nowhere to be found in nature. He ironically ends with the plea for readers to keep his poem, and thus his love, alive: "If there's just one condensed reader left / Who can figure out the abridged alphabet, / After you're dead and gone, / In this poem you'll live on!"[75] In this satirical sally at the fast-read culture of *Reader's Digest* (like high fructose corn syrup, sugary and easily digestible with negligible nutritional benefits) that would abridge the alphabet if it could (leaving us with poets like Billy Collins), the worry is that we become, like our webbannersoundbyte-bumpersticker-billboard–10-o'clock-news culture, a wasteland of condensed readers. Thus "trained," as Mark Twain's Connecticut Yankee, Hank Morgan, would have it, we are left nearsighted and insulated from our full intellectual potential—the depth of our diving—and its attendant range of feeling of intense highs and lows.

Insight through immersion into this literary world of the marathon reading that defies the very conventions of consumption intimated by the novel's own structure becomes the dividend for endurance. Indeed, the marathon reading of *Moby-Dick*, like Shea's ultramarathon reading of the *OED*, is a breach of normal consumption patterns, a highlighting not only of the body's connection to print culture but also of postconsumer ethics in a culture fetishizing specialization. For as serious, deep, and wide-ranging as those insights can be—Shea finds the full range of human experience and emotion in this dictionary, as in any great literary work, like *Moby-Dick*—both literary stunts are burlesques of bourgeois consumption patterns.

Literary marathon readings especially function to subvert traditional consumption patterns of the novel, the ultimate middle-class commodity that sprang into existence with the unprecedented expansion of leisure, privacy, and entertainment. Shea mocks that bourgeois print culture—its controlled, piecemeal perusing—every bit as much as the *Moby-Dick* Marathon reading explodes the stuffy, parlor-culture notion of classical literature with the toughness and idiom of whaling. But the irreverence, the sheer violation of convention here, comes ironically through a gesture of profound respect. It hurts to read the *OED* for ten hours a day for a year, just as there are distinct rough patches inevitable to listening to *Moby-Dick* for an entire day. This rebellion against accepted reading practice thus becomes a spectacle in itself, so painfully against the grain of what humans can mentally and physically stand, a type of performance publicly recognized at the marathon reading's closing ceremony in the awards that go to the survivors of the full event, and for Shea, in the publication of his own triumphant tale. Kafka's "Hunger Artist" bears an interesting relation here in terms of the defiance of accepted consumption patterns that transforms into publicly acknowledged performance art. Yet unlike Kafka's protagonist, who pushes asceticism to starvation, the ultimate reflection of self-denial, Shea reads the whole *OED* because he loves words; we hear all of *Moby-Dick* at once because we love the novel. (My own personal pleasure lies in its kinetic and physical energy.) Shea and we Melvillians give ourselves what we want, only perhaps too much at once, like Ahab. Herein lies the crossing of the line in print culture, another of the lines Wyn Kelley so eloquently illustrated in her lecture at the 2009 reading on the equatorial metaphor in Melville, the border between convention and madness. But crossing that line in reading practice is nonetheless an act of love, bridging on obsession, that transcends proper notions of consumption and time, two factors that make the entire reading experience as physical as it is intellectual, as cultural as it is ideological, as rebellious and fanatical as it is reverent and almost worshipful.

The critical history of the adoration of the world's favorite free verse poet, *Worshipping Walt: The Whitman Disciples* (2008) by Paul Robertson, offers a perspective of iconic American authors that makes the *Moby-Dick* Marathon reading appear but a chapter in the history of Melville hero worship. Yet the reading is as much about the novel as it is about the author and indeed carries with it a painstaking experience in language and reading that is both at the very core and at the lunatic fringe of print culture. For an ideal vantage point to see the enthusiasm for Melville and his great novel, my assignment to read "The Gilder" positioned me on the periphery of the nether regions of the middle third of the novel, and at the beginning of the end, "penetrating further and further into the heart of the Japanese cruising ground."[76] Neither in the witching midnight hour nor in the celebrated opening and closing of the narrative, my spot was nonetheless poised at the brink of Ahab's final confrontation with the whale. For an all-night reader, physically and mentally, this was one of the toughest phases of the marathon reading, as the end was not in sight, yet the wear of twenty-three hours of reading had taken its toll. Few remain on this Sunday morning in this alternate place of worship at 9:30 AM, a time when pastors all over New Bedford, let alone the entire eastern time zone, are clearing their pipes for *their* weekly oratorical performance. Our dramatic finish, shortly after noon, did not conflict with theirs, as clergy and their flocks were free to wander through the doors of the New Bedford Whaling Museum after their rites in order to witness the close of our sacred ritual.

But prior to that exalted finish, the sun up for only a few hours on the frosty January New England morning, the mostly sleepless night left the hearty few all-night marathoners in ragged shape. They hunkered in their pews, curled up over the novel, or blissfully asleep, having succumbed to an auditory dream of the White Whale. Morale at its lowest, this was the equivalent of miles twenty through twenty-two of the athletic marathon, too early to start a finishing kick, yet late enough to feel weary beyond comprehension. I think of Shea, his *OED*, and endurance, and the ebb and flow of hero worship, at the quietest, loneliest moment in this momentous party for Melville, this adulation of his greatest work. Unlike the boy in Joyce's "Araby," however, I will see the lights go back on in this museum that is our cathedral, and in the corresponding atmosphere of the soul.

Twenty-two and a half hours into a twenty-five-hour reading marathon offers the truest glimpse of the spirit of the readers. Will they last? Are they still engaged with the text? Do they smile—laughter takes too much energy now for all but the delirious—at Melville's wit, still a pervasive force in the novel even at this point? Do they wince at his brutal images? Are they aloft with Ishmael's discursive fancy? All have faded in and out of focus throughout the night, ebbing and flowing from the giddy and anxious opening line, and the excitement of the stroke of midnight that brings with it the prospect of raising the sun—and the dead—along with the White Whale. At 9:30 AM Sunday, the night is behind us and Ahab's teardrop of "The Symphony" prefacing the breathless, frantic chase is but a dream of a high-noon showdown still hours away.

My surest gage of the morale of the all-night readers, so I thought, was to be Mark Wojnar, the prophet living an alternative lifestyle who was due to arrive for the seventy-seventh reading spot. As mentioned in the previous chapter, Whittemore had alerted me to his status as veteran marathoner and Melville authority, if not mystic guru. As fate would have it, he never came. Like Bulkington in "The Lee Shore," he was a brilliant thought that never came to fruition, a character with great potential left in an embryonic state of creation. Like Bulkington, Wojnar's story lives on among the crew as a kind of legendary sailor who endured considerable hardships in life and for whom *Moby-Dick*, like landlessness for Bulkington, was a life force. This hard-core marathoner had attended the full duration of eleven of the last thirteen readings; despite his absence from the 2009 gathering, the novel surely continues to play a sustaining role in his life. I bowed my head to wish him well, this, the Bulkington of marathon readers, embodying the spirit of the sea in all the freedom and adventure it holds.

Wojnar has historically had trouble finding consistent employment, and he may be struggling today. In January 2009, the month of the reading in which I participated, unemployment reached over ten percent in some states, like Michigan, as our wracked economy has lead to soaring suicide rates, the most sobering fallout from the recession. A place of worship is a natural place to go during such hard times and, in fact, is Ishmael's last stop before heading out to sea, as he, like most whalers shipping out, stops for a sermon at the Whaleman's Chapel. The reading also makes it a priority, as we relocate across the street to read chapters 7 through 9, "The Chapel," "The Pulpit," and "The Sermon." Once inside, we are treated to a phenomenal performance of Father Mapple's sermon, which in *Moby-Dick* becomes an inadvertent self-parody, raising more questions than it answers for the confused Ishmael, and even pointing toward the egalitarian militancy of Ahab. A minister himself by trade, Edward Dufresne made a theatrical entrance with self-aggrandizing flourishes. Dufresne could not repress a smirk at the audacity of manning a bow-shaped pulpit. The delivery was accordingly campy, theatrical—the congregation sings the hymns in unison—and tongue-in-cheek, the only interactive literary theatre unadapted, unabridged, and unexpurgated from the original performed in the world, a *Rocky Horror Picture Show* for literati. Memorials like those Ishmael spots on the walls in the chapter "The Chapel" are intact, dating back to the 1830s, ranging all the way through 1917, 1945, 1970 (erected by the New Bedford Seafood Council), and with one as recent as 1979, the names growing increasingly multiethnic, especially Latino, as the years progress through the twentieth century. In what should be a life buoy of a sermon that becomes a confusing mess for Ishmael, the true spiritual stability hangs on the walls in the memorials, the years reaching up through the twentieth century, a confirmation that we are not alone at sea in this thing called death.

Ishmael's narrative functions as a life buoy differently for different readers. Peter Whittemore, for example, finds in *Moby-Dick* a revolutionary force and thus an inspiring story exposing the treachery of tyranny. For others, the novel's sustaining function lies more in its capacity to act as social glue bonding families. At 4:40 AM during the reading, a time when morale is low as standby readers are summoned with alarming regularity to replace the increasing numbers of no-shows and when spirited readings are rare, George Vezina approached the podium, flanked by his son, Spencer Vezina, at the podium next to him. With a voice that sounded like Norm on *Cheers* (another New England icon), Vezina read his passage and yielded the stage to his son. As he passed behind him, his burly open hand patted his son's shoulder reassuringly, with the kind of love and support Captain Vere shows toward Billy Budd at the youth's crucial moment of utterance. There, there, boy, take your time, the gesture said, sympathizing with the youth's moment just prior to facing the world with language and voice to bare the soul on the public stage. It was a subtle gesture, yet resonant with meaning in its poignancy and tenderness at a time when the crowd had nearly reached its nadir of eight readers and six spectators by 5:10 AM.

The Vezinas represented one of many father-son duos either reading or listening at the *Moby-Dick* Marathon. About fourteen hours earlier, I encountered Nephi Tyler, a baseball-capped youth in jeans and a sweatshirt, by far the youngest spectator in the lobby at the time, casually waiting for his father, Walter Tyler, to finish his 2:40 PM reading. Affable, yet rugged and anything but bookish, Nephi spoke of the significance of *Moby-Dick* in his relationship with his father. "I hadn't intended on coming down here," he said, "but I saw the atmosphere and thought, this is unique." I asked if his father's participation in a marathon reading of a novel like *Moby-Dick* was crazy. "No, no, no," he assured me, as his perfunctory endorsement blossomed into a wide-eyed belief in the importance of his father's place here. You do not understand, his demeanor seemed to say, his voice lowering in earnestness. "He loves this; he carves whales, that's his thing. He's a southerner, a Mississippi transplant and was in the navy. He married my mom who was from New England," he said, swinging freely into the biographical details, as an image of a humble Jay Gatsby in military uniform transgressing the sociocultural iron curtain that separates North from South to court the elite Daisy Buchanan sprang into my mind. "Since he was in the navy, this whole world of *Moby-Dick* and the Whaling Museum fit him perfectly." Nephi then shared an anecdote that stands as the single most archetypical, quintessential example of *Moby-Dick*'s role as a source of vitality in the lives of its readers, the epitome of how Melville lives now in print culture, an answer, finally, to the question of how old books live on. The intimacy, the depth of meaning and compassion, is deeply moving in how Nephi's

> brother fixed up a house in Fairhaven; it was an old historical grange building, and we had a dedication rite for it. My Dad carved a whale for it that we raised up, in what was like an official ceremony; then he read a chapter from *Moby-Dick* about the Seamen's Bethel.

As for where to find answers to the *Moby-Dick* Marathon's sudden spike in popularity, he said, "You'll have to open the book and find out; if you read the book it will grow on you; I work on the waterfront, too, so the history is kind of personal as well." Someday will Nephi read here at the Marathon? "Oh, yeah, for sure," he said with an easy smile. The waterfront worker feeling the fiber and grain of history in his bones through his New England surroundings could tell of his father's pride in his brother's work—literally restoring New England memory with hammers and nails—and in his own carving, and inflected through the voice of Ishmael through a makeshift, yet no less "official" and profoundly sacred, ritual dedication, one with more lasting meaning than many that occurred within church walls. For here was a dedication to the renovated house, a dedication to the history of New England, and a pride in the bricks and mortar of the Seamen's Bethel intoned by a Newport seaman from Mississippi. This is Americana at its best, print culture at its profoundest and most believing, expressing its deepest reverence to the seamless connection to the past and the building promise of the future. Melville lives? Melville *lives*.

Illustration of Moby-Dick breaching, by Rockwell Kent. Copyright © 1930 by R. R. Donnelley and Sons, Inc., and the Plattsburgh College Foundation, Inc. All rights reserved.

·6·

The Breach

Exulting in the Whale

*M*OBY-DICK IS IN MANY WAYS a series of highs and lows. The previous chapter explored the darkest depths of those lows and methods of surviving them both in the novel and among Melville's contemporary readership as represented at the marathon reading. Moving from somber situations and contemplative considerations of death, we now turn to the highs, moments in the novel and marathon reading of pure ecstasy. Calculated considerations of risk and mortality dissolve like so much sea spray in the whale's breach, a moment of sudden bursting transgressive energy, in which a creature that lives miles under water rockets through the water's surface, majestically arching into the air. It is almost impossible to witness such a sight firsthand indifferently; powers of observation are virtually overloaded with excitement at the spectacle of a sixty-foot-long sixty-ton creature, the largest mammal on earth, executing its most audacious feat. Even Charles Darwin broke from objective scientific data collection on his famous voyage aboard the *Beagle* off the coast of Tierra del Fuego in 1838 to register shock at "a curious spectacle of very many Spermaceti whales . . . jumping straight up out of the water; every part of the body was visible excepting the fin and the tail. As they fell sideways into the water, the noise was as loud as a distant great gun."[1] Arthur Conan Doyle, creator of Sherlock Holmes, similarly recalled how a breaching right whale in the Arctic in 1880 stunned him, as "a general gasp of astonishment made me glance up and there was a whale *in the air*."[2] Certain passages in *Moby-Dick* render the same unmistakable aesthetic joy. The whale, of course, must eventually plunge back down where "the first man of the *Pequod* that mounted the mast to look out for the White Whale" on his own "peculiar ground . . . was swallowed up in the deep."[3] More than just a foreshadowing of those lows that await, more than just the figurative manic zenith of a bipolar episode, the irresistible euphoria of a breaching whale stands for playfully performative exuberant creativity, embodying the uplifting spirit of the marathon reading itself.

The White Whale and Melville himself both breach out of the narrative waters of *Moby-Dick* with brash assertions of individuality and defiant displays of power fueled by surplus stocks of vitality. The *Moby-Dick* Marathon reading is a ritual group reenactment of precisely those moments, ostensibly among the event's keenest pleasures. Riding the waves of Melville's best riffs, hearts race and adrenaline flows with the kinetic physicality of his exalted prose. The author decisively drops the perfunctory narrative mask of the garrulous Ishmael and shouts at the top of his lungs, reveling at the height of his creative powers like Muhammad Ali taunting a challenger with reckless fun in a show of beautiful bravado and terrible power. As readers, we also "rise and swell with [the] subject," just as Melville's handwriting "unconsciously . . . expands into placard capitals." Subtle shading and muted tones be damned, "Give me a condor's quill!" he roars. "Give me Vesuvius' crater for an inkstand! Friends, hold my arms!" for "so magnifying is the virtue of writing on a liberal theme! We expand to its bulk," he writes, noticing by chapter 104 the sheer immensity and concentration of his work thus far. "To produce a mighty book, you must choose a mighty theme," he reasons, in an attempt to explain his magnificent ambition.[4] With the whale providing an ample canvas and the world's oceans offering plenty of sea room to work with, at this late stage in the novel, Melville is all too aware of his own accomplishment, of the taxing yet colossal momentum he has established, as its arc swings back to the decks of the *Pequod* for the final chase. He can sense the work's impending denouement building out of his last diversion off the path of the main narrative, as the evidentiary bones from the discussion of whale evolution in "The Fossil Whale" become the whalebone of Ahab's prosthesis, which leads to a consideration of that leg's construction in "Ahab and the Carpenter," a chapter that effectively returns to characters in dialogue on board the *Pequod*, and thus back to the business of hunting the White Whale with "Ahab and Starbuck in the Cabin."

This chapter traces Melville's authorial creative energy generated in 1850 and channeled through to 2009, exploring the sources of that energy from its various manifestations in *Moby-Dick* to the aesthetic reactions in the contemporary entertainment industry and among my fellow marathon readers and audience. No one expects a perfect work of art; we admire it for its daring ambition and willingness to breach out of the waters of conventional literature and society, out of safe insularity. We encounter an ambition that Melville himself was aware of in the process of composing *Moby-Dick* itself, as he was aware of the inspiration he drew from his friend and longtime editor, Evert Duyckinck, and from his close companion and literary partner in crime, Nathaniel Hawthorne. At the heart of this authorial ambition is Melville's sense of play, ever present in his works, which hinges on a deadly serious desire to produce nothing less than the literature of an American Shakespeare.

One Shock of Recognition

THE SUMMER OF 1850 was white-hot with creativity for Herman Melville. The interdependence between his passion as a reader in search of beautiful, transcendent literature and his extreme power and ambition as a writer was particularly evident in his praise for Hawthorne's literary genius in his 1850 essay, "Hawthorne and His Mosses." Partly a playful stab at review writing, with which Melville was all too familiar since his career had hinged on reviews for the past five years, the piece engages in the conventions of the typical book review in wide circulation at the time. (Melville's April 1851 letter to Hawthorne, a mock review of *The House of the Seven Gables*, also attests to his fascination with the form and, like "Mosses," ranges into vast metaphysical conjecture and signature wild discursiveness to which he pleads guilty, admitting "[I] began with a little criticism extracted for your benefit from the 'Pittsfield Secret Review,' and here I have landed in Africa.")[5] Meandering asides and lengthy summaries of Hawthorne's sketches bring Melville to a final prediction about the likely place of *Mosses from an Old Manse* in the arc of Hawthorne's career. Melville boldly proclaims the volume of short tales will be Hawthorne's magnum opus, but not without hopes the author might outdo even this massive achievement. "I pray Heaven that Hawthorne may *yet* prove me an imposter in this prediction," he writes.[6] The qualification reveals Melville's anticipation of Hawthorne's next breach, his hope for a stunning reemergence of creativity into broad daylight, wherein still more submerged potential might be realized now, "not entirely waiting for their better discovery in the more congenial, blessed atmosphere of heaven." Like a whale watcher anticipating the bursting forth of the dark mass silently gliding under water, Melville clings "to the strange fancy, that, in all men, hiddenly reside certain wondrous, occult properties — as in some plants and minerals — which by some happy but very rare accident . . . may chance be called forth here on earth."[7] He eagerly awaits a revelation of more and even greater hidden creative powers in Hawthorne that echo natural processes, "as in some plants and minerals," forceful and miraculous yet presently unseen. His chief worry is that Hawthorne's potential will go to the grave with him, his talents lost to the "blessed atmosphere of heaven."[8]

Melville ends "Mosses" anticipating a "shock of recognition" beyond even the Shakespearean standard of quality he affixes to Hawthorne's tales. This is, in part, because Melville himself was attempting to outdo Shakespeare with the composition of *Moby-Dick*. The self-referential nature of the essay reveals Melville's desire to be ranked among such authors as Hawthorne, a feat he believed was attainable through the publication of *Moby-Dick*. Melville envisions his friend, and himself by extension, dramatically joining ranks with the highest circle of literary "genius, all over the world, [which] stands hand in hand, and one shock of recognition runs the whole circle round."[9] The vision of joining Hawthorne in the circle of global genius held such a prominent place in Melville's imagination that a full year later he would write Hawthorne invoking the same image of "men like you and me and some others, forming a chain of God's posts round the world."[10]

In Melville's schema, full recognition of a creative breach like *Mosses from an Old Manse* calls for the American readership to adopt a standard of literary excellence, which at the time was totally alien to them. As reviewer of Hawthorne's short story collection, Melville presents himself in "Hawthorne and His Mosses" as a model for a new antebellum readership, in part to reform old literary biases to improve the conditions of his own novel's reception, which he expected to be potentially problematic. He specifically encourages both critical and popular audiences to eschew their current derivative literary standards for a new appreciation of the darkness and originality in their own writers, exhorting them to jettison all comparisons to Europe and fearlessly promote their own incomparable geniuses to the entire world. Such was Melville's hope, or even fantasy, for the reception of *Moby-Dick*; his faith in a magnificent future would never reach the heights of those expressed in "Mosses," except in the pages of the novel itself. It is hard to imagine Melville writing anything like "Hawthorne and His Mosses" after 1851, when it became painfully obvious that his magnum opus had failed commercially and critically, crushing all hopes for a worldwide shock of recognition of the singular dark genius of his wicked book broiled in hellfire. But in 1850, his monumental dream was still alive, as "Mosses" testifies to his careful construction of a new ideal of authorship to accommodate it. However steeped in the nationalistic pride of Young America, Duyckinck's literary coterie, Melville felt compelled to reconceive of American authorship on a global scale to suit his transnational epic novel. He saw himself occupying, with Hawthorne, "God's post around the world"; ". . . all over the world," an authorial role aimed at a universal audience rather than one immersed in the self and narrowly defined by American interests only, or worse, confined to the quirky inner world of New England whaling.

Melville's notion of authorship, however grandiose, never fell into the salient solipsisms of the rank narcissistic quagmire in which the protagonist of *Pierre* wallows. Melville would satirize Pierre's authorial ambition as distinct from his own rush of creativity that became *Moby-Dick*. The fictional Pierre differs distinctly from Melville in that he has no Hawthorne and thus no muse or model worth emulating. Instead, Pierre is driven by the desire to appease his dead father's memory and somehow erase the patriarch's shadowy sin of adultery, which Pierre unwittingly replicates, or even consummates, in a tragic Oedipal spiral. Pierre will never breach, given such self-absorbed egotism, which Andrew Delbanco attaches to "the image of the hermit artist indifferent to a world that generously returned that indifference . . . the blocked stupendously pretentious writer [as] . . . Romantic author imagining himself as high priest charged by God to bring forth Truth."[11] In Pierre, Melville indeed may have mocked any inclination of his own toward such an authorial self-image, but the distinct difference lies in Melville's more outwardly focused social connections that fueled the production of *Moby-Dick*. Critics, Delbanco included, have been tempted into making a one-to-one correlation between Melville and Pierre. Yet Pierre not only lacks an inspirational Hawthorne figure or a supportive Evert Duyckinck, both of whom were instrumental during the composition phase, he also does not turn to great literature for solace during his darkest hours the way Melville so consistently did.

Pierre cares little for the thoughts of others, whereas Melville was a voracious and, as "Hawthorne and His Mosses" attests, enthusiastic reader. Melville's friendship and literary connection with Hawthorne arose out of his ecstatic reaction to his fiction; Duyckinck provided essential fuel for his creative fire precisely because he allowed Melville unlimited access to his private library, the largest in all of New York in the 1840s and 1850s. Emory Elliott recognizes reading as the essential difference between Pierre and Melville, noting that "Pierre never does think in philosophical or spiritual terms about his cause or situation" and that he is the subject of the narrator's persistent mockery of his lack of "talent, preparation, and connections" in the face of his outsized ambition.[12] Melville's broad and deep reading enabled the spectacular breach of *Moby-Dick*, a work of consequence totally outside the powers of Pierre and drawing on an enormity of outside source material[13] from science to religion.

Melville's reading, which tied him so closely to Hawthorne and Duyckinck, was the key to his writing, and it gained him access to the antebellum print culture out of which his authorial ambition grew. Indeed, the function of literary coteries is driven as much by reading as by writing: the more its members read each other's works, the more they could cross-pollinate their creative talents and bring forth a mutually beneficial result, a sort of literary version of successful international trade in the free market. As such, Melville's voracious reading from Duyckinck's library and Hawthorne's fiction are well represented in *Moby-Dick*, a novel capable of breaching into the open air precisely because it generated much of its force and momentum from such materials. This economy of literary energy suggests that an author like Pierre who feeds upon the airy vapors of his own insular intellect cannot break through the surface, whereas Melville himself sustained his writing with vigorous reading, especially that of his two heroes Hawthorne and Shakespeare, each heartily (re)canonized and valorized in "Hawthorne and His Mosses."

A century after Melville composed *Moby-Dick*, Jack Kerouac would also draw profound reservoirs of creative energy from his literary circle, the Beat Generation, breaching in homage to their electrifying affect on his imagination. Kerouac rejoiced in an ecstasy rooted in the present that transgresses social codes, releases pent-up energies, and totally transcends the excessive self-consciousness and hypercritical doctrinaire theorizing that tyrannizes so much of our lives and decisions. An open gush of creative force, *Moby-Dick* is what Kerouac might have always wanted to write (but for him, according to Truman Capote, it was all just typing) in one all-night feverish dash, scrolls of paper unrolling out of his manual typewriter in the authorial equivalent of the twenty-five-hour reading. Kerouac would have loved to breach with such artistry as Melville, such manic intensity and concentrated vision in a dream of everlasting creative energy drawn from "the mad ones, the ones who are mad to live, mad to talk, mad to be saved, desirous of everything at the same time, the ones who never yawn or say a commonplace thing, but burn, burn, burn, like fabulous yellow roman candles exploding like spiders across the stars."[14]

Evert Duyckinck introduced Melville to some of the greatest artists and writers of their generation, initiating the young author to bohemian New York City on October 6, 1847, during a celebration for the opening of several new rooms at the Art Union. Duyckinck recalls the night's magic beginning with "Herman Melville dropping in, I carried him along, introducing him to Mr. Bryant and others. One of [Thomas] Sulley's bathing nymphs suggested Fayaway [the native beauty of *Typee*]. [Charles] Lanman introduced me to [William S.] Mount, the humorous painter . . . Mount and Melville were delighted with the living tableaus."[15] Melville, true to his nature, was drawn to the physicality ("living tableaus") of the art and enjoyed Mount's witty conversation, which potentially matched his irreverent, racy, and pungent humor. Even among the well-mannered aesthetic elite, Melville could find the "mad ones" for whom Kerouac would yearn a century later.

Duyckinck's diary entry describing the event is among his longest, as it lovingly passes through the evening's events. Careful not to paint the outing as complete debauchery, "this occasion was purely canonical," he defensively adds, noting that the "punch [was] a liquor nowhere spoken against in Scripture," exposing his doctrinaire side that would later temporarily alienate him from Melville.[16] The entry nonetheless glories in plenty of sumptuous art, food, and big names to feast upon with an amusing anecdote about an overexuberant and unmistakably intoxicated speech made by George Colton of the *American Whig Review*, complete with Irvingesque caricature as the man "rivaled an infuriated Dutch windmill in the flourishes of his arms" while delivering an equally circular story.[17] Melville's connection to the literary and art world through Duyckinck at the time provided a stimulus that eventually led him to Hawthorne and Shakespeare, just as Kerouac drew from the Beat Generation his living muse and confidante, Allen Ginsberg, and a reverence for Buddhist scripture to ignite his roman candles.

Breaching with the Whale

"WE ULTIMATELY READ," as Melville did, and as we do now at the nonstop reading of his greatest work, "as Bacon, Johnson, and Emerson agree, in order to strengthen the self, and to learn its authentic interests," according to one passionate reader.[18] Melville's novel could not have been produced without the considerable strength amassed through his reading. Further, if reading ought to be "experiential and pragmatic," the marathon reading provides an ideal venue for experiencing the novel communally, yet very much individually, and in the ideal setting of the New Bedford Whaling Museum, resplendent with the accoutrements of whaling.[19] At the marathon reading, we not only "affirm a memorable reading experience," as do so many blogosphere pundits hashing out the merits of their favorite literature on the Internet, we create a new one in a live setting, not so much to be celebratory or nationalistic, but to witness together how the novel can "disrupt mainstream pieties."[20] We emerge stronger for that experience, poised to breach in our creative, personal, or professional lives.

Saturated with an aesthetic sublime integral to his simultaneously beautiful and terrifying depictions of whales breaching and raising their flukes skyward, the psychology of reading fiction like Melville's is characterized, in the words of George Hagman, by a "powerful discharge of desire and aggression without catastrophe," much like the play of leviathan himself. The sublime "can portray the results of discharge without the destruction of self or loved one. Death, sexuality, aggression, loss of self, vulnerability and isolation are embraced and overcome, although not by being negated or denied. Paradoxically, the experience of these terrors in the sublime," he explains, "is vitalizing and self-confirming, not disorganizing."[21] This formulation speaks volumes of why readers rank such chapters as "The Tail" among the most satisfying of the novel. The tail's "amazing strength" abets, rather than constrains, the "graceful flexion of its motions; where infantileness of ease undulates with a Titanism of power, [as] those motions derive all their appalling beauty from it." Strength and beauty are fused here, a key to Melville's aesthetic, in which power, usually also beautiful, contains the stuff of mass destruction and instant death: "Could annihilation occur to matter, this were the thing to do it."[22]

Moby Dick's own breaches come primarily in battle with Ahab as acts of defiance toward the enraged sea captain who hunts him. They are beautiful and terrible, shocks of recognition in their own right through their sudden emergence into plain sight. As such the breach echoes the familiar Gothic trope of the sudden revelation of the monster from the abject depths for which Poe had an affinity. The aesthetic experience of witnessing a breach swings through "an emotional state of arousal and tranquility," as Hagman describes, whereby "what is internally threatening is safely put outside the self. There is an externalization of fantasy, desire, and fear . . . an experience of vulnerability from a position of safety."[23] Fear and desire, terror and beauty all fuse in a volatile yet ultimately satisfying cocktail that bears the distinctive contours of an erotic experience. The elements of fantasy, desire, and arousal all focus on one condensed climactic moment of the breach followed by repose. The interpenetration of the sexual and aesthetic response together forms a larger enamored condition that identifies the erotic within the beautiful. Thus eros cannot be denied its prominence in the beauty of art (if the text, like vocal music or orally read literature, is a figure or anagram of the erotic body) and nature. In this way, "art has rescued [beauty] from the sphere of abstract concept and embedded it in the realm of sensuousness," as Herbert Marcuse writes.[24]

Herein lies the erotic in Melville's aesthetic, also visible in much of Hawthorne's favorite theme of creativity that depends on observation. Such observation for Hawthorne involves primal desire and spectral gratification from the aesthetic, voyeuristic perspective. Ever covert and shy, Hawthorne's narrators are not given to such outpourings as Ishmael. Instead, their sexuality and erotic desire show through their storytelling capacity. Miles Coverdale of *The Blithedale Romance* and Holgrave (who narrates one chapter) of *The House of the Seven Gables* are prime examples of author figures whose surges of creativity reflect an erotic dimension. The most notable instance occurs in the *The House of the Seven Gables* when Holgrave tells Phoebe the story of Alice Pyncheon with "the insight on which he prided himself, [as] he fancied he could look through Phoebe" with his daguerreotypist's penetrating gaze.[25] The aesthetic experience of telling the tale for Holgrave becomes an emphatic expression of his submerged passions for Phoebe visible in "the young man's earnestness and heightened color [that] might have led you to suppose that he was making love to the girl!"[26] Desire here is as sexual as it is professional, interestingly enough, as Holgrave shares his plan to "publish [the story] in a magazine" with Phoebe, whose ignorance of his obscure literary reputation prompts his resigned sigh, "Well; such is literary fame!"[27] The breach here is at once literary, creative, and erotic, with "Holgrave plunging into his tale with the energy and absorption natural to a young author."[28]

The erotic overtones of Hawthorne's image of authorship—plunging youthful vitality; natural energy and absorption—call to mind Melville's erupting Vesuvius and outsized phallic authorial power figured in the Condor's quill. The whale's breach functions as a metaphor for creativity evoking not only sexual climax but also birth (a bursting forth from the dark amniotic waters) as conception and creation become one. In "Mosses," Melville's image of bursting out of a vice with abrupt transcendent force is not unlike the spectacular whale's breach. The image in that case specifically dramatizes a sudden liberation from the shackles of patronage and the politics of critical reception that might misjudge, cloud, or otherwise interfere with a writer's ascent based on merit. "Not that American genius needs patronage," he writes, qualifying the zealous, and even shameless promotion of Hawthorne to his readers through his Carolina cousin's staunch, if semi-literate, dedication to American literature. Careful to avoid the appearance of pandering for patronage, Melville adroitly shifts tack to the even more bombastic assertion that Hawthorne's genius will leapfrog over the complex social matrix of the literary marketplace—its readers, reviewers, and publishers—that to Melville, too often screen out true successes. As such, he imagines Hawthorne diverting the same market forces that hamper most professional authors. Hawthorne's talent, he urges in an image of sexual potency echoing male climax, contains "that explosive sort of stuff [that] will expand though screwed up in a vice" of such constraints, "and burst it, though it were triple steel."[29] Tellingly, the vice represents the double pressure to express the self and sell the self that has seized so many of America's best young writers since the invention of the double-cylinder steam press and ever more efficient mail delivery transformed the literary vocation into mass market entertainment and our very first form of show business. It took a special kind of potency, a unique literary genius, Melville believed, to achieve this feat.

Rejecting the notion of arduous labor and protracted struggle, Melville nurtured the fantasy of spontaneous victory over both mass market and critical readerships. The vision was essential for the development of the astonishing ambition and objective that drove the composition of *Moby-Dick* and his larger sense of authorship in 1850. Sheila Post-Lauria's *Correspondent Colorings: Melville in the Marketplace* (1996)[30] has convincingly established Melville's use of popular forms in his writing to win over the mass market, a finding that Anna Hellen has usefully expanded in her 2001 essay, "Melville and the Temple of Literature." But the real tension so painfully expressed by the mid-1850s through his tortured and speechless author figure, Bartleby, the Scrivener, lay in the wedding of such commercial ambitions to the lofty literary aims of joining the ranks of Shakespeare of Stratford and, as the hot-souled Virginian vacationing in Vermont argues, Hawthorne of Salem.

Melville finishes the essay by reemphasizing this dream of mass-market and canonical success. Hawthorne's works "should be sold by the hundred-thousand; and read by the million," while also being "admired by every one who is capable of admiration."[31]

Breaching the popular and critical divide was a feat only Charles Dickens ever really achieved during the antebellum era. Dickens of course was British, which disqualified him from Melville's American nationalistic standard. Melville scathingly dismisses Washington Irving as a derivative British sycophant, though he enjoyed huge success with educated elite readers as well as with the masses. Melville's own "shock of recognition" of Hawthorne's genius responds to the fiction's uniqueness he assumed derived from its liberation from European influence. Yet Kant, Hegel, and German romanticism held enormous sway over antebellum New England writers, including Emerson. French philosopher Charles Fourier's proto-feminist insights saturated Hawthorne's writings. Nonetheless, Melville exhorts American authors to develop in opposition to foreign influences and without their patronage or support, thus envisioning a fantasy not only of writing one's way out of the obstacle-laden American literary market but also of building strength beyond the necessity of British endorsement that fueled Irving's success. Leo Bersani has found that the same aesthetic declaration of independence from Europe signified by *Moby-Dick*'s radical departure from the Victorian novel was Melville's ultimate expression of how "American literature can be great not by being as good as or even better than European literature; it must be, in the full force of the term, incomparable."[32] It is not that American authors will rise to attract European patronage according to Melville's rhetoric, but that they will transcend its necessity altogether in total self-reliance.

Melville's list of opponents in "Hawthorne and His Mosses" comprises the forces against which he wrote in 1850. In an exhortation to excellence that will stop at nothing in the pursuit of domination, he urged that "in some sense we must turn bully" and aggressively engage the British enemy in literary battle. The process of engaging in that battle himself drove Melville on to reach such stupendous heights in *Moby-Dick*. Failure is no impediment, he proclaims in a kind of rallying of himself to greater strength, for "if any of our authors fail, or seem to fail, then, in the words of my enthusiastic Carolina cousin," a thinly veiled extension of Melville's own exuberant voice, "let us clap him on the shoulder, and back him against all Europe for his second round."[33] The gesture here is reminiscent of chapter 7 of Frederick Douglass's *Narrative* in which he dupes white boys into teaching him to read and, in the process, determines to prove wrong their assumption that his status as slave was permanent, vowing inwardly to escape not only slavery but also the humiliation of being an object of sentimental pity. Like Melville, Douglass rejects failure as a permanent condition, the thought of which rallies him to achieve the freedom those naïve urchins believed was eternally out of his reach. Similarly, the considerable critical abuses and insults Melville absorbed only fortified his will, all too potently revealed through the narrative voice of "Mosses," to make a sudden forthright and fearsome strike at greatness not in spite of, but *because of*, those international and economic forces in his way, a breaking through, as it were, the pasteboard mask of authorial failure.

Melville's other chief source of inspiration for *Moby-Dick* was of course Hawthorne, whom he genuinely loved for his darkness and psychological fearlessness. But Melville's enthusiasm for his Pittsfield neighbor imbued him with a bravado that was never Hawthorne's in the first place. Hawthorne was much more muted than this,[34] more hidden and ambiguous. Melville himself admits to underestimating "Young Goodman Brown" for its "goody two-shoes" title. Hawthorne would shy away from, rather than rise up to, the spotlight Melville so desperately wanted to shine upon him. We know this from biographical and fictional reflections of his persistent shyness, his obsessive self-consciousness, and his sensitivity to self-display and the power dynamics of voyeurism. Hawthorne was the observer, not the performer, and when he is seen it is not in a moment of swelling pride in that shock of recognition. Instead it is in a shrinking sense of galling embarrassment, like being caught masturbating, much in the way Miles Coverdale's peeping-tom vantage point of Zenobia and Westervelt is found out in *The Blithedale Romance*, much to his chagrin. Melville even acknowledges that Hawthorne is not the type to engage in self-aggrandizement and would reluctantly, at best, tolerate the glare of the exalted status he wishes for him. There is no trace of vanity, as Melville reminds us, in Hawthorne's fictional self-portraits of Coverdale and Holgrave; Melville may have felt the "shock of recognition" of genius in Hawthorne, but his "covert" qualities—the veiled, less than heroic self-portraits, the dreamy atmosphere designed to "egregiously deceive the superficial skimmer of pages"—suggest that his genius might be lost on the general public.[35]

Undeterred, Melville wanted immediate success, a sudden breach and shock of American literary recognition to burst stunningly into the light, inciting a natural, unmitigated, universal acknowledgment of genius. Melville's unbridled optimism in the potential to overcome these considerable forces—national, economic, professional—has the distinct edge of mania. Bursting free from the vise of professional authorship to instant stardom was especially appealing to a man who complained to Hawthorne, "dollars damn me; and the malicious Devil is forever grinning in upon me, holding the door ajar . . . What I feel most moved to write, that is banned,—it will not pay. Yet, altogether, write the *other* way I cannot."[36] He humorously dismisses his sentiment in "Mosses" as so much hollering, "True, I have been braying myself,"[37] with the self-effacing hyperbole that tints so many of his letters to his Pittsfield friend: "I'm rather sore, perhaps, in this letter; but see my hand!—four blisters on this palm!"[38] Yet he still shows a distinct desire to win both popular and critical favor in a vexing double ambition that has him damned by dollars precisely because of his aim to write "the Gospels in this century."[39] Winning both, according to this understanding of authorship, meant the Gospels would come at the expense of lost book sales. In his lifetime, at least, he would have neither, as critical reviews were as abysmal as sales, with some critics proclaiming that *Moby-Dick* was evidence that its author had gone mad because he could not tell a simple nautical adventure tale. He would be submerged until his breach in the 1920s, as D. H. Lawrence and Pablo Picasso, among other modernists, reclaimed him for the uncanny match of his jagged, nonlinear aesthetic and imbalanced moral universe with their aesthetic project. The premonition of the double failure was evident in the letters and even during the composition of *Moby-Dick*. He knew this was a tremendous risk, though as Post-Lauria rightly argues, his mixed-form narrative palate was in wide circulation at the time. Nor was *Moby-Dick* an attempt to write a Hawthornian novel, as one might suppose from the overflowing near hero worship of both his correspondence and "Hawthorne and His Mosses." The composition of *Moby-Dick* was a tremendously costly affair. Yet his enthusiasm for Shakespeare and his relationship with Hawthorne spurred him to a terrible and quick drive to the surface with nothing held back, engaging the full extent of his creative powers.

Playful and Profound

THE PLAYFUL quality of *Moby-Dick* constantly edges toward the powerfully profound. Ishmael, and Melville by extension, admires the humpback in the chapter "Cetology" precisely for his insatiable love of play, "the most gamesome and lighthearted of all the whales, making more gay foam and white water generally than any of them."[40] Not particularly fast or powerful, the humpback breaches the most of all whales and can do so from a virtual standstill. It generates enough force, miraculously enough, without the sudden burst of speed characteristic of minke whale and dolphin breaches. Radiating the spirit of play, humpbacks not only will breach but will "often make an additional commotion by slapping their flippers on the surface, or 'lobtailing,' when they smash the water with their flukes," according to natural historian Richard Ellis.[41]

Melville also loved the vacillation between wit and insight in Hawthorne's fiction, crediting him for including details "directly calculated to deceive" with "whatever motive, playful or profound."[42] Such "contemplative humor" Melville found so appealing was undergirded by unremitting blackness. The quiet beautiful smoothness and veiled dreamlike atmospheres in Hawthorne's fiction commonly lead to the abrupt penetration of bleak reality. Melville admires how "hushed in the noon-day repose of this Hawthorne's spell, fall of his ruddy thoughts into your soul should be symbolized by the 'thump of a great apple.'"[43] That fallen apple, funny as it is in interrupting a sylvan reverie, bears with it the pain of intrusion from the forbidden tree of knowledge, snatching a sweet heavenly dream in the biting snare of original sin hot with Calvinistic fire.

The sublime nature of the White Whale's breach in "The Chase—First Day" in *Moby-Dick* works the same way. Its silent serenity transforms into a demonic dallying "with the doomed craft in this devilish way."[44] Indeed, soon after Moby Dick is sighted, "a gentle joyousness—a mighty mildness of repose in swiftness, invested the gliding whale . . . not that great majesty Supreme! did surpass the glorified White Whale as he so divinely swam."[45] Ishmael sees in such beauty, as in his analysis of the tail's terrible grace, deeper powers to be unleashed, and thus an explanation as to why "there had been some among the hunters who namelessly transported and allured by all this serenity, had ventured to assail it; but had fatally found that quietude but the vesture of tornadoes."[46] In this context comes the first full breach of Moby Dick in the novel amid "serene tranquilities of the tropical sea, among waves whose hand-clappings were suspended by exceeding rapture."[47] The calm before the storm, the Hawthornian bewitched dream before the piercing shock of depravity, is in Moby Dick's "withholding from sight the full terrors of his submerged trunk, entirely hiding the wrenched hideousness of his jaw."[48] Then suddenly "the fore part of him slowly rose from the water; for an instant his whole marbleized body formed a high arch . . . and warningly waved his bannered flukes in the air, the grand god revealed himself, sounded, and went out of sight."[49] The clear warning from this godlike natural force takes no more than an instant to stun Ahab and crew, a bold flash of power intended to banish the hunters. Though he does not fully clear the water— only minke whales do when they breach—Moby Dick's mighty emergence and waving of his flukes are entirely consistent with the breaching behavior of sperm whales. According to Ellis, at sixty feet in length and weighing from sixty-five to 250 tons, sperm whales "cannot or don't care to clear the water completely. They usually come about three-quarters of the way out," a good forty-five feet of their mass jutting in the open air, "then twist on their long axis before reentry," a gesture appearing indeed like a warning wave of the flukes, "presumably to protect their internal organs from the shock of tons of meat and fat hitting the water."[50] Some enthusiastic whales will repeatedly breach, coming out of the water less with each successive rush in a fit of play that wears them to exhaustion, with the last exposing a scant five feet of their snouts reaching for the sky.

When it becomes apparent to Moby Dick that the ship has disobeyed his command, he returns to engage in battle. This second approach, of course, does not warn so much as it menaces Ahab, the creature grinning directly into the captain's face "with wonderful celerity uprising, and magnifying as it rose, till it turned, and then there were plainly revealed two long crooked rows of white, glistening teeth, floating up from the undiscoverable bottom."[51] From his godlike lyrical submerged presence, the whale now transforms into a gothic monster, his jaws appearing to smile in supreme control of his victims, not unlike that of Wakefield, Hawthorne's voyeuristic fiend who deserts his wife and sadistically watches her suffer. But the grace of the whale's serene swimming on the first approach is not entirely lost in his savage transformation; instead it transposes into gymnastic feline play. The whale's joyousness counters Ahab's rage in the altercation, the white birds accenting Moby Dick's attitude "with joyous expectant cries," nature's cheering section in its titanic clash with humanity.[52] After swimming supine beneath Ahab's chase boat and lying on his back, Moby Dick opens his jaws and "through and through; through every plank and each rib, it thrilled for an instant" before clamping down on the boat and shaking it about.[53] "In this attitude the White Whale now shook the slight cedar as a mildly cruel cat her mouse."[54] The whale, at this point, is only "mildly cruel," as he plays more than he pounces in an unbridled savage attack. He is not moving in for the kill, for there is too much joy in the process to be relished, making his breach at once a playful and profound fatal portent.[55]

Interestingly, the whale in this scene comes off sympathetically in contrast to the furious and monomaniacal Ahab. The whale is thrilling, even charismatic in his expert movements, gestures, and sequence of expressions, wielding with precision and play the rich range of a virtuoso. The poetry of profound play sets the whale above Ahab here. His ultimate superiority in the conflict derives from his status as a creature driven by natural instinct, untethered from psychological vengeance. He is a swimming brute exuding refinement and subtlety and catlike agility through his stunning range of tactics. Up until this point, the whale has only been known through lore expressed by Ishmael, and through the secondhand reports of other ship captains. The narrative tension anticipating his entrance is tremendous, and his first performance does not fail to satisfy.

Given the lengthy attention Ishmael gives to Ahab's humanity, the reader is not only sympathetic with the whale but develops sympathies for Ahab as well. Despite the appeal of the whale's irresistible charismatic artistry during this first confrontation, there are other moments when the reckless abandon of the novel has the feel of primitive and gleefully unrestricted momentum, the id cut loose, freeing the madman in all of us. As Stephen King told a *Playboy* magazine interviewer, the purpose of horror films is "to scream and roll around in the grass."[56] Indeed, before the whale's breach, the madman at center stage is Ahab, and his charisma is irresistible to both the reader and Ishmael. One significant reader said he gravitates to the novel for the same reason he loved it as a nine-year-old: "Ahab to me is primarily a hero, as the persona of 'Walt Whitman' and Huckleberry Finn are rival American heroes," especially in his commitment to "hunt down and kill the evidently unkillable Moby Dick," a dream with "a touch of the Quixotic in him."[57] The playful becomes profound defiance in the hyperbolic Ahab, a kind of wild attack on all that ails metaphysical life, the thrill of breaching the forbidden.

In the morally ambiguous universe of *Moby-Dick*, Ahab is both hero and villain, and in some senses he is heroic precisely because of his delicious villainy. There is a pleasure not just in Ahab's dark power, charisma, and swagger, but also in the interplay between the characteristics and the vulnerability attendant to his high-risk, high-stakes mission. We are both attracted to and horrified by Ahab's forceful powers over us; like Ishmael, our voices cry out with the rest of the crew on the quarterdeck for the death of Moby Dick. "We are captured by Ahab, even as we recoil from his monomania," one critic observed, for what appeals to us is his wild freedom, but what appalls us is his tortured inward loneliness.[58] Indeed, being profoundly alone in the world is the price of freedom, the cost of unrelenting defiance stylized to assert the self as sacred, indomitable even by fire. Ahab's early proclamation that "I'd strike the sun if it insulted me" in response to Starbuck's accusation of blasphemy[59] becomes more refined later in the novel, especially in the chapter "The Candles." He specifies his own inner fire as equally potent, if not more so, than the "mere supernal power . . . though thou launchest navies of full-freighted worlds" in the flame before him. "No fearless fool now fronts thee," he says respectfully, yet asserts his own independence: "There's that in here that still remains indifferent."[60]

David Leverenz has attached the appeal of Ahab to a desire for helplessness in the book, which defines one of the distinct aesthetic pleasures of its reading, especially aloud. Ahab's defiance of God in "The Candles" dramatizes the captain's "ecstatic yet terrified passivity," as Leverenz describes it,[61] which mirrors the delight in the desire for helplessness that characterizes the aesthetic experience of reading *Moby-Dick*, reckless and rudderless as it is. The reading experience indeed may be "ecstatic yet terrified," but I see in it a joyful immersion into the chaos of the cosmos and the whole of western civilization rather than a desire to be dominated, as Leverenz argues. It is not so much that the reader wants to be Starbuck, subdued, entranced, and acquiescent to Ahab's charismatic, flamboyant will. The pleasures of witnessing Ahab's power to entrance need not be equated with the reader's desire to be prostrate and quivering before him. Rather, it is the audacity of Ahab that has its appeal. "Who's over me? Truth has no confines" is appealing as brazen self-assertion, beyond all reason and logic, beyond all political and social consequences that warn us of its recklessness and fatal consequences.[62] Herein, the reader can find play, rather than a latent desire to be punished by his father, in the forbidden consciousness that moves with the integrated kinetic force of the whale breaking through the surface of the water. Defiance has its appeal, from Milton's Satan to Conrad's Kurtz, figures that have inspired a fascination readers have struggled to rationalize. Here again is that "externalization of fantasy, desire, and fear . . . an experience of vulnerability from a position of safety" that Hagman describes as so integral to the aesthetic experience of the sublime,[63] which I would argue also explains why readers might find inspiration in a villainous profane madman like Ahab.

The pleasures in watching Ahab's (self)destructive path lie in his role as theological outlaw. His breach is the thrill of the forbidden though diseased and deadly. His energy does not cripple but paradoxically strengthens the reader by offering an outlet for frustration at the world's ambiguities, rage at the often maddeningly elusive goals — those submerged dark masses floating in our consciousness — that direct so much of life. A former colleague of mine after teaching the novel to her frustrated undergraduates confessed her own Ahabian instincts by asking rhetorically, "At the end, don't you just want to *kill* it?" Ahab's breach is a violation and transgression, a gleeful blasphemy, a relishing of the mission of destruction that however villainous, has its heroic dimensions. By contrast, Hawthorne's evil scientists, Dr. Rappaccini of "Rappaccini's Daughter" and Aylmer of "The Birthmark," lack such appeal, while the avaricious Judge Pyncheon of *The House of the Seven Gables* is perhaps the flattest and most one-dimensional of his villains, functioning mainly as an allegorical prop. (Miles Coverdale, the narrator of *The Blithedale Romance*, confesses that he was susceptible to the persuasive force of the cold and controlling Hollingsworth, who is otherwise his nemesis; yet he never fully raises his voice in support of Hollingsworth the way Ishmael does on behalf of Ahab.) The morally ambiguous and fully developed charismatic villain indeed was not drawn from Hawthorne's aesthetic example. Ahab's fatally monomaniacal mission does however come directly from Melville's Pittsfield neighbor's palate, as all of Hawthorne's above-named characters exhibit that trait in various forms. The monomania of Hawthorne's villains, however, lacks the exultant force of will, the breaching power of Ahab; none of them would strike the sun if it insulted them. Ahab's profane violations of all that is routinely and almost unthinkingly held up as sacred provides the aesthetic jolt, the lightning bolt of energy that twists through this novel and that runs in the form of the scar inflicted by Moby Dick down the captain's face and neck, then down the full length of his body to his severed leg. Have we ever witnessed a rock star of such proportions burst on stage like this in the history of American literature? In nomine diaboli, indeed.

Contemporary Breaches

IN THE LATEST contemporary music and film inspired by *Moby-Dick*, Melville's affinity for the tension between the playful and profound has been translated with varying success. Ahab's swagger has attracted one techno-dance punk band to appropriate his character to shape their profane and defiant image. The Los Angeles-based band, Captain Ahab, picks up on the more base impulses of the novel for their raunchy performances. The presence of genital joking in the novel, along with its notoriously high levels of testosterone, have fueled this musical duo's crass and lewd lyrics with little else in the way of kinship or connection to *Moby-Dick*. Their more thoughtful musical counterpart with Melville ties is Moby, who was nominated for a Grammy for his experimental pop numbers that draw from early-twentieth-century blues archives of field cries, calls, and hollers. His connection to Melville is not so much in his musical composition as it is in his ancestral relation to the author, who is a distant uncle, many generations removed. Pop music's heavy metal brigade has also borrowed from *Moby-Dick* as far back as the 1970s with Led Zeppelin's searching instrumental tune, "Moby-Dick." More recently Mastedon, a Metallica knockoff, has titled their latest album *Leviathan* as a nod to the White Whale.

Elsewhere outside of the New Bedford Whaling Museum and the halls of higher education, *Moby-Dick* continues to make notable breaches. The new film of *Moby-Dick* now in production seizes on the novel's "action-adventure" strain which co-screenwriter Adam Cooper (along with Bill Collage) claims is "at the core" of the novel. Cooper is under the assumption that *Moby-Dick* does not have a contemporary presence beyond his own film. His tone is as hubristic as it is self-promotional: "Our vision isn't your grandfather's *Moby-Dick*. This is an opportunity to take a timeless classic and capitalize on the advances in visual effects to tell what at its core is an action-adventure revenge story."[64] Ironically most of Melville's original disapproving critics begged for more of this sort of narrative line, complaining of the excessive metaphysics of the novel. "In the popular discourse," Lawrence Buell observes of the contemporary presence of *Moby-Dick*, which I would extend to the antebellum popular culture as well, "Ishmael scarcely exists, unless one counts novelistic echoes (e.g., Kurt Vonnegut's 'Call me Jonah' to open *Cat's Cradle* [1963], Phillip Roth's 'Call me Smitty' as the opening gambit of his parodistic *The Great American Novel* [1973], or Thomas Pynchon's Tyrone

Slothrop in *Gravity's Rainbow*)," as it is "nearly all about Ahab and the whale."[65] The 2009 *Moby-Dick* Marathon reading itself has formed something of an alliance with popular culture, as participants who stayed the full twenty-five hours received neither biography nor novel, but a pop-up book version of the great book. Most of us at the marathon reading, however, gravitate toward the novel precisely because its violent conflict is socially, politically, culturally, and psychologically freighted with profound meaning resonant with our current postmodern early-twenty-first-century condition. Collage and Cooper are also apparently unaware of the considerable grassroots following of *Moby-Dick* that sees the novel in a far more sophisticated light than mere action-adventure gymnastics and pyrotechnics. Yes, action-adventure is part of the excitement that is the breach; but such a rationale is neglectful of, if not downright hostile to, any of the metaphysics behind the breach. Such depth sets it apart from the increasingly balletic and artful violence of a Bruce Willis or Vin Diesel vehicle. Cooper and Collage are clearly not being paid six figures by Universal Pictures for their grasp of the novel's critical heritage.

Timur Bekmambetov is directing the film, shot to look like a moving graphic novel. Especially relevant is one key decision the filmmakers made: the film omits Ishmael's narration, thereby placing emphasis on Ahab's charismatic leadership while downplaying his brooding existential crisis. This latest film of *Moby-Dick* will exploit the physical conflicts of the novel in an attempt to make the whale the most charismatic character of all, with details of his prior battles receiving ample attention. Interestingly, it would appear as though Melville's career has come full circle from the travel/adventure genre he clearly occupied with the publication of *Typee* that launched his career and cemented his reputation as high-seas adventure writer, a tag he could not shake, along with associated labels like "the man who lived among the cannibals." The mass market smiled on him most as the author of *Typee* and now wrenched *Moby-Dick* from the hands of high modernism, though it was D. H. Lawrence's and Pablo Picasso's darling and was hailed as the generic experimental close cousin to James Joyce's *Ulysses*. Now nearly a century after its 1920s revival, *Moby-Dick* becomes an action-adventure movie, the twenty-first-century version of the antebellum travel-adventure novel. The pre–Civil War travel-adventure novel was as ubiquitous as action-adventure movies are today. Melville for the masses operates best on the kinetic, visceral level of visual conflict, speed, and bravado, featuring a grudge match of high reputations in a spectacle of competition drawing on the culturally embedded love of sport in all its echoes and sublimated expressions of military combat.

The previous *Moby-Dick* film featured Patrick Stewart as Captain Ahab, poorly cast and vulnerable to a fault in his bearing compared to the steely rendition by Gregory Peck in the original film. Ray Bradbury wrote the screenplay for the Peck film, unfortunately, in a blur of a twenty-four-hour period (the compositional equivalent of the marathon reading) under pressure from the film's producers while holed up in a London hotel. The ethnicity of the crew and their reflection of global diversity entirely washes out of the 1950s-era Bradbury film, with Queequeg played by a white actor in make-up mouthing cigar store Indian clichés. The TNT-Stewart version, by contrast, highlights the ethnic and cultural diversity of the crew, as it begins by aptly capturing the comedy of Ishmael's xenophobic introduction to Queequeg, and later, following the tattooed cannibal throughout the narrative, filling many frames with his glorious presence. The film's attempt to capture the epic scope of the novel in a surreal light, however, falls short, as graphics and special effects used to depict the *Pequod*'s cruise through an obstacle course of polar ice caps and floating icebergs and an electric storm in "The Candles" come off as tinny and fake, an attempt at grand realistic spectacle that inadvertently exudes miniature artifice. (This was precisely the risk Steven Spielberg and George Lucas took, yet amazingly avoided, when they shot toy spaceships against cardboard black backgrounds for the battle scenes in *Star Wars*.) Despite inevitable shortcomings, all of the above mass-market breaches of the White Whale show the energy of exultation of going public with ideas, if not entirely "fresh," then certainly repackaged in the latest innovative musical or cinematic technology.

All these contemporary artistic adaptations of *Moby-Dick* call to mind the contemporary colorings of the biographical circumstances surrounding the writing of *Moby-Dick*. Much effort has gone into placing Melville's own manic exuberance during the composition of the novel into contemporary psychological frameworks. The psychological angle, of course, is best understood within that antebellum context of authorial self-definition, rather than say, a pharmaceutical lens.[66] There is no known evidence that Melville was on speed or cocaine as he wrote *Moby-Dick*, reveling in his creative surge of power. Instead, what drove him was a cocktail of testosterone, adrenaline, and endorphins, much like that which coursed through the seamen's veins in hot pursuit of whales. Delbanco makes the claim that Melville was bipolar, explaining the exultations as manic highs. Certainly the ebb and flow of the narrative and its reflective moments like "The Pipe" yield to quiet depression; the manic pitch of the three-day chase at the novel's end or the condor's quill outburst in chapter 104 are by no means sustained throughout the novel. However, Melville approached writing this novel with the astute, even awareness of a sailor aloft in the masthead on the lookout for whales, firm in his belief of never letting his philosophical reveries ("Descartian vortices"[67]) swallow him up. Likewise, Melville was disciplined enough, in this otherwise undisciplined novel, to not let his emotions get the best of him, lest he should topple from his authorial masthead and lose all connection to the whale chase.

Breaching in New Bedford, 2009

DOES THE marathon reading make this Ahab's novel? The forward rush, the unwillingness to stop for reflection, the sleepless obsession all speak to his sensibility. Yet Ishmael has his moments of euphoria and exultation. He, after all, is the one who details the transcendent qualities of the whale. Almost every member of the crew exults in ecstatic terror at some point in the novel, with time compressing and decompressing, depths plumbed, mastheads manned, in seemingly endless undulations.

My personal high point, like that of many others at the event, occurred when it was my turn to approach the podium. My voice could now go up with the rest as I made my ritual initiation into the crew of 168 readers who breathed life into every word of *Moby-Dick* in 2009. As Scott Lang said at the outset of the gathering, "People don't realize how nerve-wracking the reading is," as Melville's antebellum idiom "is almost like a different language." The exultation comes in presenting the reading first with poise (like that of the alert sailor at the masthead) and then, if possible, with "a sense of theatre." Lang, like many others, confessed he was not familiar with the dramatic readings. Ed Camara also noted the harrowing experience of reading in front of Boston's television news cameras. He added that most readers, even John O'Connor of the *London Financial Times*, worried about finding their oratorical sea legs with Melville's often unwieldy byzantine prose in which some sentences cover a full paragraph. One Internet exchange on the 2009 reading was telling in this regard, as a commenter groused that attending the reading was "one of my larger regrets. I have tried to read *Moby-Dick* about four or five times and I have never finished it. Melville's syntax is murky at best. The only reason to have a copy is if you have a problem with insomnia."[68] A woman who found his complaint to be so much whining easily dispatched this Internet curmudgeon. The energy manifest in her gamesome reply bespeaks more an attitude toward life than a matter of aesthetic taste, outshining his defeated cowardice with the upbeat reply, "Hey! Moby Dick is a great book—syntax, shmyntax. It's poetry!"[69] The terror of reading one of the most intimidating prose lines in the history of American literature presents a challenge making the successful execution of this public-speaking tightrope walk especially satisfying. For any successful reading engages in the sublime beauty of bringing Melville's lyrical prose to life, not unlike the deft, almost gymnastic, obstetrics of Queequeg delivering Tashtego from certain death in the whale's head into the bright sunshine of the *Pequod*'s deck. Terror and beauty, fear and desire, indeed, are integral to the experience of reading at the *Moby-Dick* Marathon, just as they are the essence of the aesthetic allure of the sublime. Further, beauty in Melville, as Whittemore reminded me in the wee hours of the night, often comes straight out of the profane, foul, or fetid, as in "Ambergris" and "The Spirit-Spout," the latter chapter, according to Whittemore, "an ode to snot [the whale blowing its nose] as the beauty of the world where snot becomes a poetic universal truth." Such paradoxes in the text, when read with the proper mix of awe and irreverence, render the sterling readings that make up the "fireworks" to which Lang alluded that "light up the sky" of New Bedford.

I wanted to contribute to that fireworks show, and summoning all the poise and performance left in me after a long night, I approached the podium with my entirely unrehearsed chapters to read. The thought of readers who had lit up the room during the previous twenty-three and a half hours spurred me on. Oratorical breaches were delivered with stunning brilliance as dialect matched meaning perfectly on two distinct occasions. "The *Pequod* Meets the *Rose Bud*," the chapter depicting a gam with a French ship, was read in a French accent with superb results. Another standout reading was "The Castaway," which bore the sultry intonation and slow cadence of the reader's southern accent, eerily appropriate for Stubb's galling reminder to Pip that his price in the Alabama slave market was less than that of a whale. Though a Cape Cod man, Stubb's words took on new and deeper meaning in the voice of a southern reader, enhancing the thematic presence of the southern slave market throughout this chapter.

Minutes before my turn at the podium, I drew inspiration from two African-American iconic readers, Ricardo Pitts-Wiley and Bernadet Pitts-Wiley, founders and directors of Mixed Magic Theatre, a program designed to inspire underprivileged citizens of surrounding areas through the arts, Melville's *Moby-Dick* in particular. They shone at the reading like a beacon of hope, much in the way they had for countless inner city Pawtucket citizens in need of an anchor, stability, and life force. The ease, grace, power, and resonance—Rick's voice carried a rich and sonorous bass with impressive range—of their reading, backed by their status as warriors crusading for social justice through the inspiration of this very novel supplied me with an endless source of energy. I knew better than to underestimate this speaking gig, however, and struggled to contain my exuberance.

Approaching the podium with my place marked, I began "The Gilder," the first of my two chapters. The chapter had never struck me as one that stood out in the novel, as I had given it little attention either in my teaching or in my research. Yet, here it was, glowing with new treasures, contours I had seen but not savored, details I had passed but not performed. I realized I was not in a position so much to summon it to life as I to bring what was already very much alive in it, obviously vibrating with vitality, into the microphone and out through the amplifiers. To my delight, I had miscalculated this chapter, overlooked its significance, and underestimated its playful wit and powerful function as preface to the final chase.

Right away, I felt Melville's cascading, playful rhythms, improvisational with momentum, like a Charlie Parker saxophone solo. "Often, in mild, pleasant weather, for twelve, fifteen, eighteen, and twenty hours on the stretch, they were engaged in boats, steadily pulling, or sailing, or paddling after the whales, or for an interlude of sixty or seventy minutes calmly awaiting their uprising; though with but small success for their pains."[70] His "pulling," "sailing," and "paddling" had me doing the same, and I suddenly fell into Ishmael's reverie, a fine match to any in the novel in which the rhythms of work become the rhythms of art: "These are the times, when in his whale-boat the rover softly feels a certain filial, confident feeling toward the sea, that he regards it as so much flowering earth," a feeling he extends to "long-drawn virgin vales; the mild blue hill-sides." Gradually Ishmael moves into the changeability of landscape, and from there, into the seasons of life, finally ending on a stunning insight on the indeterminacy of the afterlife. "Once gone through, we trace the round again; and are infants, boys, and men, and Ifs eternally. Where lies the final harbor, whence we unmoor no more?" he asks. Why not bask in, rather than fret about, our unknown origin and future, he finally wonders; why not forget the treachery of the sharks beneath his lovely land-surface fantasy and "let fancy oust memory," as Starbuck says, to which Stubb retorts, "Stubb takes oaths that he has always been jolly."[71] To relish the splendor of this fantasy, Stubb's soul does not require amnesia, as he happily reminds Starbuck, for his heart is eternally carefree.

Reading this, I too began to adopt a carefree, light tone, the feeling in my heart ascendant with Starbuck's willful forgetting of his troubles and Stubb's glee in never having had them in the first place. Jesus, this was good. I was dancing with Melville and playing his song, as the room began to move in merriment. I turned to my next and final chapter, "The *Pequod* Meets the *Bachelor*," realizing the close tie between the chapters, the skillful introduction of the theme of blissful ignorance prefacing the meeting with the lads on the *Bachelor*, celebrating in an eternal floating party their embarrassment of riches. "Not only had barrels of beef and bread been given away to make room for the far more valuable sperm, but additional supplemental casks had been bartered for, from the ships she had met; and these were stowed along the deck, and in the captain's and officers' state-rooms," the ship literally bursting at the seams with wealth.[72] I am struck as I read this aloud how here is an example in which Melville figures capitalist pursuit—as in so many other instances of the novel going back to Starbuck's initial plea to chase dollars and not one blasphemous creature—as a cure for the ills of monomaniacal obsession, as a healthy and normal pursuit of acquisition for sustenance, a game in which one can be absurdly lucky, and thus glad, like the mates aboard the *Bachelor*, or duped like the Frenchmen of the *Rose Bud*, the capitalist losers of the tale. Only the "moody" crew of the *Pequod* that has taken on its captain's demeanor is left with the depression and anxiety of a displaced pursuit of another man's revenge precisely because it has deviated from its original business objective. Free of worry about the whale—"We don't believe in him at all!"—the crew of the *Bachelor* can return home with casks full and carefree hearts in stark contrast to the *Pequod*'s empty casks, abandoned capitalist pursuit (exchanged for the pursuit of Moby Dick), and tortured souls, the former a "full ship and homeward bound ... sailing before the breeze" and the latter "an empty ship, and outward-bound ... stubbornly fighting against it."[73]

I finished the reading fully absorbed in Melville's study in contrasts, in the *Pequod*'s lingering jealousy of the *Bachelor*'s eternal state of liberation, the revelers' easy freedom from the chains that tether Ahab's crew to the White Whale. Having disappeared in time, I "found the hole in the page," as Stephen King says of his best writing stints in which he disappears into the story world totally oblivious to real time. Departing the podium, I was shocked and a little embarrassed at how this entrance into Melville's world, for this one time, was not solitary. Previously, such immersion came in the solitude of reading or writing about *Moby-Dick*, or in teaching it, where immersion was never total but oddly distanced, in which the novel remained at one remove given the demands for constant clarification (a bit like making love in a wetsuit, as all the motions are there, but the feeling isn't). But behind the podium, I left real time for story time, entered Ishmael's world and emerged not as if out of a solitary experience or looking up at the faces of lost undergraduates, but seeing instead an audience of believers right with me who had shared every step of this delicious reverie.

The breach is a metaphor for sudden creative expression that compresses time to the quick, bringing it directly in line with the present, making the now nothing short of eternal. As in an athletic marathon, the marathon reading demands a present-ness of those in attendance. It collars us, pulls us in, drops formalities with the initial self-introduction of "Call me Ishmael," setting us on familiar terms from the very first utterance of the novel. There is an attitude with which a group of people gather round a reading of an entire novel from beginning to end. There is a silence in their listening that internalizes and acknowledges the profoundness of those words. There is a willingness to hear it all in one day without talking back to it out loud, but to let our responses resonate in our souls and seep into the roots of our very beings. This is a gesture that says yes, this book matters, and yes it is bigger in some ways than all of us, or any of our singular responses, be they celebrations or quarrels with it. There is the sense that if we live this one day of our lives with this book, we might be privileged enough to gain the grandeur of that scope. It is a time that condenses time, compresses it to ungodly heights of urgency and profound depths of anguish, all dives and breaches. In it we visit nations and cultures for all times, not to colonize or control but to live them in just one day in which we are all, like Thoreau at *Walden* pond, "anxious to improve the nick of time, and notch it on my stick too; to stand on the meeting of two eternities, the past and the future, which is precisely the present moment; to toe that line."[74]

To receive the novel in one day is to make the present of the narrative more present, its drama and trauma more direct and intimate, more palpably with us. Between the eternity of the past—"and the ocean rolled on as it had thousands of years before"—and that of the future toward which we strive and hurtle, the twenty-five hours is not real time so much as it is an infinite present at which we all "toe that line."[75] It becomes a time in which we encounter the world's enigmas, its tangled power structures, and face our personal fears and triumphs, all in the voice of Melville's manic poetry. It is to that poetry—and its special connection to the poetics of sound foregrounded in reading *Moby-Dick* live—that we now turn.

Conclusion
Poetry in and beyond *Moby-Dick*

*T*HE SOUND OF THE *Moby-Dick* Marathon reading is a democratic pastiche of voices intoning the prose poetry of Melville's narrative. Thus
far, as a way of uncovering the essence of the marathon reading experience
I have highlighted Melville's more lyrical expressions of the romantic allure
of a nonlinear and risk-laden quest, the political hierarchy once at sea, and
finally the crushing lows and exultant highs of the novel. Sound connects all
of those inspired moments, driving Melville's aesthetic power. As such, no
better context could be imagined for the fullest appreciation of the poetry
of *Moby-Dick* than in the ritual dramatization of its sound showcased at the
marathon reading.

In this conclusion, I revisit my persistent emphasis throughout this book
on the physicality of *Moby-Dick* and its marathon reading. I have observed
that the novel's habit of mind, which so systematically weds word to thing,
thought to fact, is well suited to the marathon reading's embodied presence,
its group synergy of breathed, lived experience. The conduit between thought
and thing, body and soul is sound, both as figured in the novel and as the
central focus of attention during the reading. The reading may showcase the
materiality of whaling in the artifacts that adorn the New Bedford Whaling
Museum in which it is held, and indeed readers often show a deep attachment to their personal annotated copies of the novel, but the essential focus
is the live sound of the reading itself. The sound of Melville's poetic prose
is not an untouchable airy apparition; it emphatically exists in the sensible
world, and thus takes on a physical heft in what Roland Barthes calls music's
erotic dimension, its textured "grain of voice" associated with "the hand as
it writes, the limb as it performs." This is the very point of contact between
the spiritual and material worlds, "the only erotic part of a pianist's body, the
pad of the fingers whose 'grain' is so rarely heard."[1]

Print culture finds expression in the marathon reading as audible, nuanced art, a sensory and thus physical phenomenon, however invisible, ephemeral, and lacking in tactility. The marathon reading seeks to reproduce Melville's poetic grain of voice as inflected by, and indeed refracted through, the radically differentiated voices of its readers. This rainbow of voices corresponds well with Melville's patchwork narrative structure of discursive chapters in *Moby-Dick* behind his masterful poly-vocal ventriloquism. On display in an oral performance of the novel are the disparate discourses from grand soliloquies at the bow to profane antics in the forecastle, from rollicking sailors' songs to earnest legal defenses, from marine biological scientific reports to multiperspective mystical credos. As such, *Moby-Dick* is a prime example of Barthes's assertion that "the text is a tissue of quotations drawn from the innumerable centers of culture," even more so than most novels of the era.[2] Further, Queequeg's copy of his tattoos, themselves a copy of a cosmology from his native island, which he etches into his coffin lid, effectively illustrates the way "the writer can only intimate a gesture that is anterior, never original."[3] This is precisely what the postmodern world sounds like: newly intoning the past in a radically diverse present. The beauty is in the connectedness of the chaos, in the sound that uniquely brings the book to life for one day. The temporality of the event suggests that we might be able to defy time. The lengthy commitment to an ongoing two-to-three-week relationship with the novel becomes condensed, intensified, and distilled into this twenty-five-hour period. It is a symphony defiantly playing without pause in the face of culture dominated by commercial interruption. As Robert Milder writes, "Perhaps the reverence for old [great American novels] . . . comes from the longing for a language cleansed of debasement and misappropriation . . . and for a complex, if painful, historical truth irreducible to sound bytes."[4]

Whitman scholar Ed Folsom has recently embarked on the project of writing the biography of Walt Whitman's *Leaves of Grass*, tracing the "life" of the text in its multiple revisions over decades from the first 1855 edition through its final revisions. Treating the text as a living thing, with a birth, evolution through various seasons, and eventual decline, has special relevance to reading a novel like *Moby-Dick* in one day. The assumption behind a marathon reading is that this event will happen in real time, just as the book's life did upon composition with a finite beginning and end. Thus the novel can be understood and celebrated better as an organic entity, evolving through time continuously rather than haltingly, a stellar symphony to be taken in as a whole for greater appreciation of its value as an entire, finished (if not perfected) work of art, animated by the thematic interplay and aesthetic dialogue of those various symphonic, even orchestral, movements. Folsom is doing for the various editions of *Leaves* what the marathon reading does for the disparate chapters of *Moby-Dick*: that is to synthesize otherwise scattered elements, often taken as autonomous documents, and consider them as one organic whole. So, finally, what is the organic whole that is a twenty-five-hour, rather than a two- to three-week, *Moby-Dick*?

Moby-Dick as Epic Prose Poem

MUCH HAS been made recently of Melville as poet since the release of Hershel Parker's 2008 *Melville: The Making of the Poet* and numerous other studies prompted by the thirty-three years of verse writing that occupied the author after abandoning his relatively brief eleven-year stint as a prose fiction writer upon the publication of *The Confidence Man* in 1857. The interest in Melville's poetry began with the 1991 publication of the Northwestern-Newberry critical edition of the epic poem *Clarel* (1876) that spawned a scattering of criticism restricted to specialized journals and a few obscure dissertations throughout the following decade. The turn of the century brought fresh interest in the subject, as *Leviathan: A Journal of Melville Studies* dedicated an entire issue to examinations of Melville's poetry,[5] and in 2008 Northwestern-Newberry released a reprint of *Clarel* with a new foreword by Parker, which includes the findings of his new book. Parker's book has been helpful in revising a commonly held assumption handed down from modernist critics that Melville gave up his professional identity as novelist altogether for a resigned, dilettantish life of verse writing, for which he had little talent or seriousness. Parker's encyclopedic rendering of virtually every detail of poetic influence and interest in Melville's life has reversed this widely accepted view, revealing how saturated in verse he, and by extension his culture, really was. As a definitive literary history of Melville-as-poet, it is an indispensible source book, an archive of valuable leads and connections amassed from a lifetime of research. It thus opens up a new vista on Melville that promises to persist well into the twenty-first century. So where does that leave *Moby-Dick*?

The traditional view has been that *Moby-Dick*, being Melville's most ambitious work, defined the shape of his career, creatively for the better and professionally for the worse. Critics have now made for a radical revision of this assumption in light of the fact that Melville spent more than three times longer writing as a serious poet than he did as a prose fiction writer. If this indeed leads to a new, second Melville revival—in defiance of F. Scott Fitzgerald's ominous declaration that "there are no second acts in American lives"[6]—how are we to consider his significance as poet in relation to his role as novelist? Or are we to forget the novels altogether as a relic of the prior century's obsession sparked by the first modernist Melville revival? Lawrence Buell, whose work defined the view of Melville as poet prior to Parker's monumental book, assumes that Melville took up poetry in resignation after the critical and commercial failure initiated by *Moby-Dick*, "doubtless . . . partly out of disillusionment at the reception of his serious fiction after *Moby-Dick*."[7]

Poetry was more than just an afterthought in the wake of *Moby-Dick*'s disastrous reception. The arc of Melville's career should not be understood as a building up to his great novel followed by an adjustment to its bleak rejection and his subsequent retreat into poetry. Indeed, his orientation toward writing from when he began his first novel, *Typee*, in 1844, and not just from the late 1850s, always included poetry. His work was closer to a poet's than that of a conventional novelist. In this way, Melville was a poet writing novels rather than a novelist who later wrote poetry; he did not suddenly transform into a serious poet upon the 1857 publication of his last novel. Parker reminds us that poetry meant a great deal to Melville in the years leading up to *Moby-Dick*, as indicated by the monumental influence of Channing's "The Island of Nukuheva" and Longfellow's *Evangeline* on his early writings. But the move toward poetry is the most pronounced as Melville takes up his pen to write *Mardi* in early 1849. At this time, poetry meant even more to him than it had when he was a boy reading the verse of Lord Byron with his soul on fire. The lyrical flames in *Mardi* would accelerate into a wild inferno in *Moby-Dick*, a novel showcasing his flair for poetry more than any of his prose works.[8] Melville was always writing poetry of a sort and was forever engaged in hearing and reciting verse as a continuous extension of his love of retelling his best yarns from his days at sea. The two categories are artificially sorted into a mutually exclusive binary: the need to package, promote, and sell a new Melville "revival" is somehow utterly distinct from and irrelevant to his prose fiction. Where, for example, would that leave Andrew Delbanco's biography, which contributes so much to our understanding of *Moby-Dick*'s contemporary relevance yet is unconcerned with the poetry?

Melville's prose fiction continues to be viewed as a category mutually ex-clusive from, rather than contiguous with, his poetry. *Moby-Dick* was a poet's workshop that provides a glimpse of Melville at the starting point of his poetic vocation. The only analysis of *Moby-Dick*'s relation to poetry is Christopher Sten's *Sounding the Whale:* Moby-Dick *as Epic Novel.*[9] Its useful connections between the novel's narrative structure and those of the signature epic poems of Homer, Dante, Milton, and even T. S. Eliot implies, if not explicitly argues, that Melville developed his poetic voice in *Moby-Dick*. Sten effectively revises the dominant assumption that Melville was a rare genius who may have read extensively yet lacked patience for, or even knowledge of, the epic verse tra-dition. This raises provocative implications for the concept of sounding (a form of celebration and investigation, the very thing that occupies Ishmael throughout *Moby-Dick*) as the key to the poetics of the novel. Epic poetry's narrative structure not only inspired the telling of Ishmael's tale, it also led Melville to associate his own literary labor with poetry writing.

Rather than viewing Melville's poetry as a second life—why not call, for example, his magazine writing of the mid-1850s his "second life"?—I want to consider further Parker's suggestion that antebellum "critics prepared Mel-ville to think of himself as a poet."[10] Those critics did not plant the seeds for a sudden avowal in 1857 of the poet's vocation according to Matthew Arnold's definition. Instead, I want to suggest that the poetic properties Melville's own contemporaries identified so readily in his prose fiction, which Parker abundantly documents, did not just prepare him to finally embrace the poet that lay nascent within him. Instead, he was writing a type of poetry all along in his radically unconventional fiction. On the rare occasions when they lauded him, Melville's critics, particularly the English ones, could appreciate his language in his novels as poetic prose. Amid a rain of hostile reviews of *Moby-Dick*, Melville found succor in praise, albeit uneven, from the British. Ironically, this was the very audience he robustly rejected in the defiant "Haw-thorne and His Mosses." The English were far more critically sensitive to the presence of technically rich, nuanced, and self-consciously structured prose than were their American counterparts. Even Marlon Brando could recog-nize over a century later the dearth of satisfactory American productions of Shakespeare, owing to the way Americans, compared to their transatlantic counterparts, "simply do not have the style, the regard for language, or the cultural disposition."[11]

The preponderance of praise for *Moby-Dick* was in British literary magazines, with some exceptions of course. Parker himself acknowledges Melville's prose by 1850 was "now genuinely poetic, and at times expressed in lines closely akin to Shakespearean blank verse."[12] In particular, "The Quarter-Deck" and "The Whiteness of the Whale" both stood out to one 1852 reviewer for London's *Morning Advertiser* as evidence that "we have not overrated his dramatic ability for producing a prose poem."[13] The London journal, *John Bull*, pronounced Melville provocative and innovative precisely in his ability to find "philosophy in whales [and] poetry in blubber," noting that "few books . . . contain as much true philosophy and genuine poetry as the tale of the *Pequod*'s whaling expedition."[14] Other London reviewers spotted "fine poetic elements" in the novel, "full of poetry, full of interest."[15] In the U.S., one eagle-eyed reviewer from Louisiana detected a buoyant lyricism in *Mardi*, gushing in effusive praise for "a regular Mardi-gras of a novel, to judge by the richness of its prose. Prose! It is a poem; and you can pencil out of its pages blank verse enough to set up an hundred newspaper poets, for the balls of bowling critics to roll at."[16]

Beside a few critics such as this, the first American reviewers may have been deaf to the sound of poetry in Melville's prose. One New York reviewer praised the poetry in *Moby-Dick* despite himself, concluding that "the fine madness [that] poured out in lyric flow" failed to "redeem [the] book from being too prosy [because] the natural interest of its subject has been exhausted."[17] Melville was not alone in writing prose poetry, as the culture showed distinct signs of interest in Walt Whitman's prefaces and free verse. Whitman was endorsed by key figures in the literary mass market such as Fanny Fern, as well as by those in the philosophical elite such as Ralph Waldo Emerson. Free verse, or rather blank verse of shorter line lengths than Whitman's, was most salable under the pen of Englishman Martin Farquhar Tupper, whose popular biblical moralizing in *Proverbial Philosophy* (1846) sold nearly a million copies in the United States and passed through forty large editions in England. Melville not only knew of the work, he had likely read it, because the volume was published by Wiley and Putnam, who released Melville's first novel, *Typee*, in 1846, the same year as Tupper's *Proverbial Philosophy*. Melville's mother, according to Parker, had praised Tupper for his pious didactic moralism, idealizing him "as the Christian writer her son was not."[18] Melville even brought Tupper's address with him on a trip to London, although he never found time to call on him.

Prose-poetry experimental hybrids sprouted throughout the antebellum literary landscape. Tocqueville even noticed the jagged dissonance, the odd shifts and juxtapositions in the democratic literature of the time, brazenly blending styles and forms. Indeed, Melville himself should be understood along with Whitman as a prose fiction constituent of a wave of radical free-verse poets, novelists, and journalists who assaulted Longfellowesque sentimental poetry in the late 1840s. As David S. Reynolds asserts, such "radical democrats had a special animus against rhymed verse, which they associated with the artificiality and constrictions of an effete literary establishment."[19] Tupper certainly was no radical nor even an American, but the popularity of his blank verse opened up new vistas for more radical writers like Whitman and Melville who were willing to bend the limits of poetry and prose, respectively. Thus Melville and his culture were well acclimated to such genre blending. The intermixing of prose and poetry was indeed more common to the antebellum period than one might have presumed, despite the apparent dominance of measured rhyming verse like that of Henry Wadsworth Longfellow and his legions of imitators in the poetry market. The intermixing of prose and poetry was thoroughly embedded in the culture, and poetry enjoyed a relatively large share of the popular market when Melville began composing *Moby-Dick* in 1850. It is indeed telling that Melville would turn to a hybrid of prose and poetry works at the end of his career with *Weeds and Wildings*, which included a long prose homage to Irving's "Rip Van Winkle," followed by a poetic ode to the dozy dreamer called "Rip Van Winkle's Lilacs." Upon Melville's death in 1891, this and other such mixed-genre prose poetry were found in folders in his desk, most notably a stunning poem, "Billy in the Darbies," with a headnote that had been expanded considerably. Once reassembled by archivists, that poem's expansive headnote emerged posthumously like a phoenix from the ashes as the novella, *Billy Budd, Sailor, An Inside Narrative*.

Hearing the Poetry of Moby-Dick

ANTEBELLUM reviewers and our contemporary critics have thoroughly documented the central presence of poetry in Melville's repertoire. But surprisingly little attention has been given to the auditory dimension of the poetic flair of his prose, a key feature of his most lyrical language enhanced and amplified by the live reading at the marathon in which our own voices describe the whaling experience in the language of *Moby-Dick*. The aural poetry provides the symphonic soundtrack of the novel. It cycles through its turbulent moods in the calls to watch, the creaking wood flexing to the rhythms of the sea alternating between thunderous pounding and sweet "waves whose hand-clappings were suspended by exceeding rapture."[20] The sailors and harpooners sing and dance to Pip's tambourine. The long wail from the masthead of "Thar she blows!" shatters the dreamy "Descartian vortices" of the sea's lullaby of "that rocking life imparted by a gently rolling ship."[21]

The sounds of Melville's expedition aboard the *Acushnet* were attuned to the poetry he devoured in 1849. His only book purchases for the year were a two-volume *Poetical Works of John Milton* and a seven-volume *Shakespeare*. In 1849, this poetry, along with that of Spenser, Wordsworth, Tennyson, and Browning, had gestated and coalesced with the memories of his 1841 voyage. When he began composing *Moby-Dick* in earnest by 1850, those sources fused with whaling sourcebooks and a healthy dose of Hawthorne's dark fiction for the final ingredients of the volatile concoction that ignited his imagination. He had become as serious a student of poetry as he was an entertaining and wry weaver of a sailor's yarn, and he dove into verse just as he had into the psychological darkness of Hawthorne. Miltonic echoes reverberate through *Moby-Dick* along with unmistakable Shakespearean resonances, evidence that Melville was engaging deeply in the language of poetry as he wrote. Charles Olson was the first and best chronicler of the Shakespearean effects within the novel, and Henry Pommer's early study[22] is a thorough rendering of the pervasive, yet less obvious, influence of Milton on Melville's magnum opus.

We know that the ideas and language of the great poets are in Melville's novel, but we know less about how sound factors into that poetry, especially through the spoken medium of the *Moby-Dick* Marathon reading, a venue no different in its basic arrangements than a poetry reading, albeit an extremely long one. Lawrence Buell has noted that Melville's next logical step after writing his novels was either to essay writing or poetry, a point particularly relevant to *Moby-Dick*'s prominent place in the phase of Melville's evolution of the creative use of sound and tone. Buell rightly asserts about Melville's last three novels, "*Moby-Dick*, *Pierre*, and *The Confidence Man* are drawn away from conventional tale-telling and into reflection to such a marked degree as to make either philosophical poetry or nonfictional prose seem a much more logical step in Melville's development than additional works of narrative fiction, quite apart from his reversal of fortune in the marketplace."[23] It makes sense that if Melville were at the height of his powers as a prose writer, then the elements of poetry and philosophy might incline him to embrace fully either poetry or essay writing. Yet because his narrative fiction was evolving into such uncharted creative waters, he instead was on the verge of inventing an entirely new blended genre of literature altogether. It is not so much that Melville was ready to breach through the genre constraints of prose fiction. Instead he was radically innovating the concept of the novel toward a generically unprecedented creative form. *Moby-Dick*, in particular, was Melville's most exuberant surge of innovation. As discussed in the chapter on creative breaches, his narrative experimentation drove him to adopt mixed forms, which unleashed a torrent of critical wrath. His creative daring was fueled by his love of mixed sound, or polyphony, as a tool for the manipulation of subject, tone, and style to the extent that language frequently came to mean more than message.

Melville's best jazz, his sharpest chops, his most ungodly, godlike riffs occur between the covers of *Moby-Dick*. Buell, writing far enough in advance of the current hubbub over a new Melville revival based on his underappreciated poetry, had the clarity of vision to call Melville's attempts at verse precisely what they were: uneven and "at worst dully imitative of [his] own mannerisms." Buell speculated that the long neglect of his poetry was due to "the comparatively traditional character of its language and prosody relative to Whitman and Dickinson."[24] This much is true—as a prose-poet writing *Moby-Dick*, Melville did not suffer from the constraints of measured meter, and thus possessed a reckless abandon capable of cumulative syntactical gymnastics totally unavailable in measured meter. His propensity in his later verse for "the deliberate entanglement of the larger narrative continuities of [*Battle Pieces* and *Clarel*]" have not driven readers away, as Buell suggests.[25] Rather, the *combination* of knotty—and indeed naughty, particularly in terms of reader expectations—narrative structure and constrained meter may very well have repelled them. But complex self-referential narrative alone has been a virtue in Melville that is well suited to modernist and postmodernist sensibilities. Most contemporary readers, at least the serious ones like those at the marathon reading, find complexity part of Melville's allure, his challenging nature that "remained unsimple and hard to the end."[26]

Part of what makes Melville hard, what makes him postmodern, is his literary ventriloquism, the capacity to assume a stunning range of voices, tones, and attitudes. The central role of sound in poetry is brought to light by Marjorie Perloff's sense that "poetry has come to be understood less as the lyric genre than as a distinctive way of organizing language—which is to say the language art. Poetic language is language made strange, made somehow extraordinary by the use of verbal and sound repetition, visual configuration, and syntactic deformation."[27] Melville is a virtuoso composer in command of these techniques, in addition to the use of "language perhaps quite ordinary but placed in a new and unexpected context."[28] The chapter "Stowing Down and Clearing Up" features the burly sailors, for example, adopting the tone of housewives as they tidy up the decks to pristine spotlessness in an irreverent celebration of the satirical effects of gender inversion. "The Symphony" employs a female voice aboard the all-male ship, but this time it is that of "the gentle thoughts of the feminine air," placing Ahab at center stage in one of his most tenderly painful moments, quietly feminizing the craggy captain with a gentleness to match his earlier, almost maternal warmth in scenes with Pip.[29] In a moment torn from the pages of the sentimental fiction so popular at the time, the sky becomes the consoling female figure in "the fair girl's forehead" which "did seem to joyously sob over him, as if over one, that however willful and erring, she could yet find it in her heart to save and bless."[30]

The pivotal moment is as sonically significant as it is visually gripping, for the silence is broken by a most delicate and slight sound of Ahab's tear dropping "into the sea; nor did all the Pacific contain such wealth as that one wee drop."[31] The repetition of sound performs the movement of the tear, onomatopoeically rendering Ahab's pain in "w" syllabants with variant assonance in a brilliant progression that sounds like rhythmic crying and woe as "wealth . . . one wee" culminates in the tiniest yet heaviest of sounds in a single "drop." The quietness of this anguish is juxtaposed by Ahab's wails of agony, especially in the chapter "The Candles." This shaping and sounding of the "w" consonant harkens back to "Etymology," which opens the novel and valves of narrative utterance by phonetically pointing to the pronunciation of whale in various languages: hval, wal, hwal, hvalur, a sound round and rolling, a pun on "wail," an expression of despair, notably full of breath, like the whale's own spouting, free of hard consonants, but instead an expressive, shaped long vowel. The mood breaks when Ahab notices Starbuck watching him in his anguish; or does it? Before Ahab voices his pain to Starbuck, silence prevails over the scene with the quiet sky soothing him as his metaphorical absent wife. His teardrop in the ocean tenderly punctuates the moment, itself a figure of smallness in the immense, vast ocean, a trope rendered later amid the radically violent sounds of Ahab's head floundering in the frothing waters of the enraged White Whale like a vulnerable tiny bubble.

Ahab's sentimental speech that follows is almost a song, an aching bluesy lament in "The Symphony," a chapter self-consciously titled for the significance of sound. Its rhythms echo those of *Othello*'s cracked and painful speeches lamenting the loss of the former wife he thought he knew. The fractured syntax, "God! God! God!—crack my heart!—stave my brain!—mockery! mockery! bitter, biting mockery of grey hairs, have I lived enough joy to wear ye," calls to mind the chaos of Othello's heart that also emanates from that "one dent in my marriage pillow."[32] The tone shifts yet again, as Ahab pulls Starbuck near for sympathy in his darkest hour, his first mate seizing the opportunity to soften the captain as he begs to return home so that he too might see his wife and son. The bleak coda of this chapter's orchestral maneuvers ends with Ahab's speech, a helpless soliloquy in the face of the "hidden lord and master . . . recklessly making me ready to do what is in my own proper, natural heart, I durst not so much as dare." His speech ends, and Fedallah's silent "reflected, fixed eyes in the water"[33] ominously tyrannize the victim's image of the teardrop that initiated "The Symphony," a grand poetic movement from silence, to tears, to painful lament and bargaining, finishing with the murderous fixity of Ahab's mission figured in Fedallah's unflinching stare. The next chapter fittingly is "The Chase—First Day."

"The Symphony," crucially poised immediately before the savage three-day conflict with the whale, bears significance not only in its figurative use of sound but also in the poetry of its shifting tones as it is read aloud, occupying what Japanese German poet Yoko Tawada calls the "crevice between sound and language."[34] Read continuously through to the next chapter, the sound effects are particularly stunning, as they bring to light a reference to separate spheres of ideology in which a longing for home appears to be coded female in contrast to the male business of the chase. The binary breaks down as soon as it appears, however, as we realize that we have just seen Ahab and Starbuck searchingly look into each other's eyes for the warm glow of the domestic hearth, as the man who threatened to strike the sun if it insulted him drops an anguished tear in a vast, indifferent ocean.

Calling attention to the structures of sound it employs, "The Symphony" dramatizes the recursive feedback in its very nature, a back and forth process carrying on like a series of echoes, as in this exchange between Ahab and Starbuck or the one in the novel's climactic three-day chase, a series of thrusts and parries, calls and responses. The sea yarns Melville spun throughout his own oral culture were enhanced by the print culture of poetry that surrounded it.

When hearing *Moby-Dick*, we are reminded of the poetry Melville recited and heard most of his life and of his abundant reading of the great poets that characterized his participation in print culture. Our own experience of listening to the novel embodies the inextricable bond between print culture and oral culture in which "voice and print are inseparable."[35] In this way, as Craig Dworkin observes of the poetry of sound, "no sound pattern is inherently meaningful" but instead relies on "certain referential statements from the poem—what one might think of as the conventional meaning of its 'message.'"[36] "The Symphony" means to express Ahab's suffering at the hands of his obsession and his subsequent inability to flee it and embrace Starbuck's compassionate proposition to return home. Those referential statements are then referred back to the sound pattern, "which then loops back to reinforce and foreground particular themes in its message."[37] Herein lies the poetry of the passage, so beautifully amplified in a live reading in which its "grain of voice," as Barthes has it, achieves the heft of full expression and palpable presence.

Sounding the Whale

MELVILLE assumes the whale to be silent, since the creature's underwater voice was of course undetected by antebellum whalers, who took his odd nasal snorting upon surfacing to be his only sound. Today's underwater recording technology has documented whale communication, a song in its own right, with melodic coherences and measured cadences, that lends itself to a nonverbal sort of poetry. Melville was gripped by the power of whale communication, however silent he assumed it to be, which he could perceive in "The Grand Armada," a chapter depicting mother whales nursing their young. The lyricism of the scene is profound, as the communal gathering of two or three pods of whales over the water's surface functions to protect with "wondrous fearlessness and confidence" the sacred maternal intimacy below "in those watery vaults, [where] floated the forms of nursing mothers of the whales, and those that by their enormous girth seemed shortly to become mothers."[38] The preverbal bond between mother and newborn takes on a silent form of communication with the aesthetic significance of the natural poetry of the whale's song, an aesthetic wonder like that of Shelley's "Sky Lark." Ishmael observes how the baby whales "calmly and fixedly gaze away from the breast, as if leading two different lives at the same time; and while yet drawing mortal nourishment, be still spiritually feasting, upon some unearthly reminiscence," an echo of consciousness from the recently departed womb.[39] So new to the world are these baby whales that their gaze away from the breast seems to gesture toward the eternity of their existence prior to birth. They gaze toward another life before life wherein communication with the mother whale was utterly unmitigated in a conjoined and fully integrated symbiotic union. Andrew Delbanco has attached "a kind of holiness" to the bond, "as if each mother and nursing baby were a submarine Madonna and Child."[40] That "unearthly reminiscence" is a bleary-eyed yearning for spiritual sustenance, according to the metaphorical logic of the image, different from mother's milk, which is as innate in these creatures as in human infants. Similarly, Rebecca Harding Davis's Hugh Wolfe of *Life in the Iron Mills* (1861) describes his sculpture's profound and expressible yearning as a spiritual hunger, which Davis also assumes to be a natural human drive: "She be hungry . . . not hungry for meat . . . Summat to make her live," Hugh explains, to which the observer notes that the face "asks questions of God and says 'I have a right to know,'" a face unmistakably in wordless communication with the divine.[41] Closer to Melville's celestial embryonic figure, Henry David Thoreau would also employ a similar image of birth's intimacy with the secrets of eternity in his famous line from *Walden*, "I always have been regretting that I was not so wise as the day I was born."[42]

Thoreau's burrowing into nature inspires a lyricism in his prose the same way it does in Melville's. The closeness to the natural image transports language to the expanses above where the baby whale's dazed snout points in Melville. In Thoreau, the "sandy bottom" of Walden pond's "thin current slides away, but eternity remains. I would drink deeper; fish in the sky, whose bottom is pebbly with stars." The return to a preverbal union with nature, like the whale in the mother's womb, is imminent: "I cannot count one. I know not the first letter of the alphabet."[43] In another metaphor like Thoreau's for transcending language altogether, Ishmael describes divine expression (or exhalation) followed by inspiration (or inhalation) in the whale's spout, "a canopy of vapor, engendered by the incommunicable contemplations, and that vapor—as you will sometimes see it—glorified by a rainbow, as if Heaven itself had put its seal upon his thoughts."[44] Expression without language is thus akin to sound without words and the lyricism of nature's poetry. Melville's novel reaches toward the "ungraspable phantom of life" that John Bryant has astutely described as "inseparable from the [material] stuff of life,[45] and yet no matter how close we hold this stuff to us, we get no closer to that essence."[46] Though moments of coherence occur through them, Melville takes no smug self-satisfaction in the materials of whaling alone, its lances, harpoons, rigging, masts, cabins, and decks, its speedy chase boats and cistern and buckets. They are futile as a medium for gaining access to "that essence" of the "ungraspable phantom" insofar as they stay silent. Sounding the materials of whaling—as in measuring, investigating, trying, and finding out about—gives them voice, as it were, in the song that animates and elevates the pursuit of the White Whale to a subject worthy of poetry.

Sounding the whale in this sense is deeply connected to its lyricism and music. Melville's most lyrical prose in *Moby-Dick* thus has a special connection to its sound, which James William Johnson's definition supports. "The irreducible denominator of all lyric poetry," he writes, "comprises those elements which it shares with the musical forms that produced it. Although lyric poetry is not music . . . it retains structural or substantive evidence of its melodic origins, and this factor serves as the categorical principle of poetic lyricism."[47] The poetic voice in Melville is as distinct as it is in Frederick Douglass's narrative, for example, when the former slave's reportorial objective account elevates to the level of song, particularly in his apostrophic ode to his missing freedom via the sails on the Chesapeake Bay billowing northward toward freedom. Thoreau's singing voice is also quite distinct from his sober accounting as it rises to pitched, exalted notes usually aimed skyward toward the stars—"I prefer the natural sky to the opium eater's heaven"[48]— and clouds, as in the following reverie canoeing on Walden Pond: "In such transparent and seemingly bottomless water, reflecting the clouds, I seemed to be floating through the air as in a balloon, and their swimming impressed me as a kind of flight or hovering, as if they were a compact flock of birds passing just beneath my level on the right or left, their fins, like sails, set all around them." This swirling and euphoric image poetically blends the lofty clouds, birds, and the fancy of his flight in a balloon over the reflected clouds on the water's surface, beneath which, in a near hallucinatory effect, swim "myriads of small perch."[49] The vitality and dynamism of the image is astonishing and, taken as lyricism, approaches a symphonic feel. Thoreau was well aware of the sound of his own poetic voice as much as he was acutely sensitive to the sounds of nature he hears as lyrical song in the chapter "Sounds" in *Walden*.

Most Melvillians have their own favorite impassioned lyrical moments in *Moby-Dick* prior to the marathon reading. But part of the magic of the event is aesthetic surprise. A silent reading would not alert one to such new possibilities the way an oral reading does. "The Pacific" and "The Lee Shore" are such passages that took flight at the live reading; both stand out in *Moby-Dick* because they sing like those of Thoreau and Douglass with a lyrical texture distinct from the silent interstices, the muted isolated tones, the teardrop of wrenched, brooding lament of movements like "The Symphony." In both, the semicolon acts as a kind of line break so that the "generic classification has become less important than the poeticity of the language itself," as Perloff explains. The prose poetry's effect in "The Pacific" does not rely on what Izenberg calls the "hermeneutical payoff" for its power.[50] Instead, its power is in its rhythms, repetitions, internal rhyme, stresses, vowel sounds, and play of common consonant combinations.

Ishmael establishes the keynote of the following riff as the achievement of his private quest to greet the grand Pacific: "for now the long supplication of my youth was answered; that serene ocean rolled eastward from me a thousand leagues of blue."[51] Literally coming from the other side of the world to glimpse this new vista, he is overwhelmed with presentiment. However undercut by the fact that it is home to Moby Dick and will be the site of the *Pequod*'s demise, it vibrates with the surreal bewitching energy of chiaroscuro, the play of light and shadow frequently used by painters. Like Whitman's "Out of the Cradle, Endlessly Rocking," the poet's voice takes the rhythms of the sea for its meter:

> over the sea-pastures, wide-rolling watery prairies and Potters' Fields
> of all four continents, the waves should rise and fall, and ebb and
> flow unceasingly; for here, millions of mixed shades and shadows,
> drowned dreams, somnambulisms, reveries; all that we call lives and
> souls, lie dreaming, dreaming, still; tossing like slumberers in their
> beds; the ever-rolling waves but made so by their restlessness.[52]

The establishment of the wavelike rhythm, "and fall, and ebb and flow," sets up the cumulative syntax of the multi-clause subject. The semicolons that might serve as line breaks for the blank verse, interestingly, would create a free verse look on the page for the first two statements, both of which would spill over onto a second line. The lyricism intensifies as the statements shorten and their diction becomes more precise. His controlling metaphor of the Pacific becomes the place of "all that we call lives and souls," and his attitude toward them is sweetly sad. The descriptive distance of "mixed shades and shadows" is arrested by the alliterative cold and jarring counter-wave splash of "drowned dreams." These are deftly counterpoised by the neutral bridge of "somnambulisms" to the more buoyant "reveries." The constant movement figured in the ocean's incessant ebb and flow is gorgeously anchored by the deceptively stabilizing "still" at the heart of the passage, which of course means "continuously" in this context, rather than "unmoving." The passage may metaphorically ascribe a cause to the ocean's waves, not unlike a Native American or even ancient Greek creation myth figuratively ascribing causality to natural phenomena. But its true power cannot be fully appreciated by silently reading the passage and understanding that import. Instead, its artistry is in its voice, in the sounding (as in the acoustics of investigation or exploration) of the notion that our dreams—whether drowned ambition or reveries of hope—are like restless sleepers rolling in the ocean's tides.

The reverence in this passage that gestures toward the divine, like the sacred nursing whale facing skyward and Thoreau's stupendous balloon flight, unmistakably appears in the succeeding paragraph. "The divine Pacific," Melville writes, "seems the tide-bearing heart of the earth. Lifted by those eternal swells, you needs must own the seductive god, bowing your head to Pan."[53] The Pacific demands submission (a reflexive humility as embodied by U2's lyric, "If you want to kiss the sky / Better learn how to kneel / On your knees boy"[54]) to its mighty power and vast expanse, humbling to all but Ahab. The mysticism is justifiable to anyone who has witnessed its shores. Growing up near Stinson Beach in Marin County, California, and attending the University of California at Santa Barbara—the campus forms a peninsula surrounded by the Pacific—I have also been humbled by its massive power, in part by the occasion of my first encounter with Melville's mighty book in 1986. I could hear Melville's voice in the sea—"waves wash the moles of the new-built Californian towns"[55]—and my own restless ambition and the untold dreams of humanity rolling ceaselessly in the waves before me as I stood, head bowed, on the cliffs above Sands Beach. The poetry of the moment was inescapably rooted in the rushing sound of the sea, for "sound," as Sarah Ellis wrote in 1835, "is perhaps of all subjects the most intimately connected with poetic feeling." This is "not only because it comprehends within its widely extended sphere, the influence of music, so powerful over the passions and affections of our nature" and thus an avenue for intense reflective insight and deep emotional feeling, "but because there is in poetry itself, a cadence—a perceptible harmony, which delights the ear while the eye remains unaffected."[56]

A "Pinewood Resonance"

THE GRAIN of voice in the ocean, the whale, and Melville's narrative as spoken through Ishmael intones a variety of musical keys and pitches. The sound of *Moby-Dick*'s poetry at the marathon reading is of course mediated by the individual readers; some are stunning in their sensitivity to the poetic dyna-mism and even regional or ethnic dialect of their given passage. Even standard spoken English readings alert to the cadences of Melville's punctuation—so crucial to determining the sound effects of the novel—are profoundly mov-ing. The democracy of the event, its inclusiveness, like Melville's process of writing the novel itself, brings uneven results, as exalted lyricism, read as such, comes in rare intervals. However, the satisfaction of hearing the novel, especially in this imperfect and thus edgy circumstance, bears with it the feeling of a treasure hunt, a dicey shot at epiphany all in the hands, and voices, of the people. Readers are not screened, but universally accepted if they are eager and vigilant enough to reserve their reading slot over a month and a half in advance. Applicants, no matter how young or old, are not turned away. (The New Bedford Whaling Museum's adoption of an automated phone line scheduled to open at precisely 12:01 AM on November 15 to take reserva-tions for a single eight- to ten-minute reading testifies to the skyrocketing popularity of the event, and the premium on particular passages of the novel, especially those at the beginning and the end.)

The *Moby-Dick* Marathon reading has deep roots in both the lyric and democratic traditions of ancient Greek epic poetry. Homer after all was not a writer but a singer, a performer who memorized the *Iliad* and the *Odyssey* by virtue of their rhyme schemes. Before he was a writer, Melville was always a sailor with a story, telling and retelling his tales, sharpening his delivery on rapt listeners. Melville's knack for oral storytelling was well suited to his inclination toward poetry, which resulted in lyrical novels rich with textured free-verse prose poetry. The *Moby-Dick* Marathon harkens back to the Ho-meric tradition as an American epic in its own right performed aloud like one grand Greek prose poem. Whitman's *Leaves of Grass*, it should be remem-bered, features a democratic dynamo as its poet figure and star attraction who sings a "Song of Myself" and de-emphasizes the print trade—"I pass so poorly with paper and types"—while prioritizing the voice—"the lull I like, the hum of your valved voice."[57] It is telling that Whitman's speaker would also be so intensely democratic in light of his nostalgia for the Homeric oral storytelling tradition. Greeks invented democracy and enriched their national political identity through live performance art in satyrs, tragedies, and epics, works not so much didactic as they were problematic psychological puzzles much like those sprouting throughout *Moby-Dick*'s ambiguous moral universe. Democracy, in the Whitmanian sense of a pastiche of discordant diverse voices paradoxically coming together in one seamless chorus, bears special significance for the 2009 event since it so closely followed the historic 2008 presidential election.

Democracy and the poetry of voice played a crucial role in the veritable singing tour of the 2008 campaign for election to the presidency of the United States, as Barak Obama wooed voters with oratorical finesse and delivery unmatched since the velvety baritones of Ronald Reagan. By contrast, much of Jimmy Carter's admirable statesmanship, his peace-making inroads in the Middle East in particular, were obscured by his weak stage presence, characterized by an anemic delivery sadly unmatched to the force of his words, conviction, and integrity. Politics and American celebrity go back to the Kennedy charisma; JFK's performances at rallies and at the Democratic National Convention were theatrical extravaganzas showcasing voice and syntactical dexterity electrified by the immediacy of the live audience. His selection of Robert Frost to read at his inauguration—echoed by Bill Clinton's selection of Maya Angelou to read at his—reinforced the alliance between the political and the poetic.

At the most recent Democratic National Convention, Michael Chabon reported that Obama successfully "possessed sufficient reserves of imagination to kick oratorical ass," bringing down the house with a voice of "pinewood resonance," an instrument whose "wood could only be American," to borrow a phrase from *Moby-Dick*.[58] True to his profession, the literary novelist Chabon saw the event as constructed primarily of poetic language in all the varieties in which it is consumed at live events in American culture: "At times the convention played like an opera, loosely based on Shakespeare; a rock concert; a rhetorical full program magic show; a sporting event."[59] The analogies parallel the *Moby-Dick* Marathon reading as I have presented it in this book from athletic marathon to poetry reading, from religious ritual to symphony. Chabon reveals just how much our candidates and eventual presidents are made of words. Indeed, the greater portion of American politics itself is made up of sound, both archaic ritual and modern innovation. Authority rings out from the very beginnings of both events by giving voice to centuries old words, the poetry of which carries a presentiment of something momentous and world changing in their echo. The rhythmic cracking of an ancient gavel sets time for the music of the archaic words: "The fourth session of the forty-fifth quadrennial National Convention of the Democratic Party will now come to order."[60] Chabon especially relished the group recitation of the Pledge of Allegiance, again relevant to the Melville marathon reading as "an act of collective recollection of the past, of a time when people routinely stood up and sang together, stood up to recite pledges, credos, oaths, poems,"[61] and now, the entirety of one of the greatest novels of all time, *Moby-Dick*. Every bit a "formal, public celebration of spoken language," the marathon reading, unlike the DNC, retains its poetry and sacrifices nothing to the demand, now a perfunctory technique in political speeches, to "stay on message."[62] Obama's strength that evening ultimately lay in language his opponents called "pretty words." But to Chabon and the massive crowd that evening, on display was the lyricism of "the greatest orator of his generation," confirming beyond all doubt that "words were all we had; that writing and oratory, argument and persuasion, were the root of democracy; that words can kill, or save us."[63]

True to my depiction of the acoustic pleasures of *Moby-Dick* at the marathon reading, Obama displayed a Melvillian range of voices during his acceptance speech at the convention, a polyphony of what Chabon heard as "preacherly, plainspeaking, jocular, Lincolnesque," which he could only compare to "a regular but loose-feeling progression, like a piece of Ornette Coleman harmolodics."[64] In Melville, we hear a symphony, shifting moods and sounds from colloquial banter anticipating the jagged dark humor and irony of Eliot's *Waste Land* to the majestic thunder of Wagnerian opera, triumphant and tragic, sacred and profane, worshipful and irreverent. Like some passages in *Moby-Dick* itself, there are anachronisms at the convention, superannuated linguistic quirks oddly out of place as their sounds haunt the twenty-first-century air. The filibustering bravado prefacing each state's nomination, for example, is nonetheless necessary, albeit an arcane ritual signaling the authenticity and power of this event, precisely because it is so stubbornly unabridged, so faithfully rooted in the past.

Antebellum New England's dialect makes no sustained authentic appearance at the Melville event; *Moby-Dick* is mostly read in the present tongue, which can dance with the past in awkward ways. Like Shakespeare's Elizabethan English or Chaucer's Middle English, archaic usage remains intact, no matter how we may fumble over it or misunderstand it ("the draught of a draught" line in "Cetology" in 2008 was pronounced by an unknowing soul as the "drought of a drought") for one reason: the poetry. The novel's poetic import is untranslatable. *Moby-Dick* has been translated, of course, into innumerable languages, and indeed much of the novel can be appreciated in the hands of an extremely adept translator, part wordsmith and part Melville-channeling medium. The likelihood that none of these translations will ever be read unabridged in a marathon format is because poetry generally is essentially untranslatable, or more precisely, is what gets lost in the translation, according to Robert Frost's famous formulation. Poetry is an experience of words, not just words, and the live reading of them is essential to that experience. To this end, pedagogical theory continues to promote poetry in its various voices, from slams to live readings to recordings for analysis of expressions of the grain of voice at its heart. There is a special language in poetry, particularly the lyrical prose poetry of *Moby-Dick*, which extends our sense of what ourselves and others—ethnic, religious, cultural, political, national, social—are like, our experience of ourselves, and our range of human feelings. In Melville's hands, this becomes an uncanny language that expresses the inexpressible, like birth and death, right at the outer edges of life and language itself, far beyond their denotative capacity.

Poetry's theatrical dimension demands that it be performed live, lived and shared orally and aurally to bring out its experience of meaning beyond the words. The lore of the *Moby-Dick* Marathon reading, therefore, has circulated primarily on the Internet for its audio dimension so inextricably bound to the momentousness of its performance in time. The marathon reading, like Whitman's poetry, does not move well in type, nor for that matter in audio recordings only, much in the way a video of an entire, uncut 130-minute athletic marathon would not be of interest to most looking to relive the experience. The event in many ways is so vast, like the whale itself, as to defy being captured, recorded, and thus fully encapsulated; in this way its enigma remains forever free and untamed by celluloid or participant-observer accounts by zealous critics like me. Segments of the reading can be viewed on the Internet, but the whole reading is not available in its entirety in any recorded form for sale or even private consumption. That will likely change with time, as a camera-mounted tripod aimed at the podium from "Call me Ishmael" to "It was the devious-cruising *Rachel*"[65] might give way to hand-held recordings of the event for the most ardent of obsessed archivists. The dearth of such products testifies to how the magic lies in the experience of the event. Bootleg recordings of live rock concerts, while purportedly desirable, almost always disappoint because they are pale reflections of the lived experience. It is the rare professional documentarian who can capture the spirit of the event *and* the bulk of its proceedings. Experiencing the poetry is why we are here—poetry in all its diversity, multiple languages judiciously spicing the novel's global zest without marring its lyricism as a complete translation would.[66]

In 2009, New Bedford mayor Scott Lang, when informed that local cable television producer Ed Camara had chosen to film only the first and last two hours of the reading, vowed that the event would be filmed in its entirety in 2010. Camara's sense of the event's "prime time" indeed was accurate as those four hours were by far the most popular, yielding the greatest number of spectators and high profile readers. Yet Lang's desire to document, if not fully "capture," the mystique of the all-night reading on film attempts to do justice to its endurance factor. No one will assume that viewers will watch all twenty-five hours, but its presence will pay homage to the marathon dimension of the reading. In 2009, Camara's tripod remained rooted to the ground throughout the vast majority of the proceedings, seldom scanning the room. The photographer who covered the event with a handheld camera, by contrast, was vital and even gymnastic in his imaginative discoveries of fresh perspectives of the room. He moved among us capturing cozy couples, father-son bonding, and young tattooed, nose-ringed renegades commanding the podium, with elderly women in holiday sweaters hanging on their every word; he could be seen seeking low angles, delighting in the detail of the rows of open books and the plurality of hands lovingly cradling them. Filming the twenty-five hours unabridged might allow Camara's crew more sea room to work with, and thus free up the imaginative potential of producing more watchable, even intriguing television that taps into the visual poetry to complement and enhance the auditory lyricism of New Bedford's flagship civic celebration.

Abridgements, like full translations, seriously limit the poetry of *Moby-Dick*'s aural power, as Norman Mailer defended against his editor's insistence on shortening *The Naked and the Dead* by quoting Thomas Mann, "Only the exhaustive is truly interesting."[67] Melville's lengthy diversions, in this way, are totally essential to an authentic experience of the novel. I have had the rather unfortunate experience, for instance, of driving across the country listening to an audio version of *Moby-Dick* on CD read by film actor William Hootkins in dramatic cadences, deftly wielding a ventriloquism to match the myriad voices and characters of the novel. My inspiration would be disappointed, however, in the realization that this edition, of all six CDs no less, was abridged, hacked into arbitrary bits and pieces intended for mass audiences like Melville's original antebellum readers expecting little more than an eloquently rendered whale chase. Fingers fumbling, I jettisoned the disc, hastily replacing it with Faulkner's seventeen-hour, and to my delight, unabridged, *Light in August*, as the foothills of the Colorado Front Range receded in the rearview mirror and the high plains loomed ahead in the distance, the journey now haunted by Faulkner's slow, southern lilt, somber and lacey with dreamy intoxication, yet punctuated with percussive violence. I could then rest assured that I was in the presence of a species of prose at least approximating Melville's, potent with stiff shots of poetry, undiluted, to be savored like a good Tennessee whisky, oaky in its resonance with the American past.

Coda

AMERICA was captivated in late 2008 by the sounds of a "Grand Contested Election for the Presidency of the United States," an event in the headlines grossly overshadowing the potentially tiny whisper of the *Moby-Dick* Marathon reading, a "Whaling Voyage of One Ishmael."[68] Like these headlines facetiously and self-effacingly imagined by Melville in the first chapter of *Moby-Dick*, Hawthorne would also take a self-conscious jab at his own authorial anxiety in "The Custom House," the introduction to *The Scarlet Letter*. "What is he?" Hawthorne imagined his Puritan ancestors mockingly asking, "A writer of story-books!" The position was wholly at odds with the world-changing enterprise afoot, and the premium the nation had placed upon "being serviceable to mankind in his day and generation .... Why, the degenerate fellow might as well have been a fiddler!"[69] Today's "Whaling Voyage of One Ishmael" is the *Moby-Dick* Marathon reading on January 3, 2009, an event whose headline is totally eclipsed by the inauguration speech of Barak Obama on January 20, 2009, in Washington, D.C., marking a massive sea change in American politics and geopolitical relations. The very character of America has been forged by its presidents, from the Jacksonian democracy of the antebellum years to the Roosevelt turn of the twentieth century, to the golden jeremiad halcyon days of Reagan's 1980s and the troubled diplomacy of the George W. Bush era. And those who sing the epic songs of that character, in all its seasons of recklessness and tact, of defiance and compassion, are those minute Ishmaels who go a-whaling, those silly writers of story-books who may as well be fiddlers. Not to be underestimated, these eccentrics are our own Homers, as our epic songs are being sung now to a new era, which brings their poetry a new pitch, expanding its collective vision and diversity, singing the song of America, the songs of ourselves.

Melville lives—not only for the fashionable reason that he wrote *post-modern* fiction a full seventy years before modernism even emerged, but also because he could see an almost slapstick incongruity within his own antebellum culture that so accurately foretold our own. That he could play with those contradictions and inconsistencies, those parodies and prophecies, as lyrically as he did gives pause. This is true especially in light of how he never fell permanently into a resigned pessimism or atheism, but ceaselessly pursued his agnostic quest to shore these fragments against his ruin, as Eliot would have it. That process in *Moby-Dick* consists of equal parts sober reflection and ecstatic exultation, wrenching despair and gliding serenity. The evidence now that Melville has never mattered more, that his resonance with the twenty-first century zeitgeist has reached unprecedented heights, is visible not only in the escalating popularity of the marathon reading but also in the recent surge in works inspired by *Moby-Dick* in the film, television, and music industries, including a major motion picture of the novel currently in production. Beyond art and entertainment culture, even the political world has embraced the White Whale, as state legislators named it the official novel of Massachusetts in the fall of 2008. What draws us to Melville is his concern for the limitations of individualism and the need for restraint in a "ruthless democracy" like ours, his attention to the perils and potentialities of global trade, his prophecy of ever increasing, almost historically inevitable, transnational commercial and thus cultural exchange, and his revelation of the psychological inner life and its ongoing struggle with political context. He matters because of his sensitivity to how that political context—the captaincy of our local, national, and global lives—conditions our responses, our hopes, and our dreams and tells us how we work and why; Melville matters because he invites us to call all such conditioning, including religion, into question and to see more of the divine in a baby whale's gaze toward heaven or a cannibal's tattoos than in a fire-and-brimstone sermon by a former sea captain raging from a pulpit shaped like a ship's bow, a theatrical absurdity anticipating the stagy histrionics of televangelism. Can we hear the weaver-god amid the rush and bustle of the weaving he engages? Is he too busy creating a new political world governed by an entirely new ethos of statecraft impacting the entirety of the world's nations to hear our calls to him and our silent prayers? "Oh busy weaver!" Ishmael cries, "unseen weaver!—pause!—one word!—whither flows thy fabric? What palace may it deck? Wherefore all these ceaseless toilings? Speak, weaver! . . . by that weaving he is deafened that he hears no mortal voice; and by that humming, we, too, who look on the loom are deafened; and only when we escape it shall we hear the thousand voices that speak through it."[70] The voice of the marathon reading *is* audible despite the deafening sound of production around us, an affirmation of the "thousand voices that speak through it," an affirmation that somewhere outside the factory's open windows our reading of Melville's poetic prose does not fall on deaf ears, that our sense of classical literature's voice will find a new measure, cadence, and key to fit this dawning era. In this way, "it is with fiction as with religion," Melville wrote in his last novel: "it should present another world, yet one to which we feel the tie."[71]

·𝒩OTES·

Introduction

1. Charles Olson, *Call Me Ishmael* (San Francisco: City Lights Books, 1947), 20.

2. Chris King, "24 Hours of All *Moby-Dick*, All the Time," *New York Times* July 29, 2001, http://www.nytimes.com/2001/07/29/nyregion/24-hours-of-all-moby-dick-all-the-time.html?scp=4+sq=Moby-Dickmarathon+st=cse

3. New England seems to have a passion for literature and running, playing host not only to multiple *Moby-Dick* Marathon readings, but also to the Boston Marathon, one of the oldest foot races in North America. The true confluence between New England's love of public events honoring literature and running, however, is most apparent in the James Joyce Ramble 10-K held annually in late April through the streets of Dedham, Massachusetts. Unlike the *Moby-Dick* Marathon reading's emphasis on civic pride in their glorious whaling history, the Dedham race honors Joyce primarily to recognize the predominantly Irish community and to raise awareness about pressing contemporary issues. Race director Martin Hanley dedicates each event to an individual, from Vaclav Havel to slain *Wall Street Journal* reporter Daniel Pearl, or issue, such as the Iraq war and human rights, to challenge people to be more engaged in their world. (The link to Joyce in each year's theme is not always explicit, but those familiar with him can readily make the connections with his social and political commentary.) In the same vein, I discuss how attendees of the *Moby-Dick* Marathon relate the novel to the Muslim religion and global terrorism in chapter two of this book, also linking a live literary event to world issues. Also, the theatrics of the James Joyce ramble interestingly parallel those of the *Moby-Dick* Marathon, as costumed readers line the course and read from Joyce's work, appropriately saving *The Dead* for the last mile. See Jon Marcus, "Storybook Race," *Runner's World* 43.8 (2008): 93–94.

4. Andrew Delbanco, *Melville: His World and Work* (New York: Knopf, 2005), xii–xix.

5. "Stockwatch: New England Whaling Ltd," *The Onion* 44.28 (2008): 2.

6. More than chamber of commerce decorations or baubles, the New Bedford Whaling National Historical Park and the New Bedford Whaling Museum are the heart and soul of the town, just as Williamsburg, Virginia, has become a living shrine to colonial America, as students at the College of William and Mary can attest to the procession of tour buses that stream in and out of their community.

7. *Leviathan* is the journal of the Melville Society, headed by John Bryant, whose recent achievements on behalf of scholarly research on Melville include a fluid text version of *Typee* that allows readers online access to Melville's manuscript changes and relevant visual art. The Melville Society Archive, recently established by the society, at the New Bedford Whaling Museum under the care of curator Michael Dyer is a treasure trove of primary and secondary source materials originally held in private collections.

8. Several books have recently taken Melville studies by storm. The latest book exclusively focusing on *Moby-Dick* is by Eyal Peretz, *Literature, Disaster, and the Enigma of Power: A Reading of Moby-Dick* (Stanford University Press, 2003). It examines Ishmael as a witness to a disaster, whose discourse inspires us to "remember me, keep telling my story, and be willing to make your life an echoing of my word. But also, transform and revolutionize your life, *not by imitating me but by responding to my call or by responding to my life as to a call—leave your belongings, your home and the stable land in which you have grown, and come to sea*" (188, emphasis mine). Those at the *Moby-Dick* Marathon respond to Ishmael's call, keep telling his story, and internalize that experience enough to make our lives an echoing of his word. At the other end of the spectrum from this literary theoretical academic work is Eric Jay Dolin's *Leviathan: The History of Whaling in America* (New York: Norton, 2007), an (almost too) comprehensive historical survey that draws only slightly on Melville's work, yet impressively delves into the real lives of some obscure sea dogs as well as celebrated captains, and as such informs part II of this book on the social matrix of the *Pequod*. My conclusion draws from two outstanding sources, Hershel Parker, *Melville: The Making of a Poet* (Chicago: Northwestern University Press, 2008) (hereafter, Parker *Poet*) and Robert Milder, *Exiled Royalties: Melville and the Life We Imagine* (New York: Oxford University Press, 2003) that have inspired further exploration of Melville's much-neglected poetry, which is currently enjoying a vigorous renaissance reaching well beyond the ivory tower of academia, as evidenced by the carefully assembled website hermanmelvillepoet.org. Further, Northwestern Newberry editors have indicated that they would like their next major Melville publication to be a book-length study of his epic poem, *Clarel*. My conclusion treats the reading as an indication of Melville's poesy, as the spoken voice is so deeply connected, especially in the American tradition, to verse.

9. Jay Leyda, *The Melville Log: A Documentary Life of Herman Melville, 1819–1891*. Vol. II. (New York: Harcourt, 1951), 592.

10. Herman Melville, *Moby-Dick; or, The Whale*, ed. Harrison Hayford, Hershel Parker, and G. Thomas Tanselle (Evanston and Chicago: Northwestern University Press and Newberry Library, 1988), 393. (Hereafter, NN *MD*).

11. NN *MD*, 456.

12. In this way the reading closely echoes long-distance running, for it requires a "quiet, inner motivation, and doesn't seek validation in the outwardly visible," as Haruki Murakami describes it in *What I Talk About When I Talk About Running* (New York: Knopf, 2008), 20. The process of reading lends itself to inner rewards similar to those of running, especially "the satisfaction of having done his very best—and possibly having made some significant discovery about himself in the process [which is] an accomplishment in itself," 20.

13. NN *MD*, 6.

14. NN *MD*, 72.

15. Jack Stewardson, "Moby-Dick Marathon Draws Attention to Book, Museum," *South Coast Today: The Standard Times* January 4, 2000.

16. In Lawrence, Kansas, the Christian art gallery and bookstore, Signs of Life, holds an annual marathon reading of the Bible every June. More than 100 volunteers read passages for thirteen hours a day for a week, finishing in about eighty hours. Store owner Clay Belcher says the reading has the virtue of rendering a broad view of Biblical history that is normally doled out piecemeal on Sunday mornings. More visibly, a Bible reading marathon has been held for twenty-one consecutive years at the U.S. Capitol (www. debiblemarathon.org/Home.html). *Lord of the Rings* and *Moby-Dick* have also been read at Portland State University for fundraisers in the mid-1990s. *Ulysses, Moby-Dick, Lord of the Rings*, and the Bible make for a curious combination of works indeed, indicating that print culture tends to hold its most revered literary classics on the same plane as its most beloved popular fantasy, all with the canonical aura of the Bible itself. In recent decades, the two books most likely to be sharing space on readers' shelves are the Bible and any novel by Stephen King or J. K. Rowling. In many ways, (some) classical and religious literature has become popular culture, though no marathon readings of the Torah or the Koran have been sighted.

17. Quoted in King, 1.

18. King, 2.

19. Quoted in Sarah Guille, "Ship Out with Herman Melville: *Moby-Dick* Marathon Offers Some New Twists in Second Year," *South Coast Today: The Standard-Times* January 1, 1998, http://archive.southcoasttoday.com/daily/01-98/01-01-98/c01lio88.htm.

20. By 1850, New Bedford's fleet of 288 whalers dwarfed Nantucket's mere 62. On the global scale, the U.S. boasted 735 of the 900 whaleships worldwide, Dolin, 212–213, 206.

21. Quoted in Guille, 1.

22. Quoted in King, 1.

23. Dolin, 214, 206.

24. "The fact is," Melville groused, "almost everyone is having his 'mug' engraved nowadays; so that this test of distinction is getting to be reversed; and therefore, to see one's 'mug' in a magazine, is presumptive evidence that he's a nobody." Melville was acutely aware of the risks of commercial overexposure as early as this 1851 letter to his editor Evert Duyckinck declining the request for his engraving for publicity. Melville wanted to rise above this sort of garish competition to be more deeply respected as an author and thus "famous throughout the world," Herman Melville, *Correspondence,* ed. Lynn Horth (Evanston and Chicago: Northwestern University Press and Newberry Library, 1993), 180. (Hereafter, NN *Corr.*)

25. Quoted in Thomas F. Marvin, *Kurt Vonnegut: A Critical Companion* (Westport, CT: Greenwood Press, 2002), 73.

26. Henry David Thoreau, *Walden*, ed. Raymond M. Alden (New York: Longmans, Green, and Company, 1910 [rpt. 1854]), 76.

27. Quoted in Katherine Switzer and Roger Robinson, *26.2 Marathon Stories* (New York: Rodale, 2006), 58.

28. NN *Corr*, 121.

29. One of the most impressive results of this approach can be found in Elizabeth A. Schultz, *Unpainted to the Last: Moby-Dick and Twentieth-Century American Art* (Lawrence: University Press of Kansas, 1995), a dazzling compendium of illustrations, paintings, and sculptures inspired by Melville's great novel.

30. Salman Rushdie, "Is Nothing Sacred?" *Granta* 31 (1990), 107. Eyal Peretz notes that the history of *Moby-Dick* criticism has fallen into this sort of binary trap that pits Ahab against Ishmael, commenting that, according to the vocabulary of the novel "evil is in a way beyond good and bad," but instead "occupies precisely the place of whiteness," 150. He criticizes this "too simplistic opposition between Ishmael and Ahab . . . as a continuation of what Donald Pease and other New Americanists have characterized as the Cold War tradition of Melville interpretation . . . which saw Ishmael as the pure principle of resistance against Ahab's no less pure oppressive totalitarian power. In general we might say that the either-or Ahab/Ishmael has characterized most of the critical tradition of reading *Moby-Dick*. Thus, while in the earlier phases of *Moby-Dick* criticism the critical attention was mainly paid to the figure of Ahab, in later generations the figure of Ishmael came to the fore as an opposition to Ahab," 151. Like Peretz, I am interested in the dialectic between the two, and how and what readers consciously or unconsciously exclude from the text to sort them into mutually exclusive binaries.

31. Herman Melville, *The Piazza Tales and Other Prose Pieces, 1839–1860*, ed. Harrison Hayford, et al. (Evanston and Chicago: Northwestern University Press and Newberry Library, 1995), 2. (Hereafter, NN *PT*.)

32. NN *MD*, 347.

33. NN *MD*, 486.

34. Peretz, 42.

1. That Everlasting Itch

1. Delbanco, 38.

2. Hershel Parker has characterized this phase of his life, especially as he bounced around islands of the South Pacific, as that of a "beachcomber," *Herman Melville: A Biography, Vol. I, 1819–1851* (Baltimore: Johns Hopkins University Press, 1996), 219. (Hereafter, Parker *HM*.)

3. Quoted in Parker *HM*, 166.

4. Parker *HM*, 180.

5. The purpose of his trip west with Fly was to find his fortune. But the trip was unfortunate, as his attempt to find work with the aid of his uncle, Thomas Melville, in Galena, Illinois, failed.

6. NN *MD*, 2.

7. NN *MD*, 2, 3.

8. NN *MD*, 6, 4.

9. Melville left his post as a schoolteacher in Greenbush, New York, during the winter of 1839–40 to go west with his friend Eli James Murdoch (Fly). His mother wrote on

December 7, 1839, that his teaching career was flourishing, as she was "cheered by Herman's prospects — he appears to be interested in his occupation — he has a great charge, & deep responsibility is attached to the education of 60 Scholars, which I understand is the number usual during the greater part of the year" (NN *Corr* 23). Melville did not go directly from teaching to sea, as he depicts Ishmael doing in *Moby-Dick*.

10. NN *MD*, 5.
11. NN *MD*, 69.
12. NN *Corr*, 160.
13. Olson, 12.
14. Delbanco, 40.
15. NN *MD*, 551.
16. NN *MD*, 571.
17. Delbanco, 40.
18. NN *MD*, 371.
19. Dolin, 76, 78, 88.
20. Dolin, 83.
21. NN *MD*, 637.
22. NN *MD*, 637.
23. Parker comments that Melville had thus "participated in one of the most remarkable literary phenomena of his time, the frontier training of writers, in which ordinary Americans confronted natural horrors and wonders, far from home, and came back, when they were lucky, to tell tall tales about their experiences, or truthful tales so extraordinary that stay-at-home people would take them as false" (Hershel Parker, "Historical Note IV," NN *MD*, 637; hereafter Parker "Note"). For an in-depth study of the tall tale origins of *Moby-Dick*, see John Bryant, "Melville Essays the Romance: Comedy and Being in *Frankenstein*, 'The Big Bear of Arkansas,' and *Moby-Dick*," *Nineteenth-Century Literature* 61.3 (2006): 277–310.
24. NN *MD*, 7.
25. Such instances of enraged rammings of whaleboats were not uncommon, a vestige of the evolutionary ritual whereby male sperm whales would butt heads with each other in competition for female sexual attention. The "theory is that the head of the sperm whale is designed to be a battering ram, and that the oil-filled spermaceti organ and the junk act as giant shock absorbers to cushion the blow of a collision," as Dolin notes (77).
26. NN *MD*, 7.
27. NN *MD*, 7.
28. NN *MD*, 63.
29. NN *MD*, 69.
30. NN *MD*, 69.
31. NN *MD*, 69.
32. Quoted in Parker *HM*, 182.
33. Olson, 23.
34. NN *MD*, 4.
35. NN *MD*, 33, 34.

36. NN *MD*, 35.

37. NN *Corr*, 24.

38. NN *MD*, 6.

39. NN *Corr*, 25.

40. NN *MD*, 71.

41. NN *MD*, 7.

42. NN *MD*, 51.

43. NN *MD*, 71.

44. NN *MD*, 72, 73.

45. "Yet Another Unitarian Universalist: Posts tagged 'Moby-Dick marathon'" http://www.danielharper.org/blog/?tag=moby-dick-marathon. January 3, 2008.

46. Olson, 15.

47. Olson, 13.

48. NN *MD*, 272.

49. NN *MD*, 4.

50. Stewardson, 1.

51. Stewardson, 1.

52. Wyn Kelley, "All Astir," *Leviathan* 9.1 (2007): 85.

53. NN *Corr*, 196.

54. NN *MD*, 201.

55. NN *MD*, 129.

56. NN *MD*, 200.

2. Queequeg's Ink

1. Peretz, 36.

2. Peretz, 36.

3. Peretz, 37.

4. NN *MD*, 31.

5. NN *MD*, 21.

6. NN *MD*, 21.

7. NN *MD*, 71.

8. NN *MD*, 58.

9. NN *MD*, 117.

10. NN *MD*, 61, 62.

11. I am interested in a fresh look at the positive power of globalization, especially as it brings Queequeg and Ishmael together through their shared economic interests of signing with a whaler. The definition of globalization I am working with here emphasizes that interconnectedness between Ishmael and Queequeg we see dramatized in their work environment throughout *Moby-Dick* and is derived from Charles Waugh's useful understanding of globalization which "1) uses information and transportation technology to connect with and care about people, ideas, and events from around the world, 2) recognizes the increasing interconnectedness of the local and the global, and

3) likewise understands that various aspects of life, such as technology and community, migration and economics, or communication and ideology, are far more *interdependent* than previously assumed. The key element to all approaches is obviously the degree to which people, places, ideas, and things are *connected* with one another. Globalization, in its most condensed definition, could be said to be *connectedness*: the degree to which the world is globalized is the degree to which all the various aspects of life are *interconnected*," "'We are Not a Nation, So Much as a World': Melville's Global Consciousness," *Studies in American Fiction* 33.2 (2005), 210 (emphasis mine). Significantly, Melville chose men from remote reaches of the globe to dramatize the successful joint-stock company of two in "The Monkey-Rope."

12. Leyda, 115.

13. Leyda, 116.

14. NN *MD*, 13.

15. NN *MD*, 13 (emphasis mine).

16. NN *MD*, 13.

17. NN *MD*, 58.

18. Melville's tale "The Apple Tree Table" features a protagonist who is driven mad with worry and wonder at the source of a persistent ticking sound emanating from the old table. His ruminations range the gamut of superstition and classical myth, while he fruitlessly speculates as to its cause. Of course, it is an insect burrowed deep inside the wood of the table that is the source of the sound, inspiring the narrator's daughter to wax poetic about the bug's immortal powers. "It expired the next day," the narrator flatly declares (NN *PT*, 397), comically undercutting his daughter's homiletic Christian allegory of the everlasting soul. The story follows a similar pattern to Melville's dry humor regarding Ishmael's superstitions about Queequeg.

19. NN *MD*, 85.

20. NN *MD*, 85.

21. Solomon Sallfors and James Duban, "Chaucerian Humor in *Moby-Dick*: Queequeg's 'Ramadan,'" *Leviathan* 5.2 (2003), 77.

22. NN *MD*, 23.

23. NN *MD*, 81.

24. NN *MD*, 81.

25. Owen Elmore, "Melville's *Typee* and *Moby-Dick*," *The Explicator* 65.2 (2007), 85.

26. Geoffrey Sanborn, "Whence Come You, Queequeg?" *American Literature* 77.2 (2005), 228.

27. George L. Craik, *The New Zealanders* (London: Charles Knight, 1830), 331.

28. Herman Melville, *Israel Potter: His Fifty Years of Exile*, ed. Harrison Hayford, Hershel Parker, and G. Thomas Tanselle (Evanston and Chicago: Northwestern University Press and Newberry Library, 1982), 57.

29. NN *MD*, 25.

30. NN *MD*, 431, 444.

31. NN *MD*, 480.

32. NN *MD*, 480.

33. NN *MD*, 481.

34. NN *MD*, 480.

35. NN *Corr*, 186.

36. Emily Dickinson, *Final Harvest: Emily Dickinson's Poems*, ed. Thomas H. Johnson (New York: Little, Brown, and Company, 1961), 85.

37. Nathaniel Hawthorne, *The English Notebooks, 1856–1860*, the Centenary Edition of *The Works of Nathaniel Hawthorne*, vol. 12, ed. Thomas Woodson and Bill Ellis (Columbus: Ohio State University Press, 1997), 163.

38. NN *Corr*, 213.

39. I concur with Waugh's recent claim that in *Moby-Dick* globalization is about more than domination. He writes, "Clearly, the issue of the United States as a global empire was an important part of Melville's work, especially regarding the interrelatedness of its notions of geography, power, culture, and identity. But it seems these approaches to his work are limited to a particular type of question and answer, a type that for the most part treats the great philosophic pursuit residing in all of Melville's novels in a way that would reduce it simply to an issue of domination, rather than as an issue of power that takes into account a wide variety of interaction and multiple active agents," 225.

40. Sanborn, 230.

41. Sanborn, 231.

42. Sanborn, 231.

43. There are forty Egyptological references to hieroglyphics in *Moby-Dick*, reflecting a nineteenth-century fertility myth that developed around the Nile and effected a crisis for Christianity at the time, as it invalidated the messianic theme. Melville's skepticism toward Christianity was as strong as his interest in alternative faiths.

44. NN *MD*, 58.

45. NN *MD*, 58.

46. NN *MD*, 58.

47. NN *MD*, 166.

48. NN *MD*, 145.

49. NN *MD*, 373.

50. NN *MD*, 379.

51. NN *MD*, 374.

52. NN *MD*, 48.

53. NN *MD*, 449 (emphasis mine).

54. NN *MD*, 449.

55. NN *MD*, 449.

56. NN *MD*, 449

57. NN *MD*, 450.

58. Dickinson, 85.

59. NN *MD*, 450.

60. NN *MD*, 450.

61. NN *MD*, 450.

62. NN *MD*, 450.

63. NN *MD*, 450.

64. NN *MD*, 450.

65. In "The Custom House," Nathaniel Hawthorne's preface to *The Scarlet Letter* (New York: Penguin, 1986), a similar parody of readers' demands for a material source for romantic tales emerges. All of Hawthorne's prefaces grapple with the reading public's demands for the facts behind the fiction, staunchly defending his artistic license in tones that barely conceal his ornery resentment of such an authorial predicament. "The Custom House" hands readers the material source for *The Scarlet Letter* in the form of yet another romance, much as Melville does here regarding the source of the whale skeleton data. Hawthorne says he found the original scarlet letter itself, the actual red "A" affixed to Hester Prynne's clothing, while rummaging through her long forgotten letters in the custom house. Hands trembling and cheeks flushed, he unveils the essential authenticating document with a dramatic flourish and presses it to his very own heart!

66. NN *MD*, 451.

67. Horace Holden, *A narrative of the shipwreck, captivity, and sufferings of Horace Holden and Benjamin H. Nute on the Pelew and Lord's North islands* (Boston: Russell, Shattuck, and Company, 1836).

68. Stephan Otterman, *Written on the Body: The Tattoo in European and American History* (Princeton: Princeton University Press, 2000), 199.

69. Paul Brodtkorb, *Ishmael's White World: A Phenomenological Reading of* Moby-Dick (New Haven: Yale University Press, 1965), 146.

70. Brodtkorb, 146.

71. Brodtkorb, 146.

72. NN *MD*, 141.

73. NN *MD*, 346.

74. NN *MD*, 347.

75. NN *MD*, 347.

76. NN *MD*, 306.

77. NN *MD*, 307.

78. Quoted in Parker *HM*, 878.

79. Quoted in Parker *HM*, 878.

80. Sanborn, 239.

81. Shockingly, "supply already exceeds demand" for whaling as a source of food for Japan's people, according to Douglas H. Chadwick, "Whatever Happened to 'Save the Whales'?" *Sierra* July/August (2008), 54. "Investigators found companies rendering carcasses mainly for pet food," 54. Japan and Norway are currently "harpooning more than a thousand minkes annually;" Japan is lobbying to hunt humpbacks commercially and has "used foreign-aid grants to entice other nations to join and support pro-whaling policies," 54. In retaliation, environmental activists from Sea Shepherd Conservation Society are "still racing inflatable little skiffs between harpooners and their targets," 54.

82. *Norton Anthology of American Literature*, vol. 2, ed. Nina Baym, et al. (New York: W. W. Norton and Company, 1994), 1451.

83. NN *PT*, 2.

84. NN *MD*, 347.

85. NN *MD*, 276.

3. Captain and Mates

1. Boston University's Maurice S. Lee stated the main reason for the selection was not be-cause of local color or popular reception in its time, as Louisa May Alcott and Nathan-iel Hawthorne certainly surpass Melville on those fronts, but rather, *Moby-Dick*'s capac-ity to move from local detail to a prophetic global reach. He comments that "*Moby-Dick* is at once local and global, rooted in a Calvinist, whaling mentality but also pre-post-everything (that is, Melville seems to anticipate post-modernism, post-structuralism, post-nationalism, etc.)," Roy Greene, "Q&A: Sizing up a whale of a tale," *Boston Globe* October, 10 2008, http://www.boston.com/news/local/breaking_news/2008/10.

2. Delbanco, 157.

3. NN *MD*, 161–162.

4. NN *MD*, 164.

5. Dolin, 257.

6. NN *MD*, 165.

7. NN *MD*, 165.

8. Dolin, 257.

9. Herman Melville, "Billy Budd, Sailor," *Billy Budd and Other Tales*, ed. Joyce Carol Oates and Julian Markels (New York: Penguin, 2009), 9.

10. NN *MD*, 179.

11. NN *Corr*, 191.

12. NN *Corr*, 191.

13. Parker *HM*, 832.

14. NN *MD*, 6.

15. NN *MD*, 6.

16. NN *MD*, 6.

17. Robert Milder, "Herman Melville, 1819–1891, A Brief Biography," *A Historical Guide to Herman Melville*, ed. Giles Gunn (Oxford: Oxford University Press, 2005), 29.

18. Edward S. Grejda, *The Common Continent of Men: Racial Equality in the Writings of Herman Melville* (Port Washington, NY: Kennikat Press, 1974), 10–11.

19. NN *MD*, 566.

20. NN *MD*, 566.

21. NN *MD*, 528. For an alternative reading, see Olson's commentary on Pip as Lear's fool, 67.

22. Douglass and Melville in fact knew of each other's work, were fascinated with point of view, and employed similar political critiques in service of a shared sense of racial jus-tice. "Particularly in their Civil War writings, Herman Melville and Frederick Douglass anticipate aspects of pragmatism by turning away from absolutes and their debilitat-ing extremes—dogmatism, skepticism, fanaticism, and quietism," as Maurice S. Lee observes in "Melville, Douglass, the Civil War, and Pragmatism," *Frederick Douglass and Herman Melville: Essays in Relation*, ed. Robert S. Levine and Samuel Otter (Chapel Hill: University of North Carolina Press, 2008), 396.

23. Walt Whitman, *Leaves of Grass*, ed. Sculley Bradley and Harold W. Blodgett (New York: W. W. Norton and Company, 1973), 38.

24. NN *Corr*, 190.

25. Dolin, 257.

26. NN *MD*, 6.

27. NN *MD*, 179. This is an interesting moment of confluence between Ahab and Ishmael, figures otherwise set at odds against one another throughout the novel, as John Bryant notes: "The reader is caught between Ahab and Ishmael: between the sullen tragedy of vengeance, pride, and authority and the desperate comedy of being; between autocratic sea and domestic shore; between the 'other' and the masses, demagogue and cosmopolite," "*Moby-Dick* as Revolution," *The Cambridge Companion to Herman Melville*, ed. Robert S. Levine (Cambridge: Cambridge University Press, 1999), 71.

28. John Alvis, "*Moby-Dick* and Melville's Quarrel with America," *Interpretation* 23.2 (1996), 224.

29. NN *MD*, 163.

30. NN *MD*, 163. Kathryn Mudgett has alternately interpreted this exchange as Starbuck's compensatory offer to Ahab to use the market as an outlet for his inner turmoil, an attempt to channel his anger away from his monomaniacal focus on Moby-Dick only, toward the pursuit of all whales in particular "to gain monetary reimbursement to compensate for his bodily injury," "'I Stand Alone Here upon an Open Sea': Starbuck and the Limits of Positive Law," *"The Ungraspable Phantom": Essays on* Moby Dick, ed. John Bryant, Mary K. Bercaw Edwards, and Timothy Marr (Kent, OH: Kent State University Press, 2006), 140. But Starbuck never couches his reference to the market by offering money as compensation, nor does Ahab necessarily take it that way. Rather, Starbuck's appeal to commercial imperatives points toward the broader social order in capitalist culture that might constrain Ahab's behavior. Never does he present the market as an enticing method for Ahab to quench his thirst for revenge, but as a system to which the *Pequod* voyage is dedicated. Thus Starbuck's is more an appeal to market responsibility and duty—a tacit appeal to Bildad and Peleg in this sense—than an attempt to mollify the manic captain with money.

31. NN *MD*, 163.

32. NN *MD*, 164.

33. NN *MD*, 164.

34. NN *MD*, 164.

35. NN *Corr*, 186.

36. NN *MD*, 88.

37. NN *MD*, 89.

38. Alvis, 229.

39. NN *MD*, 214.

40. John Bryant, "Preface: 'To Fight Some Other World,'" *"The Ungraspable Phantom": Essays on* Moby-Dick, ed. John Bryant, Mary K. Bercaw Edwards, and Timothy Marr (Kent, OH: Kent State University Press, 2006), xii, xiii.

41. NN *Corr*, 191.

42. NN *MD*, 212.

43. NN *MD*, 212.

44. NN *MD*, 46.

45. NN *MD*, 412.

46. NN *MD*, 212–13.

47. NN *MD*, 213.

48. NN *MD*, 213.

49. The market of course is the subject of hilarious snapshots of bizarre burlesques of human behavior, whose humor often turns on brutal detail, from Queequeg peddling shrunken heads about town, to the innkeeper's reaction to a suicide on her premises by showing concern exclusively for the property damage and lost business she incurred, to the mincer slicing spermaceti cloaked in the skin of the whale's penis. Interestingly, many of Ishmael's best reveries and philosophical insights are contiguous with the commercially driven activity aboard the ship. This speaks volumes to Melville's own professional predicament as an author who "would seek to conflate commercial and artistic aspirations," as the antebellum period was marked by an "interdependence between a commercialization of the literary text and writing as a specialized vocation released from amateurism," as Anna Hellen notes in "Melville and the Temple of Literature," *Melville "Among the Nations,"* ed. Sanford E. Marovitz and A. C. Christodoulu (Kent, OH: Kent State University Press, 2001), 335. *Moby-Dick* is thus in tune with many of the writers of the time, including the Transcendentalists, who, "rather than turning their backs on the marketplace, sought to combine Romantic aestheticism with capitalist expansionism," 335.

50. NN *MD*, 515. Wendy Stallard Flory has alternately read Starbuck psychologically, rather than politically, not as weak or cowardly but as unable to act because he is "unfortunate" and "to be commiserated with," a figure standing for Melville's own bouts of depression that could not be reversed by sheer force of will, "Melville, *Moby-Dick*, and the Depressive Mind: Queequeg, Starbuck, Stubb, and Flask as Symbolic Characters," *"The Ungraspable Phantom": Essays on* Moby-Dick, ed. John Bryant, Mary K. Bercaw Edwards, and Timothy Marr (Kent, OH: Kent State University Press, 2006), 95. "Self-blame," she writes, "is a common feature of manic depression and, although Melville would have known from his own mood swings how unavailing conscious attempts to deflect them were, he would probably not consider this as excusing what could all too easily be seen to be moral weakness," 94. This assessment indeed rescues the hint of sympathy in Ishmael's description of his paralysis of the will, but nonetheless misses the central political focus and ramifications of his inaction, which are hardly cast as unassailable.

51. NN *MD*, 213.

52. Mudgett, 132.

53. Charles Abbott, *A Treatise of the Law Relative to Merchant Ships and Seamen*, 2nd American ed. with annotations by Joseph Story (Newburyport, MA: Little & Co., 1810), 188.

54. *U.S. v. Givings*, 25 F. Cas. 1331, 1332 (1844). In this case, as Mudgett reports, the court supported claims brought by crewmembers of the *Hibernia* against their captain for forcing them to operate the ship in what they claimed were unsafe conditions, especially with regard to the ship's rotten masts. Since his violent behavior put them in immediate risk of life and limb, the court found their retaliation justifiable.

55. Mudgett, 133. Ahab's manipulation of written law to his advantage echoes his appropriation of capitalist codes of behavior to subdue his crew to his will. Ahab thinks like a lawyer, or at least an immoral one, as he "relies on the purely mechanical aspects of the law to avoid suffering the consequences of breaking it," rather than yielding to "the

moral component on which civil society and its laws are founded and act[ing] accordingly," as Mudgett explains, 136. In terms of his conduct and behavior as captain, he is within the law, and even in hunting Moby Dick, with concessions to capturing other whales along the way, which the crew does, he is not, as Mudgett claims, "in purely contractual terms," given his deviation from the purpose of the voyage, violating positive law, 138. All parties are acutely aware of his deviant designs, but he has taken great care to remain unassailable by the letter, if not the spirit, of the law.

56. NN *MD*, 515.
57. NN *MD*, 124.
58. NN *MD*, 127.
59. NN *MD*, 127.
60. NN *MD*, 118.
61. NN *MD*, 119.
62. NN *MD*, 166.
63. NN *MD*, 202.
64. NN *MD*, 201.
65. NN *MD*, 202.
66. NN *MD*, 149.
67. NN *MD*, 151.
68. Susan Garbarini Fanning, "'Kings of the Upside Down World': Challenging White Hegemony in *Moby-Dick*," *"The Ungraspable Phantom": Essays on* Moby-Dick, ed. John Bryant, Mary K. Bercaw Edwards, and Timothy Marr (Kent, OH: Kent State University Press, 2006), 211.
69. Fanning, 211.
70. NN *MD*, 152.
71. Bryant "Preface," ix.
72. NN *MD*, 145.
73. Peretz, 51.
74. Quoted in Melville, "Historical Note III," NN *MD*, 623.
75. Herman Melville, "Hawthorne and His Mosses," *The American Intellectual Tradition*, vol. I: 1620–1865, ed. David A. Hollinger and Charles Capper (Oxford: Oxford University Press, 2006), 332. (Hereafter, "Mosses.")
76. NN *Corr*, 121.
77. Peretz, 66.
78. Peretz, 75.
79. NN *MD*, 551.
80. Henry David Thoreau, *Walden and Civil Disobedience* (New York: Penguin, 1988), 368. (Hereafter, *WCD*.)
81. Robert D. Putnam, *Bowling Alone: The Collapse and Revival of American Community* (New York: Simon and Schuster, 2000), 15.
82. Jeffrey Tobin, "Barney's Great Adventure: The Most Outspoken Man in the House Gets Some Real Power," *New Yorker* (January 12, 2009), 38.

4. Harpooners and Sailors

1. Parker *HM*, 186.
2. NN *MD*, 152.
3. Significantly, Ishmael extends the status of the harpooners to an image of the *Pequod*'s crew as a microcosm of global cultures, a motley mix, "nearly all islanders" and "Isolatoes too," each "living on a separate continent of his own" yet conjoined in this common voyage. Melville has taken his crew from the four corners of the globe, assembling what Lawrence Buell calls "a funky League of Nations" at least as much as it is "Yankee-style capitalism headed for destruction," "The Unkillable Dream of the Great American Novel: *Moby-Dick* as Test Case," *American Literary History* 20.1–2 (2008), 150. (Hereafter, Buell "Dream.")
4. NN *MD*, 152.
5. NN *MD*, 152.
6. NN *MD*, 152.
7. NN *MD*, 152.
8. NN *MD*, 153.
9. NN *MD*, 27.
10. Herman Melville, *Great Short Works of Herman Melville*, ed. Warner Berthoff (New York: Harper, 1969), 466.
11. Melville, *Great Short Works*, 393.
12. Melville, *Great Short Works*, 371.
13. Fanning, 212.
14. NN *MD*, 295.
15. Olson, 21.
16. NN *MD*, 413.
17. Thoreau, *WCD*, 77–78.
18. Olson, 21.
19. Parker *HM*, 189.
20. Olson, 21.
21. Parker *HM*, 189, 190.
22. Parker *HM*, 188.
23. Parker *HM*, 188.
24. NN *Corr*, 25.
25. Quoted in Parker *HM*, 207.
26. Olson, 22.
27. NN *MD*, 173.
28. NN *MD*, 173.
29. NN *MD*, 174.
30. NN *MD*, 174.
31. NN *MD*, 175.
32. NN *MD*, 176.
33. Especially useful here is Paul Royster's comment that for Ishmael, "the rhetoric of labor is in part a defensive strategy, an ideology that allows him to cope with the

embarrassments or unpleasantness of his working-class position," noting that he "is never so happy as when he is finding in some dull, arduous, or onerous task an allegory of universal truth," particularly in chapters like "The Monkey-Rope," and "The Mat-Maker," "Melville's Economy of Language," *Ideology and Classic American Literature*, ed. Sacvan Berkovitch and Myra Jehlen (Cambridge: Cambridge University Press, 1986), 313.

34. Dolin, 276.

35. Nathaniel Philbrick's recent retelling of the *Essex* voyage is thoroughly documented with new research and a gripping narrative line, *In the Heart of the Sea: The Tragedy of the Whaleship* Essex (New York: Penguin, 2001).

36. Quoted in Dolin, 277.

37. Gordon V. Boudreau, "Herman Melville, Immortality, St. Paul, and Resurrection: From Rose-Bud to Billy Budd," *Christianity and Literature*, 52.3 (2003), 343.

38. Quoted in David Laskin, *A Common Life: Four Generations of American Literary Friendship and Influence* (New York: Simon and Schuster, 1994), 46.

39. All testimony from whalemen in this paragraph quoted in Dolin, 436.

40. Dolin, 279.

41. Dolin, 259.

42. Delbanco, 38.

43. Quoted in Dolin, 180.

44. Parker's biography of Melville notes that Briton Cooper Bush reviewed some 3,000 whaling logs and reported in *Whaling Will Never Do for Me: The American Whaleman in the Nineteenth Century* (1994) that "sexual incidents were recorded in logs of whaling ships primarily when one man complained against another for forcing or trying to force on him an undesired act. Then the offender might or might not be punished by flogging, fine, or discharge, depending on his rank or other circumstances," 208.

45. NN *MD*, 415.

46. Royster argues that during such work reveries in *Moby-Dick* "the content of Ishmael's meditations is distinctly asocial, concerning not the relations among men but those imaginary relations between the individual mind and the universe at large," 19. Indeed, Ishmael's vision reaches the stars at these moments, topping cosmological heights. But the gesture is not at all asocial in that these reveries all occur through his shipmates as coworkers in a mystical union that does not evaporate ties so much as revitalize them with greater significance.

47. NN *MD*, 416.

48. Robert K. Martin, "Melville and Sexuality," *The Cambridge Companion to Herman Melville*, ed. Robert S. Levine (Cambridge: Cambridge University Press, 1999), 188.

49. Martin, 190.

50. Martin, 190, 193.

51. Hester Blum, *The View from the Masthead: Maritime Imagination and Antebellum Sea Narratives* (Chapel Hill: University of North Carolina Press, 2008), 122.

52. Blum, 125.

53. NN *MD*, 416.

54. NN *MD*, 416.

55. NN *Corr*, 212.
56. NN *Corr*, 212.
57. NN *Corr*, 176.
58. NN *Corr*, 196.
59. NN *MD*, 444, 445, 446.
60. Dolin, 280.
61. African-American filmmaker Spike Lee recently eviscerated Clint Eastwood for his predominantly white casting of his World War II epics about Iwo Jima, *Flags of Our Fathers* and *Letters from Iwo Jima*. Historians estimate that around 900,000 black servicemen fought in the war, a fact Lee impressed upon Eastwood, whose defensive response urged Lee to call him an "angry old man," saying he "is not my father and we're not on a plantation either," John Colapinto, "Outside Man: Spike Lee's Unending Struggle," *New Yorker* (September 22, 2008), 52. Lee remarked that depictions of the grunts in war movies did not reflect their true diversity until Jim Brown's casting in *The Dirty Dozen* in 1967. Melville, it would appear, was a little over a century ahead of the film industry in this respect, as his sailors and harpooners hail from three continents.
62. NN *MD*, 418.
63. Daniel Harper, *Yet Another Unitarian Universalist*, blog, January 4, 2008, http://www.danielharper.org/blog/?tag=moby-dick-marathon.
64. Harper, January 6, 2008.
65. Dickinson, 101.
66. J. D. Salinger, *The Catcher in the Rye* (New York: Little, Brown, and Company, 1951), 13.
67. NN *MD*, 153.
68. NN *MD*, 118.

5. Survival

1. NN *MD*, 7.
2. NN *MD*, 7.
3. Sting, "Be Still My Beating Heart," *Nothing Like the Sun* (A&M Records, 1987).
4. Harold Bloom, *How to Read and Why* (New York: Scribner, 2000), 19.
5. NN *MD*, 272.
6. NN *MD*, 274.
7. NN *MD*, 274.
8. NN *MD*, 274.
9. NN *Corr*, 121.
10. NN *MD*, 7.
11. NN *MD*, 194.
12. NN *MD* 194.
13. Thoreau *WCD*, 135.
14. NN *MD*, 570.
15. John Guare, *Six Degrees of Separation* (New York: Vintage, 1990), 34.
16. NN *MD*, 570.

17. NN *MD*, 570.
18. Herman Melville, *Journals,* ed. Howard C. Horsford with Lynn Horth (Evanston and Chicago: Northwestern University Press and Newberry Library, 1989), 633. (Hereafter, *Journals*).
19. NN *MD*, 574.
20. Buell "Dream," 153.
21. Bryan Wolf, "When Is a Painting Most Like a Whale?: Ishmael, *Moby-Dick*, and the Sublime," *New Essays on* Moby-Dick, ed. Richard H. Brodhead (Cambridge: Cambridge University Press, 1986), 145.
22. NN *MD*, 450.
23. Wolf, 145.
24. NN *MD*, 107.
25. NN *MD*, 107.
26. NN *MD*, 107.
27. Jenny Franchot, "Melville's Traveling God," *The Cambridge Companion to Herman Melville*, ed. Robert S. Levine (Cambridge: Cambridge University Press, 1999), 173.
28. NN *MD*, 414, 413.
29. Bloom, 237.
30. NN *MD*, 414.
31. Bloom, 237.
32. Olson, 63.
33. NN *MD*, 489.
34. NN *MD*, 490.
35. Olson, 58.
36. Olson, 47.
37. Olson, 59.
38. NN *MD*, 36, 37, emphasis mine.
39. Thoreau *WCD*, 212.
40. Lori Merish, *Sentimental Materialism: Gender, Commodity Culture, and Nineteenth-Century American Literature* (Durham, NC: Duke University Press, 2000), 4.
41. NN *MD*, 37.
42. NN *Corr*, 195.
43. NN *Corr*, 195.
44. NN *Corr*, 195.
45. Elizabeth Hardwick, *Herman Melville* (New York: Penguin, 2000), 67.
46. Quoted in Delbanco, 135.
47. Quoted in Delbanco, 196.
48. Parker *HM*, 780–781.
49. Quoted in Parker *HM*, 58.
50. Parker *HM*, 59.
51. David Leverenz, *Manhood and the American Renaissance* (Ithaca, NY: Cornell University Press, 1989), 281.
52. NN *MD*, 477.

53. NN *MD*, 477.

54. NN *MD*, 477.

55. NN *MD*, 478.

56. NN *MD*, 480.

57. NN *MD*, 480.

58. Quoted in Delbanco, 134, 135.

59. Dickinson, 501.

60. NN *MD*, 3.

61. See renowned psychiatrist and MacArthur fellow Kay Redfield Jamison's *Touched With Fire: Manic-Depressive Illness and the Artistic Temperament* (New York: The Free Press/ Simon & Schuster, 1994), which sheds light on the hereditary nature of Melville's disorder. Relatives of Melville in addition to his father afflicted by mental illness include his brother Allan's daughter, Lucy, whose premature death at twenty-nine occurred within the confines of an insane asylum. Like his father, Melville's brother Gansevoort also was extremely deranged on his deathbed. Allan's nephew, Henry, was declared legally insane. Melville's own son, Malcolm, likely committed suicide, although the family vehemently argued that the self-inflicted gunshot wound that occurred in his room in the Melville home was accidental; see Flory, 99 n. 4, 82, 83.

62. Flory, 88. For more on mental illness in Melville, see Paul McCarthy, *"The Twisted Mind": Madness in Melville's Fiction* (Iowa City: University of Iowa Press, 1990); and Henry Nash Smith, "The Madness of Ahab," in his *Democracy and the Novel: Popular Resistance to Classic American Writers* (New York: Oxford University Press, 1978), 35–55.

63. NN *MD*, 480.

64. Flory, 94.

65. NN *MD*, 515.

66. NN *MD*, 3.

67. NN *MD*, 51.

68. My reading here does not intend to mystify Queequeg's powers as a "quasi-theological conception" of the character "shedding goodness without end, even at those times when Ishmael seems to have forgotten that he exists," as Geoffrey Sanborn has noted is a common habit among critics, *The Sign of the Cannibal: Melville and the Making of a Post-Colonial Reader* (Durham, NC: Duke University Press, 1998), 134. Queequeg certainly does not shed goodness without end, for his influence, though crucial, is limited to the fortuitous arrival of his coffin at Ishmael's side amid the wreckage of the *Pequod*. Further, the pragmatic, willful aspects of his self-resurrection take on earthy comic overtones that are hardly pious and "quasi-theological" but instead are humble, grounded, and transparent, as he is fully aware of his own limitations—which are considerable—but is empowered to operate within their parameters. His strength instead lies precisely in that he is not sentimentalized or overly idealized, as Melville goes to great lengths to mock such tendencies by making them "newly weds" in the Spouter Inn. Melville's sharp satire of such a method of characterization attacks romantic racialism in which character traits assigned to ethnic characters are lacking in

their white counterparts, so that pairings like Ishmael and Queequeg make a complete and balanced person. Stowe became infamous to twentieth-century readers for such a characterization method in *Uncle Tom's Cabin* (1852).

69. NN *MD*, 50.
70. NN *MD*, 306.
71. Elizabeth Bishop, "The Fish," *Norton Anthology of American Literature*, vol. 2 (New York: W. W. Norton and Company, 1994), 2446.
72. Bishop, 2448.
73. Nigel Reynolds, "Helpline for Fearful Fans of *Harry Potter*," *Telegraph* (February 2, 2007), http://www.telegraph.co.uk/news/uknews/1541373/Helpline-for-fearful-fans-of-Harry-Potter.html.
74. Samuel Johnson paraphrased by Adam Gopnik, "Man of Fetters: Dr. Johnson and Mrs. Thrale," *New Yorker* (December 8, 2008), 42.
75. Howard Moss, "Shall I Compare Thee to a Summer's Day?" *Literature: An Introduction to Fiction, Poetry, and Drama*, ed. X. J. Kennedy (New York: Little, Brown, and Company, 1987), xxvii.
76. NN *MD*, 491.

6. The Breach

1. Charles Darwin, *Charles Darwin's Diary of the Voyage of the H.M.S. "Beagle,"* edited from the manuscript by Nora Barlow (New York: Macmillan Company, 1933), 211.
2. Sir Arthur Conan Doyle, *Memories and Adventures* (Boston: Little, Brown and Company, 1924), 40.
3. NN *MD*, 524.
4. NN *MD*, 456.
5. NN *Corr*, 187.
6. "Mosses," 435.
7. "Mosses," 435. The messianic overtones of this quote have led Jonathan A. Cook to investigate Melville's use of Hawthorne as Christ figure in "Melville's *Mosses* Review and the Proclamation of Hawthorne as America's Literary Messiah," *Leviathan: A Journal of Melville Studies* 10.3 (2008): 62–80.
8. "Mosses," 435.
9. "Mosses," 432.
10. NN *Corr*, 195.
11. Delbanco, 196.
12. Emory Elliott, "'Wandering To-and-Fro': Melville and Religion," *A Historical Guide to Herman Melville*, ed. Giles Gunn (Oxford: Oxford University Press, 2005), 192.
13. For a thorough study of the sources Melville used for *Moby-Dick*, see Parker "Note," 635–647. The most recent examination of Melville's appropriation of sources for his own artistic purposes is in the issue of *Leviathan: A Journal of Melville Studies* dedicated to the topic of "Melville's Reading and Marginalia," 10.3 (2008).

14. Jack Kerouac, *On the Road* (New York: Penguin, 1991), 6.

15. Donald Yanella and Kathleen Malone Yanella, "Evert A. Duyckinck's 'Diary: May 29–November 8, 1847,'" *Studies in the American Renaissance*, ed. Joel Myerson (Boston: Twayne Publishers, 1978), 241.

16. Yanella and Yanella, 241.

17. Yanella and Yanella, 241.

18. Bloom, 22.

19. Bloom, 19.

20. Buell "Dream," 139.

21. George Hagman, *Aesthetic Experience: Beauty, Creativity, and the Search for the Ideal* (New York: Rodopi, 2005), 8.

22. NN *MD*, 376.

23. Hagman, 8.

24. Herbert Marcuse, *The Aesthetic Dimension: Toward a Critique of Marxist Aesthetics* (New York: Beacon Press, 1979), 67.

25. Nathaniel Hawthorne, *The House of the Seven Gables* (New York: Barnes and Noble, 2007), 159.

26. Hawthorne, *Seven Gables*, 160.

27. Hawthorne, *Seven Gables*, 163.

28. Hawthorne, *Seven Gables*, 184.

29. "Mosses," 431.

30. Much of Post-Lauria's book builds on findings in David S. Reynolds's wide body of research, a useful and relatively recent sample of which is "'Its wood could only be American!': *Moby-Dick* and Antebellum Popular Culture," *Critical Essays on Herman Melville's* Moby-Dick, ed. Brian Higgins and Hershel Parker (New York: Macmillan, 1992), 523–544.

31. "Mosses," 435.

32. Leo Bersani, "Incomparable America," *The Culture of Redemption* (Cambridge, MA: Harvard University Press, 1990), 154.

33. "Mosses," 432.

34. For an extended analysis of this characteristic in Hawthorne's politics and fiction as framed by ethical theory, see Clark Davis's *Hawthorne's Shyness: Ethics, Politics, and the Question of Engagement* (Baltimore: Johns Hopkins University Press, 2005).

35. "Mosses," 434.

36. NN *Corr*, 192.

37. "Mosses," 435.

38. "Mosses," 191.

39. "Mosses," 192.

40. NN *MD*, 140.

41. Richard Ellis, *Men and Whales* (New York: Knopf, 1991), 13.

42. "Mosses," 434.

43. "Mosses," 427.

44. NN *MD*, 550.

45. NN *MD*, 548.

46. NN *MD*, 548.

47. NN *MD*, 548.

48. NN *MD*, 548.

49. NN *MD*, 549.

50. Ellis, 27.

51. NN *MD*, 549.

52. NN *MD*, 549.

53. NN *MD*, 549.

54. NN *MD*, 133.

55. The whale's emphatically playful demeanor here is instructive in light of Ahab's strain-ing and laborious efforts to catch him. The dichotomy between labor and leisure, as William A. Gleason reports, was becoming more sharply defined in the antebellum era for two distinct reasons: the shift from seasonal agrarian labor to year-round factory work and the influx of cheap immigrant labor, both of which forced Americans into longer stints on the job than they had been accustomed to in the preindustrial era, *The Leisure Ethic: Work and Play in American Literature, 1840–1940* (Stanford, CA: Stanford University Press, 1999), 45–46. The value of play, therefore, as an aspect of leisure, now coveted more than ever, was held in high esteem. Indeed, the whale's natural instinct to play, even in battle, mocks Ahab's total incapacity for any sort of leisure, pipe smoking included, let alone regarding this fray as anything remotely related to the play of hunting or sport fishing. However psychologically rather than financially motivated, leisure never enters Ahab's laborious pursuit of the whale.

56. Stephen King, "Why We Crave Horror Movies," *The St. Martin's Guide to Writing* (New York: St. Martin's Press, 1994), 344.

57. Bloom, 235, 236.

58. Bloom, 238.

59. NN *MD*, 164.

60. NN *MD*, 507.

61. Leverenz, 283.

62. NN *MD*, 144.

63. Hagman, 8.

64. Michael Fleming, "Bekmambetov to direct 'Moby Dick,'" *Variety*, September 22, 2008, http://www.variety.com/VR1117992634.html.

65. Buell, "Dream," 155.

66. The 2005 film *Thumbsucker* (Sony Pictures; Mike Mills, Director), one of the most effective antidrug narratives of recent years, centers on a troubled, social-misfit teenager saturated with prescription and recreational drugs to compensate for his embarrassing regressive behavior. *Moby-Dick* plays an instrumental role in his turnaround, as the boy reads the novel in one long night and emerges eloquent and ennobled from it, eventually attracting the attention of the debate coach, joining the team, and winning a pivotal competition. Self-reliance is what the boy learns from his all-night reading that sparks his miraculous recovery. *Moby-Dick* is not necessarily the panacea; inner strength, however, is.

67. NN *MD*, 159

68. "Yet Another Unitarian Universalist: Moby Dick Marathon (again)," January 4, 2009. danielharper.org/blog/?p=2301#comments.
69. Ibid.
70. NN *MD*, 491.
71. NN *MD*, 492.
72. NN *MD*, 493–494.
73. NN *MD*, 495.
74. Thoreau, *WCD*, 59.
75. NN *MD*, 572.

Conclusion

1. Roland Barthes, *Image, Music, Text* (New York: Hill and Wang, 1977), 188.
2. Barthes, 146.
3. Barthes, 146.
4. Robert Milder, "A Response to Lawrence Buell," *American Literary History* 20.12 (2008), 159.
5. The issue is entitled "Melville the Poet," *Leviathan* 9.2 (2007).
6. F. Scott Fitzgerald, *The Last Tycoon* (New York: Scribner's, 1941), 189.
7. Lawrence Buell, "Melville the Poet," *The Cambridge Companion to Herman Melville*, ed. Robert S. Levine (Cambridge: Cambridge University Press, 1999), 135. (Hereafter Buell "Poet.")
8. Parker *Poet*, 67.
9. Christopher Sten, *Sounding the Whale:* Moby-Dick *as Epic Novel* (Kent, OH: Kent State University Press, 1996).
10. Parker *Poet*, 11.
11. Quoted in Claudia Roth Pierport, "Method Man: Marlon Brando's Dilemma," *New Yorker* (October 27, 2008), 45.
12. Parker *Poet*, 21.
13. Quoted in Parker *Poet*, 20.
14. Quoted in Parker *Poet*, 20.
15. Quoted in Parker *Poet*, 20.
16. Quoted in Christopher Benfey, "Melville's Second Act," *New York Review of Books* 55.11 (June 26, 2008), 49.
17. Quoted in Parker *Poet*, 21.
18. Quoted in Parker *Poet*, 97.
19. David S. Reynolds, *Beneath the American Renaissance: The Subversive Imagination in the Age of Emerson and Melville* (Cambridge, MA: Harvard University Press, 1989), 314.
20. NN *MD*, 548.
21. NN *MD*, 159.
22. Henry Pommer, *Milton and Melville* (Pittsburgh: University of Pittsburgh Press, 1970).
23. Buell "Poet," 136.
24. Buell "Poet," 136.

25. Buell "Poet," 136.

26. Walter Bezanson, quoted in Buell "Poet," 149.

27. Marjorie Perloff, "The Sound of Poetry," *Publications of the Modern Language Association* 123.3 (2008), 753.

28. Perloff, 754.

29. NN *MD*, 543.

30. NN *MD*, 543.

31. NN *MD*, 543.

32. NN *MD*, 544.

33. NN *MD*, 545.

34. Yoko Tawada, quoted in Perloff, 750.

35. Craig Dworkin, "The Poetry of Sound," *Publications of the Modern Language Association* 123.3 (2008), 756.

36. Dworkin, 757.

37. Dworkin, 757.

38. NN *MD*, 387.

39. NN *MD*, 388.

40. Delbanco, 169.

41. Rebecca Harding Davis, *Life in the Iron Mills* (New York: The Feminist Press at the City University of New York, 1993 [rpt. 1861]), 34–35.

42. Thoreau, *WCD*, 142.

43. Thoreau, *WCD*, 142.

44. NN *MD*, 374.

45. NN *MD*, 5.

46. Bryant "Preface," x.

47. James William Johnson, quoted in Perloff, 753.

48. Thoreau, *WCD*, 264.

49. Thoreau, *WCD*, 237.

50. Perloff, 752.

51. NN *MD*, 482.

52. NN *MD*, 482.

53. NN *MD*, 483.

54. U2, "Mysterious Ways," *Achtung Baby* (Island Records, 1991).

55. NN *MD*, 482.

56. Sarah Stickney Ellis, quoted in Dworkin, 758.

57. Walt Whitman, *Leaves of Grass* (New York: Penguin, 1988), 87, 28.

58. Michael Chabon, "Obama & the Conquest of Denver," *New York Review of Books* 55.15 (October 9, 2008), www.nybooks.com/articles/21830; NN *MD*, 571.

59. Chabon.

60. Chabon.

61. Chabon.

62. Chabon.

63. Chabon.

64. Chabon.
65. NN *MD*, 3, 573.
66. As one might assume, no translated marathon readings of *Moby-Dick* exist precisely because of the difficulty in conveying the sound of the poetry from the original. Gordana Crnkovic has observed exactly this effect of translation on another intentionally poetic novel, *Death and Dervish*, by Serbo-Croatian novelist Mesa Selimovic. "In its English translation," Crnkovic posited, "the elaborately sounded passages of the original virtually disappear" (Perloff, 754). One can only imagine the pale echo of the potent poetry of "The Lee Shore," "The Pacific," and "The Symphony" rendered in Serbo-Croatian, a washing-out made more obvious in an oral reading.
67. Thomas Mann, quoted in "Norman Mailer: Letters on Writing," ed. Robert S. Silvers *New York Review of Books* 41.2 (February 12, 2009), 19. Later translations of Mann have put his famous line in slightly different terms, yet one sees the relevance to a full-length reading of *Moby-Dick* in the intended sense of the entire paragraph from the preface to his 1924 mammoth 800-page novel, *The Magic Mountain*. In defense of his story's girth, Mann writes, "We shall tell it at length, in precise and thorough detail—for when was a story short on diversion or long on boredom simply because of the time or space required for the telling? Unafraid of the odium of appearing too meticulous," a presumption also driving every sentence of *Moby-Dick*, "we are much more inclined toward the view that only thoroughness can be truly entertaining," *The Magic Mountain* (New York: Knopf, 2005 [1924]), xxxvi.
68. NN *MD*, 7.
69. Nathaniel Hawthorne, *The Scarlet Letter* (New York: Norton, 1988), 9–10.
70. NN *MD*, 450.
71. Herman Melville, *The Confidence Man* (Evanston and Chicago: Northwestern University Press and the Newberry Library, 1984), 158.

· INDEX ·

scrimshaw, 104, 111–112, 126

sea, 114, 157; and current events, 210; for Ishmael, 20, 24, 28, 56, 69, 78, 131–33, 137, 147–148, 184; for marathon readers, 30, 33, 37, 92, 129, 148, 156; for Melville, 21, 23, 62, 104, 130, 133, 204; in *Moby-Dick*, 40, 46, 136, 198; for whalemen, 22, 80, 97, 106, 109, 147; sounds of, 196, 198, 203–204; and whale, 56, 80, 161. *See also* death at sea, ocean

sea eye, 114

Seamen's Bethel, 25–27, 37, 60, 94. *See also* Whaleman's Chapel

"Sermon," 94, 123, 157

sexuality, 98, 106, 112–114, 169

Shakespeare, William, 32, 83, 138, 153, 163–164, 166–167, 170, 173, 193–194, 196, 207

shipping out, 40; for marathon readers, 21, 25, 34, 40, 43; and Melville, 23–25, 28

skepticism, 53, 58, 78–80, 83

sounding the whale, 193, 200–202

space: for marathon readers, 30, 65, 153; in *Moby-Dick*, 47, 49, 53, 62–63, 88, 91, 136–137, 140. *See also* time, truth

"Sperm Whale's Head," 23

"Spirit Spout," 183

spirituality: for Ahab, 86; for Ishmael, 83, 133; for marathon readers, 60, 136; for Melville, 51, 53, 137; and *Moby-Dick*, 136. *See also* God, religion

"Squeeze of the Hand," 113–114, 116, 118

Starbuck, 69, 77, 79, 81–82, 86–91, 106, 118, 133, 147–148, 177, 185, 198–200

Stowe, Harriet Beecher, 63, 139

"Stowing Down and Clearing Up," 84, 104, 198

"Street," 23

"Surmises," 75–76, 85–87

survival, 77, 104, 134, 145–151, 157; for marathon readers, 52, 147–150, 152, 157; of whale, 150–151. *See also* death, life

"Symphony," 140, 156, 198–200, 203

tapestry. *See* lines

"Tail," 55, 168

tattoos, 40, 44, 46, 50–51, 58–59, 61, 68, 147, 149, 190, 211

Thoreau, Henry David, 23, 84, 92, 101, 132–133, 140, 186, 201–204

time, 29, 47, 106, 136, 186; for marathon readers, 29, 36, 147, 155, 182, 186–187, 190. *See also* nature, space

truth, 40, 43, 51, 91, 136–137, 147, 177, 183; for marathon readers, 52, 68, 190. *See also* God, space

Two Years Before the Mast, 21–22

Typee, 19, 28, 49–50, 54, 59, 84, 116, 167, 180, 192, 194

Walden, 23, 39, 84, 186, 201–202

weaver-god, 57–62, 136–38. *See also* God

weaving, 86, 126; for Ishmael, 58, 84, 212; for Melville, 36, 125

Whaleman's Chapel, 27, 139, 141, 157. *See also* Seamen's Bethel

whalemen, 22–23, 66, 101, 104. *See also* sailors, sea, whaling

whaler ships, 21, 97, 101, 108, 117–118

whales, 24, 55, 61, 66, 100, 110, 123, 161, 183, 198, 200; humpback, 174; minke, 174–175; right, 23, 30, 36, 67, 161; sperm, 22–24, 27, 61, 107, 161, 175; as symbols, 56–60, 161–162, 169–170, 201. *See also* capital, sounding the whale, survival, White Whale

whaling, 19, 21, 26, 45, 56, 63, 66, 73, 75, 101, 118, 202; as business, 22–23, 26–27, 44, 53, 64, 66, 81, 84–87, 100–102, 107, 109, 113–114, 139–140, 185; culture of, 100–118; hierarchy, 76, 80, 90, 97, 100–101, 108; personal benefits of, 20–23, 28–29, 84, 89, 91, 114, 140; romance of, 21–22; sounds of, 105–106. *See also* gams, New Bedford, whalemen

White Whale, 22, 25, 55, 60, 76, 81, 84–86, 107–109, 111, 116, 121, 134, 143, 150,